Meyerhold, Eisenstein
and Biomechanics

Meyerhold, Eisenstein and Biomechanics
Actor Training in Revolutionary Russia

Alma Law *and* Mel Gordon

McFarland & Company, Inc., Publishers
Jefferson, North Carolina, and London

The present work is a reprint of the library bound edition of Meyerhold, Eisenstein and Biomechanics: Actor Training in Revolutionary Russia, *first published in 1996 by McFarland.*

LIBRARY OF CONGRESS CATALOGUING-IN-PUBLICATION DATA

Law, Alma H.
  Meyerhold, Eisenstein and biomechanics : actor training in revolutionary Russia / by Alma Law and Mel Gordon.
    p.   cm.
  Includes bibliographical references and index.

  ISBN 978-0-7864-6750-1
  softcover : acid free paper ∞

  1. Meĭerkhol'd, V. Ė. (Vsevolod Ėmil'evich), 1874–1940 — Criticism and interpretation. 2. Eisenstein, Sergei, 1898–1948 — Criticism and interpretation. 3. Movement (Acting) I. Gordon, Mel. II. Title.
  PN2728.M4L38   2012
  792'.028'0947 — dc20   95-42738

BRITISH LIBRARY CATALOGUING DATA ARE AVAILABLE

© 1996 Alma Law and Mel Gordon. All rights reserved

No part of this book may be reproduced or transmitted in any form or by any means, electronic or mechanical, including photocopying or recording, or by any information storage and retrieval system, without permission in writing from the publisher.

Cover images © 2012 Shutterstock

Manufactured in the United States of America

McFarland & Company, Inc., Publishers
  Box 611, Jefferson, North Carolina 28640
  www.mcfarlandpub.com

To Jay Leyda,
for his encouragement and inspiration

Contents

Acknowledgments ix
Introduction 1

Part I. Meyerhold and Eisenstein

1. Meyerhold: From Actor to Revolutionary Director 13
2. Meyerhold: From Biomechanics to the Triumph of Socialist Realism 33
3. Eisenstein: From Engineer to Revolutionary Filmmaker 74

Part II. Biomechanics

4. Introduction 95
5. Biomechanical Exercises 99
6. Description of the Exercises 106
7. Program of Studies 124

Part III. Documents

8. Meyerhold on Biomechanics 131

   Biomechanics of Vsevolod Meyerhold by M. Korenev 133
   The Biomechanical Laboratory by M. Korenev 134
   Principles of Biomechanics by M. Korenev 135
   Meyerhold Demonstrates a Biomechanical Exercise by Erast Garin 139
   The Actor of the Future and Biomechanics by V.-Es. 141
   Biomechanics According to Meyerhold by Ippolit Sokolov 144
   Taylorism on the Stage by Arkady Pozdnev 148

viii *Contents*

    Project: Profile of the Actor Graduating from the Meyerhold State Theatre School   151
    Promptbook for "The Magnanimous Cuckhold"   160

9. Eisenstein on Biomechanics and Expressive Movement   163

    Notes on Biomechanics by Sergei Eisenstein   164
    Principles of Movement in Our Theatre by Sergei Eisenstein   167
    What Is a "Raccourci" and What Is a Pose? by Sergei Eisenstein   168
    At Rehearsals of "The Wiseman" by Aleksandr Levshin   170
    Expressive Movement by Sergei Eisenstein and Sergei Tretyakov   173
    On Recoil Movement by Sergei Eisenstein   192
    Lecture on Biomechanics, March 29, 1935, by Sergei Eisenstein   204

10. International Accounts of Biomechanics   224

    An Interview with Meyerhold at the Theatre of the Revolution by Lancelot Lawton   225
    How Meyerhold Trains his Actors by John Martin   228
    Biomechanics in Meyerhold's Theatre by André Van Gyseghem   233
    Notes on Biomechanics by Lee Strasberg   236
    Notes on Eisenstein's Lectures, 1934, by Marie Seton   238
    A Biomechanical Session by Harold Clurman   252

Part IV. Appendices

    Glossary of Biomechanical Terminology   257
    Notes   259
    Selected Bibliography   273
    Index   275

Acknowledgments

This book would not have been possible without the help of many people in both this country and the former Soviet Union. We are particularly indebted to the former members of Meyerhold's own theatre who so generously shared their experiences in working with Meyerhold. Included among them is our dear friend and colleague Stella Ogonkova, whose recollections as an actress in Meyerhold's theatre from 1922 to 1924 have proved invaluable. We are especially grateful to Aleksandr Gladkov, Mikhail Korenev, Erast Garin and his wife Kheisia Lokshina, and above all to Aleksandr Fevralsky (all now deceased), for making available to us most of the documents on Biomechanics and Expressive Movement contained in this book as well as many of the photographs of the exercises. We wish also to express our appreciation to Maya Sitovetskaya and her colleagues at RGALI (Russian State Archives for Literature and Art) in Moscow for making it possible to check the accuracy and completeness of these documents against those contained in the archives, and to Marina Ivanova, formerly of the Bakhrushin Theatre Museum, for the information she furnished in identifying some of the photographs of the biomechanical exercises. Our gratitude is owed to the Bakhrushin Museum itself for making available for study the short film clip on Biomechanics housed in their archives.

We are deeply indebted to Meyerhold's granddaughter, Maria Valentei, who has worked tirelessly to restore to her grandfather his rightful place in the history of Russian and Soviet theatre. Without her continuing support of our research and her frequent intervention on our behalf, it would have been impossible for us to have gained access to many of the most valuable documents we have drawn on in writing this book.

We are also grateful to Meyerhold's daughter, the late Irina Vsevolodovna, for arranging a demonstration of Biomechanics by her students in Leningrad, and to former Meyerhold actor Valentin Pluchek, who arranged a similar demonstration of Biomechanics by a group of young actors in

Moscow at his Theatre of Satire. Led by its director, Aleksei Levinsky, this group has in recent years reconstructed the entire body of biomechanical exercises and études under the guidance of the late Nikolai Kustov, one of Meyerhold's original teachers of Biomechanics. The opportunity to see these demonstrations and actually to work on some of the exercises under Mr. Levinsky's guidance provided many of the crucial breakthroughs in our understanding of the key principles of Biomechanics.

The authors wish to thank Naum Kleiman, curator of the Eisenstein Museum in Moscow. His encyclopedic knowledge of source materials and perceptive insights on Eisenstein's theory of Expressive Movement were of inestimable value. Our thanks also go to Nikolai Pesochinsky, whose recent research on Biomechanics has led us to many new sources.

Unexpected but valuable assistance was given to us by the late Lee Strasberg. Not only did he generously provide us with photographs of many of the biomechanical exercises and with his own eyewitness description from his visit to Moscow in 1934, but both as teacher and mentor, he enthusiastically encouraged our research and experimentation from the very beginning.

The dozens of students from New York University and elsewhere who have served since 1979 as our guinea pigs in trying to work out the biomechanical exercises should also be acknowledged here. We are especially appreciative of the loyal enthusiasm and the patience of those, including Sheila Gordon, David Brimmer, and James Curly, who have stayed with us through the countless permutations the exercises have undergone with each bit of new information we have gained during the past few years.

We are very grateful to the International Research and Exchanges Board (IREX) for enabling Alma Law to spend six months in Moscow in 1973 doing research on Meyerhold. While research for this book was supported in part by a grant from IREX, with funds provided by the National Endowment for the Humanities and the United States Information Agency, none of these organizations is responsible for the views expressed.

Finally, a very special word of thanks goes to the late Rose Raskin, whose superb knowledge of both Russian and English was crucial not only in the translation of the documents, but also in the interpretation of them.

All translations from the Russian are by Alma Law, unless otherwise noted. In transliterating Russian words and proper names, we have used a dual system. In the text we have followed more popular usage in rendering Russian names and terms. In notes and source references, we have used a modified Library of Congress system, omitting diacritical marks and ligatures. For the sake of consistency, in the documentary material we have normalized the spelling of words and such terms as Biomechanics. Brackets are used throughout to indicate information or comments by the authors of this book. Terms used by Meyerhold, Eisenstein, and others, such as Biomechanics, Expressive Movement, and Stanislavsky's Method of Physical Action, are capitalized throughout to indicate their specialized usage.

The city founded by Peter the Great was called St. Petersburg until August 1914, then Petrograd until January 1924, and thereafter Leningrad until September 1991, at which point it reverted to St. Petersburg. For the sake of historical accuracy, we have observed these changes in the text. Dates up to February 14, 1918, are given according to the Julian (or Old Style) calendar, and after that date according to the Gregorian (or New Style) calendar. Before 1900, the Julian calendar in use in Russia was twelve days behind the Gregorian; from 1900 to 1918, it was thirteen days behind.

.

Introduction

Biomechanics was a system of actor training devised by Vsevolod Meyerhold shortly after the Russian Revolution of 1917. Although not always understood, it received wide attention during the twenties and thirties as a result of Meyerhold's unique position as the foremost Soviet avant-garde director. Despite radical stylistic changes in Russian acting during the interwar period—from eccentric experimentation to Socialist Realism—Meyerhold's conception of the role of Biomechanics remained remarkably constant throughout his career. In fact, Meyerhold insisted that the mastery of Biomechanics afforded the actor all the primal elements of kinesthetic movement, the very core of the theatrical experience.

Like Konstantin Stanislavsky, his former teacher, Meyerhold had difficulties articulating his program of actor training. Critics and journalists frequently confused what these master directors did on stage with what they developed in the classroom and rehearsal hall. Both Stanislavsky and Meyerhold also had problems containing—or controlling—their pupils and disciples. Some theatrical acolytes slavishly imitated their teachers, but only in a most superficial and unthinking manner. Other students, like disgruntled children of famous artists, rebelled in adolescent rage, yet always omitting to discard the glamorous names of their celebrated parents.

Meyerhold also had a third kind of pupil, one who both perfected and challenged his teacher's theories and regime in actor training. This was Sergei Eisenstein, whose international star would one day outshine that of Meyerhold. Eisenstein, too, investigated the relationship between the psychophysical movement of the actor and expression, first in Meyerhold's workshops, where he formulated some of the most illuminating definitions of the principles of Biomechanics, and later in his teaching at the Institute of Cinematography. Eisenstein called his own work "Expressive Movement." But like Meyerhold, who became more recognized for his radical treatment of the dramatic text and his directorial wizardry than for

Biomechanics, Eisenstein's movement experiments with actors were completely overshadowed by his theory and cinematic use of montage.

While Meyerhold and Eisenstein, each for his own reasons, revolted against the Stanislavsky system and the Moscow Art Theatre style of performance, the two revolutionaries nevertheless accepted Stanislavsky's basic analysis of the special problems of the actor: inspiration and expression.

Artists — painters, writers, architects, designers, directors — normally create just at those times they feel truly inspired. Only the performing artist must create on demand, according to someone else's schedule: for instance, six nights a week at 8:10 exactly. In addition, the actor does not see his work at the moment he creates it. The performer's expressive means — his body — is inseparable from his critical faculties. Therefore, unlike most other artists, the actor is dependent on others to direct him.

Stanislavsky devoted the latter part of his life to formulating solutions to the problems of inspiration and expression. Basically he promoted the theory that the proper stimulation of the actor's mind would lead to a more truthful and profound mode of onstage expression.

Meyerhold and Eisenstein believed quite the opposite: that expression in movement — the actor's motor functions — could lead automatically to feelings and inspired emotions. They argued that the function of acting is not merely to fill the performer with hidden thoughts and feelings, but to communicate expressively with the audience. Whether an actor feels "correctly" or not becomes immaterial if the spectator cannot see and feel the result. Theatre is much more than an exercise in "truthful" emotion; it involves an entire spectrum of scenic elements, acting being one of them. The goals of Biomechanics and Expressive Movement were to train the actor in such a way as to develop and extend his expressive vocabulary, or his kinesthetic abilities, while learning to follow the exacting commands of the director.

Beginning in the mid-twenties, the term "Biomechanics" acquired almost magical properties among Western European and American journalists, theatre historians, and left-leaning intellectuals. As the world outside the Soviet Union became aware of Meyerhold's bold and innovative stage productions, more and more theatre practitioners associated Meyerhold's name with Biomechanics and scenic Constructivism. Yet without having seen Meyerhold's acting workshops or understanding their place in the program of experimental Russian theatres and studios, latter-day scholars and otherwise authoritative theatrical figures completely misinterpreted the role and function of Meyerhold's Biomechanics.

For both theatre and cultural historians, Biomechanics became an open symbol, a mere cipher of 1920s eccentricism in Soviet art. These

Sergei Eisenstein (far left) sitting with Meyerhold (center) at a rehearsal of Yuri German's *Prelude*, circa 1932 or 1933.

misguided assumptions and factually tangled analyses from the West—sometimes based on a single photograph—have been repeated for more than sixty years and are still the major source of false information on the work of Meyerhold. Altogether, these misconceptions fall into six distinct categories:

One. *Biomechanics was a machine-like acting vocabulary, or a mechanical style of acting.* The British writer Huntley Carter probably was responsible for this most common and frequently repeated notion of Biomechanics. It started with his thousand-word description of Biomechanics in *The New Theatre and Cinema of Soviet Russia*, written in 1924.[1] While referring to Taylorism and the principles of Biomechanics that treat the human body like a "mechanism," Carter failed to mention that Biomechanics was an actor training program. Following Carter's limited definition, authoritative theatre scholars like Nikolai A. Gorchakov, in his *Theatre in Soviet Russia* (1957),[2] and Edwin Duerr, in *The Length and Depth of Acting* (1962),[3] assumed that Biomechanics was a "new system of acting" or a "new kind of acting." Moreover, the fact that the movement sources of Biomechanics could be found in less mechanical origins, like Commedia dell'arte, was not well explained in Carter's definition. The reader was left with the heady impression that Meyerhold's biomechanical actors moved about the stage and interacted like robots or human machines.

Meyerhold himself fostered this misconception by directly introducing biomechanical études as "citations" in his 1922 productions of *The Magnanimous Cuckold* and *The Death of Tarelkin*. But these purely biomechanical demonstrations in the context of a performance were few and far between. To be sure, as Meyerhold himself pointed out to his actors in 1933, there were in all of his productions certain segments that could easily serve as biomechanical études—Goncharova's death scene in Meyerhold's 1931 production of Yury Olesha's *A List of Benefits*, for example.[4] But the vast majority of the performers' gestures and physical activity in all of his productions were only based on the principles of Biomechanics, not on the replication of the exercises. In fact, Meyerhold believed that the outward appearance of Biomechanics should (and would) completely disappear from his actors' movements on the stage, leaving only their kinesthetic effects to act on the spectator.

Two. *Biomechanics was the only source of actor training in Meyerhold's theatre and was utilized only by his performers.* Meyerhold conceived of Biomechanics as a psychophysical program to be taught at his studio beginning in 1922. Through his biomechanical exercises, an actor would learn to communicate with the audience by the most dynamic and visually powerful means. Boxing, dance, pantomime, and physical culture were also taught at Meyerhold's studio. But these were purely physical skills for bodily development and scenic demonstration. Biomechanics was predicated on a deeper, more scientific foundation that involved the entire corporeal presentation for theatrical expression.

It was Meyerhold's hope that Biomechanics would supplant other less efficient forms of actor training in the Soviet Union that were either totally internal or physically based. In the early twenties, and even as late as the thirties, many amateur and agitprop troupes adopted Biomechanics as teachers from Meyerhold's workshop became available. The Proletkult, the Theatre of the Revolution, and Aleksei Granovsky's State Jewish Theatre (GOSET) were among the best-known theatres that taught Biomechanics.

Three. *Biomechanics is related primarily to scenic Constructivism in the early twenties.* Western scholars have generally analyzed and dissected Meyerhold's direction by means of published reviews of his productions, Soviet texts, and publicity stills. These materials unearth style and social content, but they rarely reveal stage movement or rehearsal technique. Some aspects of Biomechanics can be deciphered in photographs, but many more remain hidden.

Of the two dozen theatrical productions Meyerhold directed after *Tarelkin*, fewer than half of them could be construed as Constructivist in design. Yet Biomechanics remained the thread and backbone of actor training for virtually every production that Meyerhold created after 1922. It is misleading to suggest, as James Symons does in his 1971 book *Meyerhold's Theatre of the Grotesque*, that with his production of Ostrovsky's *The Forest*, Meyerhold abandoned "purely acrobatic Biomechanics" for a "more humanized and realistic" form of production.[5] For Meyerhold, Biomechanics was not a "style." It schooled the actor in tragedy as well as comedy, agitprop as well as highly realistic productions; it was equally useful for contemporary Soviet political melodramas and grand opera.

More recently, Robert Leach in *Vsevolod Meyerhold* (1989) asserted that Meyerhold's Biomechanics was "never fully explained or codified by Meyerhold,"[6] that it was "little more than a compendium word to cover all elements of acting which he taught and wished to utilize in productions," and that it is "better understood as a kind of philosophical underpinning of [Meyerhold's] actual programme."[7] Like a number of other Western writers, many of whom have relied solely on sources published in English, Leach's interpretive translation of the word *otkaz* as "rejection" and *rakurs* as "silhouette" demonstrates a basic lack of understanding of Meyerholdian and Japanese movement techniques.[8] From 1922 onward, even as he experimented with different exercises and études, Meyerhold referred to Biomechanics' role and usage in specific and unchanging terminology. Furthermore, although Meyerhold never insisted on a fixed number of exercises and études, the actual physical work in Biomechanics continued to revolve around the same twelve core exercises and études that had been developed in Meyerhold's first directors workshop.

Four. *Biomechanics and Stanislavsky's Method of Physical Action were similar concepts.* The personal rapprochement between Stanislavsky and Meyerhold at the end of the thirties has fostered the erroneous notion among some Western theatre scholars that what has come to be known as Stanislavsky's Method of Physical Action took the form of, or at least was inspired by, Meyerhold's Biomechanics. Unfortunately, this oversimplification ignores the motivation, theatrical function, and practical objectives of each technique.

At the end of his career, Stanislavsky experimented with the use of physical actions during rehearsals because of an intense dissatisfaction with actors and their uninspired approach to character work. While young performers seated around the director's table could often construct elaborate and analytically dazzling biographies and psychologically justified actions for their roles, once they mounted the stage, few of their bookish ideas manifested themselves in theatrically viable schemes.

Stanislavsky discovered empirically that drawn-out intellectual preparation by the actor rarely pushed the rehearsal process forward. In fact, he came to conclude that the less the performer knew about the play's overall meaning or emotional core, the more likely it was that a director could exact a deep, spontaneous reaction from him. The Method of Physical Action has little to do with body behavior or training. It was a means to manipulate the work of the actor during rehearsals in helping him to achieve a genuine sincerity and belief in the role he was playing.

Meyerhold created Biomechanics primarily as a kinesthetic training device. The entire stage picture could be revitalized through a more expressive use of the human figure in movement. A graduate of Meyerhold's workshops was able to execute physical actions on the stage with greater agility and poise. True, like Stanislavsky's Method of Physical Action, Biomechanics followed no special style. But while one can refer to a biomechanically-trained actor, there is no such thing as a Method of Physical Action–trained actor.

Five. *For political reasons, Meyerhold abandoned Biomechanics in the 1930s.* Historians have assumed that as Meyerhold publicly accommodated himself to the Soviet government's demand for Socialist Realism in art, he dropped his program of biomechanical training. Like many other public figures in the Soviet Union in the 1930s, Meyerhold often felt compelled to say one thing in public for official consumption and another in private. But as documents recently made available to the authors now prove, Meyerhold remained faithful to Biomechanics as the cornerstone of his program of actor training. In June 1933, Meyerhold and his performers spent four days discussing nothing but Biomechanics. In his concluding remarks to his actors on that occasion, Meyerhold once more affirmed what he had frequently said in the past, that he would never abandon Biomechanics.[9] Meyerhold and his assistants continued to study and refine the scientific foundations of Biomechanics until the theatre was closed down in 1938. Finally, as dangerous as it was to do so in the mid to late thirties, both Meyerhold and Eisenstein continued to speak of Biomechanics and to make it a fundamental part of their programs of actor training.

Six. *So little is known about Biomechanics that it is nothing but a historical symbol of antinaturalistic modernism.* Both scholars and theatre practitioners have declared that Biomechanics is a fascinating idea that disappeared with the death of Meyerhold. Writing in *Travail théâtral*, Christine Hamon asserted that little remains other than "accounts by students or actors, sometimes written long after performances, and notes of meetings which treat Biomechanics in terms that are vague or too polemical" to be of much use.[10]

Concurrently, Jerzy Grotowski, at his Polish Theatre Laboratory, and his pupil Eugenio Barba at the Odin Teatret, claimed to "reinvent" Biomechanics during the sixties and early seventies. Other groups, like Stockholm's Teater Schahrazad, created weirdly distorted and abstract versions of it—somewhat resembling Grotowski's *corporals*—which they taught throughout Europe in the late seventies.

In fact, Meyerhold's Biomechanics was not lost to history, nor is its resurrection dependent on the playful imagination of Western avant-garde troupes. After the Stanislavsky system was officially adopted in 1939 as the sole program of actor training for all theatre schools in the Soviet Union, no other system of actor training could be openly utilized or even discussed as an alternative. Edward Braun, one of the few Western scholars to have fully understood and appreciated the significance of Biomechanics, has noted, "[Biomechanics'] practical success was largely responsible for the introduction of some form of systematized physical training into the curriculum of every Soviet drama school."[11] But it is important to point out that this training has focused primarily on generalized physical culture and on the development of movement skills (such as fencing or dancing) rather than, as Valentin Pluchek has noted, "on training the actor's psycho-physical apparatus."[12]

Even after Meyerhold was formally rehabilitated in 1955, Biomechanics, along with the teachings of Mikhail Chekhov and Grotowski, could only be studied in unofficial groups. Nevertheless, Meyerhold left behind film clips, photographs, notes, detailed descriptions and loyal teachers whose memories still retained the psychophysical imprint of their youth. In the last few years, as a growing number of theatre practitioners in the former Soviet Union have come to appreciate the importance of alternative programs of training for actors, there has been a renewed interest in Biomechanics. The fruits of this new surge of interest are only now beginning to become evident in Russian research and practice.

Until Meyerhold's official Soviet rehabilitation, and the publication of several books on his life and work more than a decade later, the only material on Biomechanics available in the West was a few descriptions to be found in scattered accounts by journalists, theatre directors, and tourists who visited Russia in the twenties and thirties (several of which are included in the documentary section of this book), and an assortment of photographs of the exercises. The material that emerged in the Meyerhold publications following his rehabilitation served to whet the appetite of the curious, but was hardly sufficient for a full understanding of Biomechanics, much less a reconstruction of the exercises and études.

The situation was exacerbated by the fact that many of Meyerhold's former actors and assistants (Igor Ilinsky and Aleksandr Gladkov, for example), still traumatized by years of enforced silence, either dismissed

8 *Introduction*

Biomechanics altogether, or deliberately played down its significance by subscribing to the simplistic notion that there was little difference between Stanislavsky and Meyerhold's teachings — they were merely working from opposite ends of the same tunnel.[13]

In writing about Meyerhold and his system of biomechanical training, Soviet theatre scholars have also found themselves subject to the same constraints as the theatre schools in teaching Biomechanics. Nothing was allowed that might in any way cast a shadow on Stanislavsky's position as the "father of Soviet theatre." Up until the advent of glasnost under Mikhail Gorbachev, there even existed a quota system whereby the number of books published on Meyerhold could not exceed the number dedicated to Stanislavsky.

Still, the available new material was enough to launch the authors of this book on a search whose objective was precisely that: to gather all the existing documents on Biomechanics, and to attempt to reconstruct the exercises. This quest began appropriately enough in 1974, the one-hundredth anniversary of Meyerhold's birth, when Mel Gordon wrote an article on Biomechanics for *The Drama Review*, in which he made the first attempt to reconstruct the exercises based on available descriptions and interviews.[14] During the same period, while in Moscow researching Meyerhold's productions in the nineteen-twenties, Alma Law uncovered intriguing archival material on Meyerhold's Biomechanics.

Our two pursuits converged in the late seventies when we began working with a group of New York University acting students to reconstruct some of Meyerhold's biomechanical exercises. The unexpected interest in our demonstrations from the New York theatre, art, and dance community inspired us in our attempts to recreate more of the exercises as well as to explore how Biomechanics translated into performance. The latter led us to our scenic recreations of Meyerhold's *The Magnanimous Cuckold* (1922), shown at the Guggenheim Museum in 1981, and more recently of Meyerhold's productions *The Death of Tarelkin* (1922) and *D. E.* (1924).[15]

It was the discovery in a private Moscow archive of Sergei Eisenstein's writings and lectures on Biomechanics and other movement training that led to our including here his preliminary study of Expressive Movement because of the important insights it offers on the theoretical sources of Biomechanics.

Books on the performing arts tend to follow certain established categories and corresponding formats. They either primarily instruct the reader in a specific theatrical craft (like acting), record the artist's work, provide a critical analysis, theorize about the function of stage art, assemble related documentary materials, or describe a cultural or biographical moment in the theatre's three-thousand-year-old history. Rarely does a performing arts book attempt to embrace more than one dominant shape or structure, although play anthologies usually contain some dramatic criticism and theatre histories will often place manifestos and selections of other documents in an appendix.

The present work, *Meyerhold, Eisenstein and Biomechanics*, is intended to be an exception. To a degree, it encompasses all of the different traditional approaches of books on acting and performance history. There is much scholarly description and analysis by the authors, but that frequently acts as connective tissue between (rather than a substitute for) some of the most exciting documents in twentieth-century theatre. Newspaper accounts and transcribed materials from public and private archives detailing classroom assignments and productions are mixed with excerpts from letters and personal diaries and eyewitness descriptions both by actors who worked with these two great innovators and by Russian and foreign theatre specialists. From the multiple perspectives of Russia and America, the cultural annals of Soviet art take on a more intense and significant meaning, especially when reflected against new biographical information on Meyerhold and Eisenstein.

Also in the present work are many detailed descriptions and photographs of the biomechanical exercises. More important than the exercises themselves, however, are the basic principles of movement that Meyerhold and Eisenstein pioneered and which are presented here for the first time.

Since few of the documents in this book have appeared in any publication, the authors have attempted to publish each in its fullest form. Normally, overlapping or seemingly repetitive facts would be edited out. The integrity of some documents, however, demanded that we retain them in their original version.

The book is divided into four parts. Part I traces the history of Biomechanics in relation to Meyerhold's and Eisenstein's aesthetic development. Part II is made up of documentary materials: the theoretical foundations of Biomechanics and Expressive Movement, with descriptions of the basic biomechanical exercises and études. Part III consists of descriptive accounts and interviews by British and American journalists and theatre practitioners. In Part IV are a glossary of biomechanical terminology, notes, bibliographical information, and the index.

Part I
Meyerhold and Eisenstein

Chapter 1

Meyerhold: From Actor to Revolutionary Director

> *As a director, I began by slavishly imitating Stanislavksy. Theoretically, I was no longer accepting many of his earlier methods of directing; I was critical of them. But in practice, when I began my work, I at first timidly followed in his footsteps.*[1]
>
> V. E. Meyerhold

Few artists have left as profound a mark on the twentieth-century theatre as has the Russian director Vsevolod Meyerhold. With ample justification, he has been called the Picasso of the modern theatre. Like the great Spanish painter, Meyerhold was also a visionary, a ceaseless experimenter with new forms and techniques, the leader of an aesthetic revolution. Taken as a whole, Meyerhold's work in the theatre, encompassing everything from circus tricks and acrobatics to Kabuki and Charlie Chaplin, is an encyclopedia of modern theatrical history. Many of his productions are an entire "school" in themselves. In fact, there are few devices and innovations regarded as avant-garde in today's theatre that Meyerhold did not think up and put to use at some time during a career spanning some forty years.

Meyerhold possessed a seemingly boundless imagination. He never paused long enough to perfect what he had already introduced. Instead he constantly rushed onward to experiment anew. He left it to others to pick up and further develop what he had tried and discarded. "After all," he said, "life is short, and if you repeat yourself there's much you won't manage to do."[2]

In the twenties and thirties Meyerhold's theatre became a mecca for foreigners visiting Moscow. Open rehearsals at which the master himself starred in a cascade of "demonstrations" of one or another scene, became one of the obligatory stops on any tour of the Communist capital. There was hardly a figure of importance in the arts at that time who did not come to see the renowned director—Edward Gordon Craig, André Malraux, Diego Rivera, Erwin Piscator, Mei Lan-fang—and many, including Bertolt Brecht, stayed on to study at his theatre. In an article on the Russian Theatre written in 1935, after spending five weeks in Moscow, Craig observed, "Stanislavsky and Danchenko are adored: Tairov is loved: and Meyerhold—Meyerhold amazes everyone, they both adore and love him." Calling Meyerhold the "great experimenter," Craig added that he wanted to visit Moscow again just to see Meyerhold's work in its entirety.[3]

During his travels abroad, Meyerhold made the acquaintance of countless other leading musicians, writers and artists, including Darius Milhaud, Fernand Crommelynck, Fernand Léger, and Picasso, who tentatively agreed to design the sets for a production of *Hamlet* at the Meyerhold theatre. As his fame spread in the 1930s, Meyerhold also received invitations to direct abroad as well as to write articles for foreign newspapers.

In manner and appearance, Meyerhold was a caricaturist's field day. Thin and slightly stoop-shouldered, he had a huge Cyrano-like nose and dust-gray hair that was inclined to fly in all directions. Though his bearing suggested a much taller person, Meyerhold was, in fact, of only average height. He was quick and sharp in his movements, yet at the same time extremely graceful. Meyerhold possessed phenomenal energy and never spared himself at rehearsals. He rarely sat for long at his director's table. He would prowl the auditorium studying the mise en scène from all angles. And he was constantly leaping up on the stage to demonstrate a particular movement, a dance, a bit of pantomime, even a fall down the stairs. Aleksandr Gladkov recalled one rehearsal in 1937 of the mass scene from Lidiya Seifullina's *Natasha* when Meyerhold, then sixty-three, jumped up on the stage sixty-one times.[4] In an instant, Meyerhold would transform himself into a young servant girl, an old woman, a nervous suitor, or a drunken husband. And somehow through it all he remained unrumpled and unsoiled. He would return to his director's table looking as elegant as when he had arrived at rehearsal.

Meyerhold was a complex person, a mixture of sharp contradictions. He had an unquenchable thirst for the new in life as well as in his work in the theatre. "Life has to be stirred up often," he would say, quoting Gorky, "so that it doesn't turn sour."[5] He could be capricious, suspicious, and unforgiving. Never one to be indifferent, his relationships with people followed a pattern of extremes, from warm friendship to sharp and often slanderous attack. "I love passionate situations," he once said, "and often create them myself in life."[6] But even those who suffered most severely from his thrusts never lost their respect for his remarkable genius. "Only those who had never known him," Gladkov once remarked, "could remain his enemy."[7]

Meyerhold's Early Years

Meyerhold was born on January 28, 1874 (old style), in Penza, where his father, Emil Fedorovich Meyergold, owned a prosperous vodka distillery. Meyerhold's parents, who were German Lutherans, baptised their eighth and last child Karl Teodor Kazimir.[8]

Located about 350 miles southeast of Moscow, Penza was founded in 1666 as a fortress. But by the end of the nineteenth century it had become a typical provincial town with a population of under 60,000 inhabitants. When Meyerhold was staging *The Inspector General*, it was his memories of Penza that he drew upon in recreating the stagnant atmosphere of Gogol's provincial Russia.

As Meyerhold recalled later, his father was a man of Western culture having little in common with the merchants of a small Russian town. He was a tall, powerful figure with strong passions and an avid taste for fine wines and the companionship of women. German was the language spoken at home, and on his desk Emil Fedorovich kept an an autographed portrait of Bismarck.

Largely ignored by his father, who had little time for or interest in the youngest family members, Meyerhold's early years were relatively carefree. He and his brother Teodor spent much of their free time with the distillery workers, swimming and going fishing with them, and in the summer, among the peasants on the estate belonging to his father. The frequent fires in Penza, which like most provincial towns at the end of the last century, was largely composed of wooden buildings, and the surreptitious visits to Orthodox Church services disguised in servants' clothing provided additional excitement for the two brothers. The annual fair held on the square adjacent to the Meyerhold house introduced the future actor and director to a rich kaleidoscope of spectacle: the folk *balagan*, larger-than-life marionettes, jugglers and acrobats, trained bears, organ grinders with parrots, jesters and barkers with their drums and bells.

But it was only a matter of time before Emil Fedorovich would turn his attention to his youngest sons, and they would feel the full force of his despotic personality. Demanding total respect from his offspring,

Meyerhold's father did not hesitate to raise his hand to his children because of a low grade, or even because he didn't like the way they looked at him. One time when reproached by his mother for not loving his father—"You must love him!" she insisted—Meyerhold replied, "I must hate a father like that."[9]

It was characteristic of Meyerhold even then to pursue what he was interested in with an unrelenting passion and to remain indifferent to everything else. He was not, in fact, a very good student. Three times he had to repeat a grade in the gymnasium, taking eleven years to complete the eight-year course. When Meyerhold was in Novorossisk Prison following the Revolution, he wrote in his notebook among excerpts from Pushkin, "I want to do important things, only important ones. What everyone else is able to do, I do worse than anyone."[10]

During his years at the Penza Gymnasium, Meyerhold spent as much time as he dared going to the theatre. He saw many of the great performers of that day, including Ivan Kiselevsky, Aleksandr Lensky, and Nikolai Rossov. Actors, both resident and touring, were also frequent guests at the Meyerhold dinner table. Among them was Vasily P. Dalmatov, whom many years later Meyerhold would direct at the Alexandrinsky Theatre. All his life Meyerhold treasured a photograph of the actor which he had autographed for Meyerhold's father.

Theatre was not the only influence on the young Meyerhold. He was a voracious reader and spent many hours devouring the German and Russian books in the family library as well as revolutionary and other illegal literature then in underground circulation. The reproductions of museum masterpieces in the richly illustrated German journals his parents subscribed to also awoke a passion for art that remained with him the rest of his life. In later years Meyerhold became an avid collector of art reproductions. Whenever he returned from abroad he always brought back many albums of them.

Meyerhold's mother, Alvina Danilovna, loved music and often organized musical evenings at which members of the family, as well as guests, performed. Meyerhold very early learned to play both the piano and the violin. For a time he secretly dreamed of becoming a virtuoso violinist, and he practiced for hours on end. Many years later he remarked that only his failure to pass the competition for a position as violinist with the university orchestra had prevented him from becoming a professional musician instead of an actor. Throughout his life Meyerhold continued to love music. He rarely missed a concert, and there were always musicians present in his apartment (where at one time he had two grand pianos). They included Vissarion Shebalin and Sergei Prokofiev, as well as Dmitri Shostakovich, who also lived with Meyerhold for a while.

Meyerhold made his theatrical debut on February 14, 1892. Then eighteen, he played Repetilov in a production of Aleksandr Griboyedov's *Woe from Wit* staged by the "Lovers of Dramatic Art." (His brother Fedor played Chatsky, and his future wife, Olga Munt, Sonya.) Meyerhold also worked on the production as assistant to the director, and under a pseudonym he even wrote a review of it in which he described his own performance as "not bad."[11] Performing on the stage only served to feed a love for the theatre that had begun much earlier, well before Meyerhold was old enough to accompany his mother to sit in the family box. In fact, some of his earliest memories were of mimicking himself before one of the numerous mirrors gracing the walls of the Meyerhold compound. Later, Meyerhold and his youngest brother would borrow one of their mother's shawls as a stage curtain and spend hours acting out scenes at home that they had seen in the theatre. At the end of 1893 Meyerhold wrote in his diary, "I have talent, I know that I could become a good actor.... This is my most cherished dream, one I have thought about almost since I was five."[12]

Less than a week after Meyerhold made his theatrical debut, his father died following a long and painful illness. Long since alienated from his father, Meyerhold vowed he would not follow in his footsteps. Somehow he would escape the smothering atmosphere of this provincial town, leaving behind everything connected with his past. When the family gathered in council after Emil Fedorovich's death, to learn that the vodka factory was on the verge of bankruptcy, Meyerhold announced that he was not at all interested in the family's financial situation, and that he was planning to take Russian citizenship and to marry Olga Munt. His announcement immediately brought the full wrath of the family down on him. Only his oldest brother Artur, who had been disowned by his father for marrying an actress, and Teodor, with whom Meyerhold had been especially close, remained silent. But first Meyerhold had to finish his schooling, and it would be another two years before he would pass his final examinations.

These final two years in Penza were difficult ones for the young Meyerhold. He was by nature high-strung and sensitive, and the combination of family strife, concern for the fate of his brother Teodor, who already showed signs of becoming an alcoholic, and his reading of Dostoevsky "from cover to cover," filled his mind with despair to the point of considering suicide. Later he would tell Aleksandr Gladkov that he never considered staging Dostoevsky because the writer was too closely connected with one of the darkest periods of his life.[13]

Thus it was that in June 1895 at the age of twenty-one, Meyerhold broke with his past completely by changing his nationality to Russian and embracing the Orthodox religion (both to avoid German military conscription and to be able to marry Olga Munt). At that time he chose the name Vsevolod in honor of one of the favorite writers of his generation, Vsevolod Garshin. And to make the break with his family complete, he also changed the spelling of his last name from Meyergold to Meyerhold.

Apprenticeship in the Theatre

When Meyerhold arrived in Moscow on August 30, 1895, to study law at Moscow University, his first stop was the Maly Theatre to buy a ticket for a performance of Aleksandr Ostrovsky's *The Last Sacrifice*, starring the great tragedienne, Maria Ermolova. For Meyerhold, studying law was largely a means of postponing the choice of a career. During his first year in Moscow, he spent every spare minute at the theatre and concerts or visiting the Tretyakov Art Gallery. The notebook he kept reveals how Meyerhold the future actor constantly took precedence over the future lawyer. Interspersed among the lecture notes are lists of books on the theatre, names of plays, as well as lines from Pushkin.

When Meyerhold went back to Moscow in January 1896, following Christmas vacation, he immediately applied for permission as a student to marry. Upon receiving an affirmative answer from the Minister of Enlightenment, Meyerhold returned to Penza where on April 17, 1896, he married Olga Munt. By then Meyerhold had already decided to leave the university at the end of the school year.

After a summer spent in Penza acting with the Narodny Theatre, in the fall of 1896 Meyerhold entered the Moscow Philharmonic Society Drama School, where he studied under Vladimir Nemirovich-Danchenko. In March 1897, actors, directors, playwrights, and impressarios came to Moscow from all over Russia to attend the First All-Russia Conference of Stage Workers. In spite of a heavy course load, Meyerhold didn't miss a single session. Later, he would recall in particular Lensky's speech in which he noted the low cultural level of the Russian theatre and called for more education for actors.

At the final examination the following year, Meyerhold was one of only two students to receive a silver medal, the other being Anton Chekhov's future wife, Olga Knipper. After graduation from the Drama School, Meyerhold was invited to join the new Moscow Art Theatre (initially called the Moscow Popular Art Theatre) then being organized by Stanislavsky and Nemirovich-Danchenko. At the time, Meyerhold was twenty-four years old.

Meyerhold spent four years with the Moscow Art Theatre. He played Prince Shuisky in the theatre's inaugural production of Aleksei K. Tolstoy's *Tsar Fedor Ioannovich*. His performance as Treplev in the Art Theatre's première of Chekhov's *The Seagull* marked the beginning of Meyerhold's close friendship with the playwright.

By the fourth year it was clear to Meyerhold that his days were numbered. Nemirovich-Danchenko, who had praised Meyerhold highly when he graduated from drama school, now regarded him with growing animosity as a troublemaker. And Meyerhold, deprived of any new major roles, was becoming more and more frustrated. Still, it is unlikely that he would have made the break with the Art Theatre at that time if he had not felt that he was being forced out when the founders reorganized in 1902 and they did not invite him to become one of the shareholders in the new company.

Novice Director

In February 1902, Meyerhold left the Moscow Art Theatre. Almost immediately he was invited to form a new theatre in Kherson together with two other lesser members of the Art Theatre, Aleksandr Kosheverov and his wife, Maria, who had the means for financing it. But before launching his new career as a director, Meyerhold made his first trip abroad, to northern Italy, where it was not so much the theatre that interested him, although he did see Tommaso Salvini perform, as it was the colorful street life and the life of the workers.

Meyerhold spent three seasons in the provinces, first in Kherson and then in Tiflis. In all, he staged some 165 plays (the first 85 of them with Kosheverov), including all of Chekhov's dramatic works as well as most of the rest of the Moscow Art Theatre repertory. He began, as he once said, "by slavishly imitating Stanislavsky...."[14] But Meyerhold quickly moved on from the realism that was and would remain the hallmark of the Moscow Art Theatre to experiment with new theatrical forms.

Meyerhold was a leader in the symbolist movement as it swept through the Russian theatre at the beginning of the century. By the end of his first season in the provinces he had already staged his first production of Maurice Maeterlinck, the Belgian Symbolist, with a performance of *The Intruder* at an "evening of new drama."

In December 1903, he began trying out nonrepresentational stage techniques in his production of Stanisław Przybyszewski's *Snow*, a production which the Symbolist poet, Aleksei Remizov, praised as "a symphony of snow and winter."[15]

Theatre Studio on Povarskaya Street

In 1905, Stanislavsky, aware of the limitations of the Moscow Art Theatre's "representation of coarse realism" in staging the Symbolist playwrights, invited Meyerhold to return to Moscow to head his new experimental Theatre Studio. During its brief existence before the studio was closed following the 1905 revolution without ever giving any public performances, Meyerhold continued his exploration of theatrical stylization. For Gerhart Hauptmann's *Schluck and Jau*, Meyerhold discarded naturalistic stage settings in favor of just a few significant details, often of exaggerated proportions. In his production of Maeterlinck's *Death of Tintagiles* he made use of a static bas-relief staging inspired by the altar paintings of Hans Memling. Meyerhold also experimented, albeit with disastrous results, in using stylized declamation and what he called the music of movement, gesture, and pose. This marked the first of Meyerhold's attempts at creating a new form of theatre in which music would serve not merely as accompaniment to the action but as an integral structural and aesthetic principle.

The Theatre of the Future

Meyerhold's experience with the short-lived studio only served further to convince him of the unsuitability of traditional acting styles for the new theatre he dreamed of creating. Georg Fuchs' book, *The Theatre of the Future*, which Meyerhold read in the spring of 1906, inspired him to begin moving away from the Symbolist theatre in other directions. During a brief season in Poltava that summer, he took a first step toward destroying the barrier between spectator and performer by eliminating the stage curtain in several of his productions, including Ibsen's *The Ghosts*. He also began making freer use of the stage space, removing the footlights and covering over the orchestra pit to extend the acting area out into the auditorium.

Influenced by Fuchs' observations about the central importance of rhythmical movement in the Japanese theatre, in his production of Arthur Schnitzler's *The Cry of Life* Meyerhold also experimented with the dance-like movements of the Japanese actors. Like Fuchs, in 1902 Meyerhold had seen the Japanese actress, Sada Yakko, perform during the first-ever Western tour by a company of Japanese actors. Although Otojiro Kawakami's company could hardly be considered authentic Kabuki theatre (Meyerhold would not see that until the late 1920s), their performances had a profound effect on Meyerhold. It marked the beginning of a life-long interest in Asian theatre, and judging by the frequency with which he referred to it, certainly one of the central influences on his work as a director. Seven years later, in a speech delivered on February 19, 1909, criticizing the non-professionalism of contemporary dramatic actors, Meyerhold would cite Yakko's performance as "showing the meaning of genuine stylization on the stage, the ability to economize one's gestures and reveal all the beauty of one's pattern of action."[16]

More innovations followed during the two stormy seasons (1906–1908) Meyerhold spent at Vera Komissarzhevskaya's theatre in St. Petersburg as he attempted to solve that inherent contradiction between two-dimensional scenic backdrops—what Adolph Appia appropriately called "dead stage pictures"—and the three-dimensional actor. In staging *Sister Beatrice* (1906), Meyerhold moved the performers to the very edge of the forestage. He brought paintings by Hans Memling and Botticelli to the theatre to show his actors the kind of bas-relief arrangements and distinct gestures he was trying to achieve. His production that same year of Blok's *The Fairground Booth*, in which he himself played Pierrot, marked the beginning of Meyerhold's life-long interest in the techniques of Commedia dell'arte. For Leonid Andreev's *Life of a Man* (1907), Meyerhold hung the entire stage with drapes to create a "grey, smoky, monochromatic expanse," and he introduced area lighting, perhaps for the first time on the Russian stage.

In the spring of 1907, Meyerhold spent several days in Berlin with Fedor Komissarzhevsky. While there, he saw the première of Max Reinhardt's production of Maeterlinck's *Aglavaine and Sélysette*. It was his first opportunity to see the work of the renowned German director, and even though he was greatly disappointed, he did draw a number of important lessons, the most significant of which was the realization that the term "stylized theatre" was not the sole property of Symbolist drama. Rather it is "a technique of staging" that could be applied to any form of theatre from Shakespeare to Ibsen and Chekhov to Wagner.[17] In Berlin, Meyerhold also met Edward Gordon Craig, whose work at the time was not at all known in Russia. So impressed was he by Craig's ideas that he translated from the German two of his articles, "On Stage Decor" and "Some Words on Directing and Stage Design."[18]

At the Imperial Theatres

In 1908, following his dismissal by Komissarzhevskaya, who accused him of trying to turn her theatre into a "director's laboratory," Meyerhold was invited by Vladimir Telyakovsky to join the Imperial theatres in St.

Petersburg. From then until November 1918, Meyerhold worked as a stage director and actor at the Alexandrinsky Theatre and as a director at the Marinsky Opera. During his tenure with the Imperial theatres, Meyerhold staged his first opera production, Wagner's *Tristan und Isolde* (1909), and such other memorable productions as Molière's *Don Juan* (1910), and Gluck's *Orpheus* (1911). In these productions Meyerhold further developed his notions of theatrical stylization and the freer use of stage space. For *Don Juan*, he removed both proscenium and curtain, and he flooded the auditorium with light in order to unify actors and audience into a single entity. Meyerhold kept stage properties to a minimum; borrowing from the Asian theatre, he introduced proscenium servants to carry them on and off as needed.

Meyerhold's appointment to the Imperial theatres also marked the beginning of his close collaboration with the artist Aleksandr Golovin. Together they created some of the most breathtakingly beautiful productions ever seen in the Russian theatre. For *Masquerade*, on which they worked on and off for over five years, Golovin not only designed a series of opulent gossamer curtains for each of the ten episodes, but every last object used on stage as well, including the playing cards. This production, which had its première on the very eve of the February Revolution in 1917, marked the apotheosis of Meyerhold's pre-Revolutionary "Petersburg" period. Reinstated in the Alexandrinsky (later the Pushkin) Theatre's repertory in 1923, *Masquerade* remained in the repertory until 1941. After the sets were destroyed by fire at the beginning of World War II, *Masquerade* was performed several times in a concert version, with Nikolai Yuriev still playing the leading role, as he had in the very first performance.[19]

At the end of 1912, Meyerhold's first book, *Vs. Meyerhold: On the Theatre*, was published.[20] A collection of articles and notes, many of which first appeared in journals and anthologies between 1907 and 1910, it sums up his first ten years of experience in the theatre. The first book ever to be written by a Russian theatre director, it was also the only book Meyerhold wrote dedicated to a theoretical examination of his views on theatre. In it, Meyerhold presents his version of the work of the short-lived Theatre Studio on Povarsky Street. In summing up the experience gained from it, Meyerhold emphasized "the impossibility of building a new theatre on old foundations."[21] He went on to conclude that new forms of stage presentation can only come about by first training new actors. It was a lesson that Stanislavsky also drew and it is hardly coincidental that on the heels of the Studio's failure, he began formulating the first version of his system of actor training.

In his book Meyerhold laid out for the first time the basic principles that would guide his work throughout the remainder of his career:

1. The primary role of the director as the "author" of a theatrical production. He creates the performance text, determines its overall style and himself works out every stage action.

2. The recognition of the stage and auditorium as a single organic whole and the audience as an active participant in the theatrical performance (in opposition to Stanislavsky's "fourth wall," intended to exclude the audience from the creative process).

3. The central importance of movement in the theatre.

As Meyerhold wrote in 1914:

> Movement is the most powerful means of expression in the creation of a theatrical production. Deprived of words, costumes, footlights, wings, theatre auditorium, and left only with the actor and his mastery of movement, the theatre would still remain theatre. The spectator would learn the thoughts and motives of the actor by his movements, his gestures and his facial expressions.[22]

4. The importance of stylization as the basic principle of all art, including the theatre. Throughout his career, Meyerhold never failed to use any opportunity to attack naturalism based on the "exact representation of life." In leaving nothing to the spectator's imagination, Meyerhold argued, naturalism destroys the very mystery that draws people to the theatre. Although the concept of stylization first arose in relation to the Symbolist theatre and the "theatre of mood," Meyerhold understood very early that they were not synonymous. As he would point out to a group of graduating student directors in 1936, "All art, including naturalism, realism, impressionism, expressionism, and any other 'ism' — all art is basically stylized."[23]

In 1913, Meyerhold went to Paris at the invitation of Ida Rubenstein to stage Gabriele d'Annunzio's *Pisanelle*, which had been written especially for the Russian ballerina. Meyerhold broke no new ground in this, his debut abroad. But it did give Western audiences and critics a chance to view his work for the first time. With decor by Leon Bakst, choreography by Mikhail Fokine, and a cast including more than two hundred extras, the production was an enormous critical success.[24]

When Meyerhold returned to St. Petersburg in July after a little more than two months in Paris, he took back with him, in addition to a fistful of rave reviews, a rich kaleidoscope of new impressions. He was enchanted by the poet Apollinaire, who had served as his guide to historic Paris. Shunning the fashionable theatres, Meyerhold concentrated on acquainting himself with such popular entertainment as the Médrano Circus and the Spanish Tavern in Montmartre. He also met and heard Marinetti lecture and saw a performance by the "Fairy of Light," Loie Fuller.

Doctor Dapertutto

Parallel with his work at the Imperial Theatres, Meyerhold continued to pursue his experiments with new theatrical forms and acting techniques. At first he staged productions in a variety of venues, including the short-lived "Lukomore" and the "Tower Theatre" in poet Vyacheslav Ivanov's apartment where he staged Calderón's *Adoration of the Cross*. It was the first of a number of productions Meyerhold would direct in exploring the conventions of different theatre traditions, in this case the Spanish theatre. Meyerhold's next foray was into Commedia dell'arte, with a production of *Columbine's Scarf*, an adaptation of Arthur Schnitzler's pantomine *The Veil of Pierrette*, at the House of Interludes. Finally, in 1913, Meyerhold organized his own studio on Troitskaya Street (it moved the following year to a building on Borodinskaya Street). Here, under the pseudonym Doctor Dapertutto, Meyerhold began laying the foundations for his program of actor training.

This was not Meyerhold's first attempt to organize a studio. From the very beginning as a director in the provinces in 1902, Meyerhold considered actor training as an integral part of his work in the theatre. As already noted, the failure of the Theatre Studio on Povarskaya Street strengthened his conviction that only through actor training could a new form of theatre be achieved. In January 1908, Meyerhold, in order to earn some extra money, began conducting a course entitled "The Auditorium of V. E. Meyerhold" at the music school operated by K. I. Daneman.[25] In the discussion of his productions included in his book *On Theatre*, Meyerhold also mentions the "Petersburg Studio" he organized in his own home in which during the 1908-1909 season the composer, Mikhail Gnesin, taught a course based on the theory of "the musical reading of drama;" the ballet teacher, Valentin Presnyakov, taught plastic gymnastics, and Meyerhold himself, movement and expressiveness.[26]

But it was only with the organization of the Studio on Borodinskaya in the winter of 1912-1913 that Meyerhold was able to realize his first systematic program of actor training. Included were courses in Commedia dell'arte taught by Vladimir Solovyev, and in "Musical Reading," taught by Gnesin. Later, Meyerhold invited a dancer from the Marinsky theatre, Aleksandr Chekrygin, to teach dancing and the circus performers, Giacomino and Donat Donato, to teach acrobatics. But central to the curriculum was Meyerhold's own course on movement training. As early as 1907, he had attacked the naturalistic theatre for ignoring movement as an expressive means in the theatre and for not including physical culture as a basic subject in its theatre schools.[27] Now, with his own studio he was able for the first time to work out a broad program of movement training.

Prelude to Biomechanics: The Sixteen Études

Together with Vladimir Solovyov, Meyerhold devised a series of sixteen études abstracted from a variety of theatrical traditions, including Commedia dell'arte and the Elizabethan and Asian theatres. These études, and others that the students themselves devised, were intended to teach the students a number of specific principles of scenic movement: Guglielmo's law of *partiere di terreno* (literally, "apportionment of the terrain," or what Meyerhold would later call "having a good eye"); how to move in certain patterns (circle, square, or triangle); how the alternation of the numbers of even and odd characters on stage affect the style of acting; the relationship between movement and the shape of the acting platform or proscenium boundaries; the traditional "antics appropriate to the theatre," involving the contrast between the space-and-time realities of the stage and life; the relationship between the metric basis of music and movement (including the idea of pauses in movement); working with stage properties; and generally the effects of acting on the spectator (the difference between large and small gestures).[28] These études, some of which were performed publicly on February 12, March 2, and March 29, 1915, in conjunction with other pantomimes and sketches, laid the foundation for what ultimately became Biomechanics.[29]

Although the only detailed documentation we have of the études are a course description of the class conducted by Meyerhold and Solovyov, and those few that were demonstrated in 1915, the titles and brief generic descriptions themselves provide the reader with some information as to their possible use in actor training:

1. Two Baskets, or Who Got the Better of Whom. An étude composed of "antics appropriate to the theatre."
2. Two Jongleurs, an Old Woman with a Snake, and the Bloody Climax under the Canopy.
3. Ophelia. An étude of the mad scene from *Hamlet*.
4. The Story of the Page Who Was Faithful to His Master and of Other Events Worthy of Presentation. An étude treated in the style of a sentimental, late seventeenth-century story (performed on the main stage; training in slow motion).
5. Arlecchino, the Vendor of Bastinadoes. A pantomime in the style of the French harlequinade of 1850 ("antics appropriate to the theatre").
6. Fragment of a Chinese Play — "The Catwoman, the Bird, and the Snake." (The use of Chinese scenic conventions as might be interpreted by Carlo Gozzi; use of mise en scène to create illusion of more characters than actually appear.)
7. The Two Esmeraldinas. A sketch from a Commedia scenario.
8. Collin Maillard. An étude performed in profile in the manner of Lancret's paintings.
9. The Street Jongleurs. A pantomime in the style of the popular perfor-

mances of late eighteenth-century Venice (use of stage audience to guide emotions of real audience; acting on two levels; "antics appropriate to the theatre").
10. From Five Chairs to a Quadrille. An étude in the manner of the 1840s.
11. The Baker and the Chimney Sweep. An étude.
12. The Loss of the Handbags.
13. The Cord.
14. Three of Them.
15. Three Oranges, the Astrological Telescope, or What One's Love for the Stage Masters May Lead To. A circus *buffonade* (use of trick properties; "antics appropriate to the theatre").
16. How They Carried Out Their Intentions.[30]

With these sixteen études, Meyerhold attempted to create a limited and precise system that would encompass all the fundamental expressive situations an actor would encounter on the stage. They differed from his later Biomechanics in a purely functional manner—the Sixteen Études pertained mainly to Meyerhold's pre-Revolutionary studio work, which was a synthesis of many traditional theatre conventions, while Biomechanics, based on physiological principles of movement, was designed as a more universal system for many kinds of theatre. No doubt Solovyov's and Meyerhold's failure to discover actual Elizabethan or Commedia training techniques heavily influenced their decision to create such a system. Yet, even beyond their format, the Sixteen Études bear other resemblances to Biomechanics, for example, in the circus *buffonades* and in the use of shouts and cries instead of words.

Valery Inkizhinov's arrival at the studio on Borodinskaya in October 1916 undoubtedly also played a role in the early development of what was to become Meyerhold's system of Biomechanics. As one of the studio members, Aleksandra Smirnova-Iskander, recalled, "He captivated all of us, and especially Meyerhold, with his virtuoso acrobatic and plastic technique. The flexibility and dexterity of his movements were supernatural, calling to mind the plasticity of a tiger, of a cat."[31] Together with Inkizhinov, Meyerhold began working out various exercises based on acrobatics essential for the actor. Later, when Meyerhold formed his State Higher Theatre Workshops (GVTM) in 1921, he would invite Inkizhinov to teach Biomechanics there.

Theatrical October

Meyerhold had nothing but disdain for the "languid indifference" of the bourgeois audiences that filled the Imperial theatres before the 1917 Revolution. More to his liking were the wounded soldiers who attended rehearsals at his studio. Their enthusiastic response prompted him to write that "they constitute the very audience for which the new theatre, the truly popular theatre is intended."[32] Still, it would be misleading to suggest that Meyerhold immediately embraced the Bolshevik cause. Like the vast majority of the artistic intelligentsia, he was hostile to the Leninists and the aims of the Bolsheviks. Aside from a brief foray into propaganda theatre following the outbreak of war in the autumn of 1914, Meyerhold had remained largely apolitical in his theatrical work. He consistently rejected the use of the theatre as a platform for solving social and philosophical problems. As he stated in an interview in 1913, defining the role of the theatre, "Such a theatre destroys its own theatricality.... The stage is a world of marvels and enchantment; it is breathless joy and strange magic."[33]

In the chaotic days following the February Revolution, Meyerhold took an active part in the formation of a Union of Workers in the Arts, an organization whose main objective was to establish complete autonomy in the arts. Meyerhold also participated in meetings and debates, including one on "Revolution and Theatre," held on April 14. In an impassioned speech he expressed his belief that the theatre was by its very nature revolutionary. Again condemning the "sleepy, indifferent [audience] in the parterre," he asserted that "only with the arrival of the proletariat in the parterre would the theatre take on a new life."[34]

Throughout these months of uncertainty, Meyerhold continued to direct at the former Imperial theatres.[35] With the lifting of censorship, he was able for the first time to stage all three parts of Sukhovo-Koblyin's trilogy: *Krechinsky's Wedding*, *The Case*, and *The Death of Tarelkin*. Of these, the most successful was *The Death of Tarelkin*, which premièred just three days before the Bolsheviks took power in October 1917.[36]

Following the October Revolution, and apparently with some persuasion from Vladimir Mayakovsky, Meyerhold did not delay long in supporting the artistic program of the Bolsheviks.[37] When the newly appointed People's Commissar of Enlightenment, Anatoly Lunacharsky, called a meeting in November of one hundred twenty leading members of the Petrograd artistic community to discuss the reorganization of the arts, only five people turned up: Natan Altman, Aleksandr Blok, Ryurik Ivnev, Mayakovsky, and Meyerhold. Aside from being the oldest and the most experienced, he was also the only theatre practitioner present.[38] Meyerhold's shift to the left was interpreted by many of his fellow artists as a blatantly opportunistic maneuver. But for Meyerhold, allying himself with the Bolsheviks was undoubtedly not so much a matter of ideological affinity as it was an opportunity to realize freely the ideas he had been developing over the years for transforming the bourgeoise theatre. "I joined up with the revolution," Vladimir Blyum recalls Meyerhold telling him in 1920, "because with one blow it had cut all the knots which up to then had to be torturously untangled."[39]

Meyerhold had never felt at home working in the hostile atmosphere of the Imperial theatres. As he told Smirnova-Isksander, one of the members of his studio on Borodinskaya, on meeting her outside the stage door of the Alexandrinsky Theatre in the fall of 1915, "Not once in all my years of employment . . . have I gone in or come out of that door without a feeling of fear and apprehension that I might be stabbed in the back with a dagger."[40] Perhaps now, at last, he would be able to bring together under one roof in his own theatre his experimental work in training actors with his professional activities as a director, something he had always had to keep separate while affiliated with the Imperial theatres, even to the extent of adopting the pseudonym of Doctor Dapertutto for his studio work.

In August 1918, Meyerhold became a member of the Communist Party, and Anatoly Lunacharsky appointed him deputy head for Petrograd of the Theatrical Department of the People's Commissariat of Public Enlightenment (Narkompros). For the first anniversary of the Revolution, Meyerhold staged in three short weeks Mayakovsky's *Mystery-Bouffe*, with set designs by Kazimir Malevich. Shortly afterwards, on November 16, 1918, Meyerhold resigned his position as director at the Marinsky Theatre, thus ending a decade of association with the Imperial theatres.

One of Meyerhold's first decisions as deputy head of Narkompros, was to organize in collaboration with Leonid S. Viven a broad program of "Courses in the Mastery of Stage Production." The objective of this sixteen-month program was, "the creation of new cadres of well-prepared actors, the raising of the level of acting forces in the country, and the dissemination of special knowledge related to the techniques of acting."[41]

Included in the program was an ambitious regime dedicated to the "Technique of Stage Movement." Its emphasis on physical training clearly indicated the direction in which Meyerhold was now heading:

    1. Gymnastics—not directed at a one-sided development of physical strength, but at the development and strengthening of flexibility and agility:
        a. Exercises with sticks and bottles;
        b. Equipment exercises: horses, parallel bars, trapezes, steps, vertical bars;
        c. Jumping—high jump, leap from a height, broad jump;
        d. Gymnastics with a partner.
       Recommended Sports:
        1. Running
        2. Discus throwing

3. Horseback riding
   4. Equestrian acrobatics
   5. Lawn tennis
   6. Sailing
   7. Skiing
 2. Fencing (foils, swords)
 3. Juggling
   a. Training of the hands in handling objects.
   b. Strengthening of the torso.
   c. Training in concentration.
4. Dancing:
   a. Classical exercises.
5. Stage Movement:
   The Course in Stage Movement:
   a. Formulates, especially in the conditions of the Theatre of Drama's special stage objectives, exercise material for the student in a series of other classes.
   b. Tests and develops the emotionality of the student.
   Work:
   a. The laws of movement;
   b. Schematization of movement;
   c. The achievement of rhythm in movement;
   d. The development of a sense of time;
   e. The establishment of a connection between emotions and movements;
   f. Improvisation of movements (without a theme, to a theme).
6. Supplementary Subjects:
   1. Music
      a. Elementary course;
      b. Play on some instrument;
      c. rhythmic gymnastics.
   2. Singing: *Solfeggio*, chorus, solo, duet.
   3. Drawing: Ability to draw from memory: position, pose, face, costume, plan, etc.
7. Scientific-theoretical Subjects:
   1. Anatomy and physiology (basic principles).
   2. Theatrical science and scenic science.
   3. The establishment of analogies between various forms of art. The place of theatre as a synthesis of the arts among other arts.
   4. Pantomime, dance (general information).
   5. Versification.
   6. Psychology of emotions (basic principles).

Among the teachers was a Dr. A. I. Petrov, a teacher of anatomy and biomechanics who, in Vivien's words taught gymnastics "according to a new system."[42]

Meyerhold eagerly threw himself into his new teaching activities until ill health forced him to leave Petrograd in May 1919, to undergo treatment for tuberculosis in Yalta. When the White Army took over Yalta, Meyerhold joined his family, then living in Novorossisk. While there, Meyerhold was imprisoned and barely escaped execution by the Whites. For a time following his liberation by the Red Army, Meyerhold stayed on in Novorossisk, even managing to produce one play, Ibsen's *A Doll's House*.

Meyerhold remained in the Crimea until the autumn of 1920, when Lunacharsky summoned him back to Moscow to become head of the Theatre Department (TEO) of the Commissariat of Education. Meyerhold immediately took over editorship of the theatre journal, *The Theatre Courier*, and began calling for the revolutionizing of the entire theatrical system, which at the time was in a state of complete disarray.

In addition to assuming these duties, Meyerhold also took over the Free Theatre Company. Combining it with the remnants of two other defunct theatres, he renamed it the R.S.F.S.R. Theatre No. 1. As a demonstration of his vision of revolutionary theatre, Meyerhold began rehearsing *The Dawns*, an epic verse drama by the Belgian Symbolist poet Émil Verhaern. Meyerhold planned the production as a political meeting with a chorus in the orchestra pit and actors planted in the auditorium to stimulate audience response. Flyers were floated down from the balconies and announcements were made that shouting and whistling were allowed during the performance. While the production, which premièred on the third anniversary of the October Revolution, proved to be something of an embarrassment for the Communist critics, including Lenin's wife, Nadezhda Krupskaya, workers and Red Army soldiers filled the theatre at every performance. It ran for more than one hundred performances.

Meyerhold saw his production of *The Dawns* as a manifesto against the pre-Revolutionary theatre. Choosing the Red Banner as the theatre's emblem (as the seagull was for the Moscow Art Theatre), he called for a transformation of the actor's psychological makeup. "No pauses, no psychology and 'experiencing' either on the stage, or in working on a role.... A lot of light, joy, grandeur and infectiousness, light-hearted creativity, involvement of the audience in the action and in the collective creation of the performace—this is our theatre program."[43]

Meyerhold also became interested at this time in the work in physical culture the Red Army was doing. It had initally attracted his attention in Petrograd during preparations for the mass spectacles to celebrate the first anniversary of the Revolution. In Novorossisk and later in Moscow, Meyerhold lent his support to Nikolai I. Podvoisky's program of the theatricalization of physical culture entitled *Vsevobuch* (*Vseobshchee voennoe obuchenie* [General Military Training]), based on the work of the

All-Russia Red Stadium. At a meeting, "*Vsevobuch* and Art," held on December 9, 1920, Meyerhold proclaimed:

> The artistic world must rally around the new army and lay down the principles of a new, proletarian culture. Only on new stages can that new theatre we are timidly seeking in laboratory work be born. For the creation of the new theatre, living material capable of performing a revolutionary repertoire is essential. Movement is the basis of theatrical spectacle. First movement, then emotion leading to the word, and then the word itself. And in the mass spectacle, first an enormous silent wave, the spreading of movement, a great accumulation of emotion and finally the great word.[44]

Shortly after delivering this speech, Meyerhold took over the Theatricalization of Physical Culture (Tefizkult), a Subdivision of the Theatrical Department (TEO) of the Main Political Education Committee (Glavpolitprosvet). The organizers of Tefizkult envisioned a broad program that would unite the R.S.F.S.R. Theatre No. 1 (the former Zon Theatre) with the Second State Circus (the former circus of the Nikitin brothers) and the garden of the former Aquarium (all adjoining each other on Triumphant Square [now Mayakovsky Square]) to form a Tefizkult Village. Their objectives were to develop a "new system of work gymnastics (theatrical sports training of the work gesture)," to form a laboring mass to take part in mass spectacles, to establish the basis for the scientific organization of labor, and finally, to lay the foundations for a proletarian theatre "closely tied to the principles of physical culture."[45]

Efforts to create a Tefizkult Village came to naught when the Moscow District Party Committee turned the Aquarium over to the Maly Theatre for the summer. Because of a lack of funding, Meyerhold's plans to realize the objectives of Tefizkult with a mass spectacle in honor of the Third Congress of the Komintern also remained on the drawing boards. Entitled "Struggle and Victory," this monumental spectacle designed by Aleksandr Vesnin and Lyubov Popova was to have taken place on Moscow's Khodynsky Field, with 2,300 Red Army soldiers, 200 men on horseback, 16 cannons, five airplanes, tanks, motorcycles, searchlights, military bands, choirs and gymnasts taking part.

Meanwhile, Meyerhold did succeed in staging a second version of Mayakovsky's *Mystery-Bouffe* as a popular political review incorporating acrobatic and circus antics by the circus performer, Vitaly Lazarenko, whom Meyerhold invited especially for the production. This time Meyerhold eliminated the proscenium entirely, setting the action on a series of platforms connected by steps with a ramp leading down into the audience. The production opened on May 1, 1921, to negative reviews by critics who objected to its futuristic obscurantism. But *Mystery-Bouffe* was a great success with audiences that found the cartoon-like characterizations of the

"Unclean" and Igor Ilinsky's clowning in the role of "The Conciliator," or Menshivik, enormously appealing. It played to some 120,000 spectators in the five months of its existence.

In June 1921 the Moscow Soviet ordered the closing of the R.S.F.S.R. Theatre No. 1 as a money-losing operation and on September 6, 1921, it went out of business, one of the victims of Lenin's New Economic Policy (NEP). The advent of NEP also marked the end of Meyerhold's self-proclaimed Theatrical October and left the leading Bolshevik director without a theatre.

Chapter 2

Meyerhold: From Biomechanics to the Triumph of Socialist Realism

> *In my Biomechanics, I was able to define in all twelve or thirteen rules for the training of an actor. But in polishing it up, I'll leave perhaps no more than eight.*[1]
>
> V. E. Meyerhold

The closing of the R.S.F.S.R. Theatre No. 1 was a serious blow to Meyerhold's reputation, but in the long run it proved a blessing. By then Meyerhold was already aware that the Futurist movement in the post–Revolutionary theatre, inaugurated by his own productions of *Mystery-Bouffe* and *The Dawns* had reached a dead end. But what was to take its place?

As director of a newly-created State Higher Directors (later Theatre), Workshops (GVRM-GVTM), in the autumn of 1921 Meyerhold gathered together some one hundred young students and began training them as future actors and directors.[2] Meyerhold's inclusion in the curriculum of a course new to theatre schools — Biomechanics — and his decision to develop in the Workshops the principles of scenic Constructivism gave some hint of the revolution he was about to launch.

Four years after the Revolution, with the demise of the mass spectacle movement, the decline in the general quality of the proletarian theatres became increasingly obvious. "Stereotypes, clichés, psychosis, formlessness" is the way one writer characterized the performances of these proletarian groups performing in factories and clubs.[3] Although Meyerhold continued to place the utmost importance in the development of amateur and semiprofessional workers' troupes as both an educational and social tool for the masses and as a bulwark against the bourgeois academic theatres, he too was deeply dissatisfied with their clumsy and ineffectual attempts at acting.

Lacking any formal training, many of the new mass actors simply mounted the stage and gracelessly declaimed speeches, very much in the manner of a provincial melodrama protagonist without regard to the mise en scène, stage size, or audience. The irony lay, Meyerhold felt, in the fact that the theatre, whose social function was to educate and promote the socialist and scientific reconstruction of Russia, had retreated to archaic and basically primitive forms. Whereas other sectors of Soviet society were already going through a process of rapid collectivization and industrialization, the theatre continued to cling to the past.

If the theatre was to survive and play a dynamic part in the future Soviet culture, then it too would have to be transformed by the same factors that were guiding the rest of Soviet life. Thus, drawing on the scientific methodologies that were then current in Soviet industry and culture (Taylorism) and in Soviet psychology and education (reflexology), Meyerhold began formulating his own scientific foundations for actor training, "the laws of Biomechanics."

Taylorism

The work of Frederick Winslow Taylor, the American industrial engineer who pioneered the study of scientific management at the turn of the century, became widely known throughout Europe in the early 1900s, including Russia, where Taylorist experiments were first conducted following the 1905 Revolution.[4] Although initially hostile toward Taylorism, by 1914 Lenin himself, held up Taylor's principles of scientific management as a primary example of those achievements of capitalism, which, however, brutal and exploitive in intent—the augmentation of work output and resulting profits—represented a grand and revolutionary approach to the entire work process worthy of Soviet emulation.

Investigating each work unit on a production line, Taylor came to the conclusion that the worker's physical movements were among the least efficient in the entire work process. In factories and mills, the worker would often engage in superfluous and awkward motions, causing a premature strain in his muscles and generally lowering his work output. Analyzing the execution of each work task according to precise motions, which he timed and regulated within fractions of a second, Taylor sought to find the most efficient movements and gestures for each kind of activity. Calling his study "motion economy," Taylor had soon to take into account such nonlinear and unmechanical factors as work rhythms, balance, muscular groupings, fatigue, and "rest minutes." Through trial and error, Taylor developed a system of "work cycles," each involving a whole network of movements and pauses, allowing the laborer to produce the greatest output with the least amount of strain.

Although Taylor seemed to relish the variance and multiplicity of detail in his movement analyses, many of his American followers sought to delimit and abstract certain principles from his study of motion economy in order to make them more universal. (Frank and Lillian Gilbreth had already discovered in 1912 sixteen fundamental hand movements [*therbligs*] that were cross-occupational.) After Taylor's death in 1915, several such generalized tables began to appear. From these, seven fundamental Taylorist principles on the use of the human body in the work process evolved:

1. Smooth, continuous, curved motions of the hands are preferable to straight-line motions involving sudden sharp changes in direction.
2. Both hands should begin and complete their actions simultaneously.
3. The two hands should never be idle at the same time, except during work pauses.
4. Motions of the arms should be made in opposite and symmetrical directions, and should be made simultaneously.
5. Hand and body motions should be confined to those muscles that require the least amount of exertion (usually the fingers, forearm, and shoulder).
6. Movements involving single contraction of a positive muscle group are faster, easier, and more accurate than movements caused by sets of antagonistic muscles.
7. Rhythmic movements are, generally, the most efficient.[5]

Aleksei K. Gastev, the foremost Soviet Taylorist and head of the Central Institute of Labor (TsIT), founded in 1921, went even further than his American counterparts in the reduction of Taylor's principles. Taylor's theories of scientific management had already become a subject of heated debate among Russian scientists and intellectuals even before the Revolution. Under the name Scientific Organization of Labor (NOT), Gastev's version of Taylorism won further endorsement by both Lenin and Trotsky following the First All-Russian Initiating Conference on the Scientific Organization of Labor, convened in January 1921.[6]

A poet as well as a trade unionist, Gastev represented a special utopian strain in Bolshevik culture. Frequently cited as an unrelenting "Fordist," Gastev called for the mechanization of every aspect of Soviet life. Not only the workplace, but the field and living quarters of every worker were to be subject to the scientific dictates of motion economy. And whether or not a worker was of proletarian or peasant origin meant little to this "Ovid of engineers, miners and metal workers."[7] Gastev maintained that once a worker attained perfect mastery over the handling of (a) the hammer, (b) the knife, and (c) the pick, he would be able to operate any piece of machinery, no matter how complex. All Soviet citizens, according to Gastev's exhortations, had the capacity to become super-efficient, to merge with the machine. In fact, at his Laboratory No. 7 in Moscow, Gastev designed an apparatus to "force" mechanical productivity from each worker.

This basic idea—the single, outwardly simple, yet complex and difficult pedagogical device—had a special appeal for Meyerhold, whose Biomechanics became synonymous with Taylorism in the theatre, with Meyerhold being hailed as the "Taylor of the Theatre." Although Meyerhold was happy to ride the wave of Taylorist popularity in the early twenties, there were significant differences between Gastev's objectives as a social engineer in transforming workers into efficient producers and Meyerhold's Biomechanical training for actors whose primary objective was not worker output, but the achievement of maximum expressiveness on the stage.

Reflexology

Shortly before 1900, several schools of "objective psychology" arose independently in America and Russia. While differing in their findings and temperament, they shared similar sentiments toward the introspective trends in psychology, which they vigorously attacked. Rejecting the notion of the soul outright and minimizing the significance of the intangible unconscious, the "objectivists" looked for other ways of explaining behavior.

Unable to exorcise his states of severe depression through his own mental faculties, William James, the American psychologist, began to investigate the actual visceral nature of emotion. Many of the folk maxims that prescribed seemingly irrational, secondary actions for the reduction of unpleasant emotional states—such as, "Whistle when you pass a graveyard" or "When you're so angry that you can't speak, just count to ten"—he surmised were nothing more than the application of effective reflex reactions. Experimenting on himself, James concluded that emotional consciousness and its transitory states were directly linked to the physical body; in fact, the body's automatic response to stimuli itself was the emotion, preceding the mental perception of the emotion. Using the dictum, "I saw the bear, I ran, I became frightened," James attempted to demonstrate the physiological basis of his theory. The act of running, not the bear, caused the fright. Or as Meyerhold put it: to trigger the sensation of fear, a person would only have to run—with his eyebrows raised and pupils dilated. Regardless of what the person was stimulated by or thinking, an automatic reflex signifying fear would be felt throughout his body. Surprisingly, James shied away from any formalized theory or system, believing that while certain patterns of muscular activity elicited certain emotional states, each of these states varied with the individual body and were, therefore, infinite and unclassifiable.

In Russia at this time, Vladimir Bekhterev had already begun his research toward the discovery of the precise laws that govern human reflexive action and behavior, or reflexology. Like James and Ivan Pavlov, whose studies of conditioned reflexes in animals were linked to his own, Bekhterev rejected the old subjectivist psychology as intuitive and unscientific. Working with children and groups of criminals, he formulated his theory of "associated motor reflexes": all human behavior can be explained by the pattern of reflexes produced by the environment in the individual's nervous system. Once fully developed, Bekhterev maintained, the science of reflexology would eventually replace psychology, since all human motivation and behavior could then not only be understood and predicted according to immutable laws of biology and sociology, but instantly changed under laboratory conditions.

In 1908 Bekhterev founded in St. Petersburg the Psychoneurological Institute, which he headed until his death in 1927. Although he himself was unable to provide a large body of supportive data, his theories were widely circulated among physiologists, psychologists, and educators even before the Revolution.[8]

Pyotr Lesgaft and His Program of Physical Education

The father of modern physical education in Russia, Pyotr Lesgaft began his career in 1861 at the St. Petersburg Academy of Medicine, where he taught anatomy.[9] In 1874, Lesgaft was placed in charge of the physical training of military cadets. Following two summers spent studying physical education programs in Western Europe, he began developing his own program of physical education for military schools.

Simultaneously with his pedagogical work for the military, Lesgaft also turned his attention to developing programs of physical education for civilians. As secretary of the "Society for the Encouragement of the Physical Development of Student Youth" which he founded in 1892, Lesgaft began propagandizing programs for the physical development of children and young people. He also established the "Courses for Teachers and Supervisors of Physical Education" (or Lesgaft's "Higher Courses" as they came to be known), the first civilian program for instructors in physical education. In the wake of the 1905 revolution, Lesgaft was charged with fomenting student unrest and his teaching activities were curtailed. Nevertheless, two years after his death in 1909, these "Higher Courses" were allowed to reopen and following the October Revolution, in 1919 they became the foundation for the Lesgaft State Institute of Physical Education.

Fundamental to Lesgaft's program of physical education was his theory of the close relationship between physical and mental development. An opponent of special gymnastic equipment, he argued that its use dulled the emotions. Lesgaft also opposed those systems of physical training based on the rote repetition of exercises, as well as those in which participants passively carried out the commands of instructors, all of which, in Lesgaft's view, called forth movements unconnected with thought. "Each movement must be explained in advance, including how it should be carried out and for what purpose," he noted.[10] Only in this way, Lesgaft believed, does a person learn to force his actions to obey clear, distinct thoughts while at the same time training his thoughts to express themselves in motivated actions.

Lesgaft strongly advocated providing physical education instructors and athletes with a firm foundation in functional anatomy (including a knowledge of biomechanics). Only through the unity of physical and mental development, he argued, could a person learn to efficiently control his body. He also stressed the importance of a gradual program of physical training, beginning with very simple movements and moving on to exercises of increasing complexity. In subsequent stages of training, the student learns to harmonize his movements in time and space and in relation to objects around him. Thus, as James Riordan notes in summarizing Lesgaft's philosophy, "At each stage of physical education, different, increasingly complicated, pedagogical aims are pursued, the main purpose being to teach the [student] consciously to master the movements of his body and to attain the best results with the minimum energy and time expenditure."[11]

Meyerhold and the "Laws of Biomechanics"

In Meyerhold's Constructivist vision of the theatre as factory and schoolroom—the use of the fastest and most efficient methods (Taylorism) to produce a predetermined audience reaction (reflexology)—we find a total emphasis on work output, i.e., the manufacture of effects in the spectator, creating a desired state of mind. Allowing for the fact that there were a finite number of effects and states of mind, the Constructivist director-engineer was free to calibrate the theatrical components at his disposal (dramatic text, performing space, scenery, properties, costuming, lighting, styles of acting, speech, music, tempo, etc.) in virtually inexhaustible combinations, toward a single goal. In this, the Constructivist director worked much like Taylor, who approached each task differently, seeking a unique strategy for the execution of economic and efficient movements.

On the other hand, Meyerhold, like Gastev, was searching for certain core movements that would train the new precision worker in the efficient execution of all of his prescribed tasks. Even the training system itself would have to be a model of economy: a concise, but comprehensive, program that would require a minimum amount of time to learn. (The number of biomechanical exercises varied from seven to more than twenty, generally staying at twelve or thirteen.) Just as Gastev created a whole series of paradigmatic working movements from the perfect execution of a seemingly unsophisticated task like swinging a pick, which was unlike any of the complex machinery Gastev's workers were being trained to operate, Meyerhold fashioned each of his biomechanical exercises to contain complex bundles of physical activity that superficially appeared to be simple and unrelated to the Constructivist acting styles. Yet, every exercise was to be a fountainhead of lessons in the development of expressive movement, culminating in a system that utilized every essential principle in scenic movement that an actor might encounter.

Taking stock of his extensive theatrical background, Meyerhold selected and refined his biomechanical exercises from a host of sources that he found most dynamic or "theatrical" — circus, music hall, boxing, gymnastics, military discipline, the Chinese theatre, and Kabuki, as well as those theatrical cultures from which he devised the Sixteen Études in his pre–Revolutionary studio work on stage movement. Dividing each gesture of the études into exact movements, Meyerhold was able to apply both Taylorist principles of motion economy and James' emotion theory to the actor, causing him to experience automatically an entire gamut of emotions due to a constantly changing arrangement of his musculature. This would also enable the actor, like the Lesgaft-trained athlete, to establish precisely the relationship between his physical actions and his own inner feelings. As Meyerhold told Harold Clurman in 1935, "Each exercise is a melodrama. Each movement gives the actor a sense of performing on the stage."[12]

One of Meyerhold's students recalled:

> Meyerhold began with the technique of stage movement, gesture, and the control of objects on the stage. The exercises developed into études, and from

études into pantomimes. Thus, from the exercise "Shooting the Bow and Arrow" the étude "Hunting" evolved and from it a pantomime which was used to train each "generation" of the Studio.[13]

Other elements of Taylorism and reflexology were directly incorporated into Biomechanics. Meyerhold's conception of the "acting chain" (Intention; Realization; and Reaction, Recoil, or Point of Repetition) was closely modeled after Taylor's "working cycles" and functioned similarly. Also Pavlov's conditioning experiments were employed mainly with sound stimuli to perfect the actor's state of "reflex excitabilty," his ability to realize an externally prescribed task with the minimum amount of forethought.

The Term "Biomechanics"

No clear evidence has been found indicating precisely when Meyerhold gave the name "Biomechanics" to his system of movement training for actors, or where he derived it from. It is characteristic of Meyerhold that he never publicly stated the source himself.

As "the science of the action of forces, internal or external, on the living body," the term "biomechanics," was already in scientific usage in Russia as well as in the West by the beginning of the century. As already noted, Lesgaft included it in his courses on physical education and at least one book on the subject had already been published in St. Petersburg as early as 1910.[14]

The generally-held notion is that Meyerhold took the term "biomechanics" from Aleksei Gastev.[15] But there seems to be no solid evidence to support this. To be sure, the two men knew each other, although it is not quite clear just when they first became acquainted: in St. Petersburg in 1917–1918, or later, after Gastev moved to Moscow in 1920. In any case, because of their mutual interest in some form of scientifically-based physical training, their paths frequently crossed in the 1920s. In 1921 Gastev was listed as one of those "directing the work" of Meyerhold's Directors Workshops.[16] Although there is presently no evidence that Gastev took an active part in the Workshops' program, he was, as his son Aleksei recalls, a devoted fan of Meyerhold's Theatre and frequently attended performances there.[17] Both men also sat on the board of Platon Kerzhentsev's League of Time.

As an early enthusiast of Taylorism, Gastev's initial interest had been mainly focused on developing a "methodology of organization" and the training of "social engineers." It was only later, as the head of the Central Institute of Labor (TsIT), founded in September 1920, where Gastev began his research in Motion Economy, that he speaks of biomechanics as a methodology for training of workers. The the word itself first appears in his article, "How Work Should Be Done," in *Pravda*, June 11, 1922, that is, some time after Meyerhold began using the term.

This is not to suggest that the reverse was necessarily true, that Gastev took the term from Meyerhold. Rather, the most plausible hypothesis is, as Gastev's son has noted, that they were both drawing on the same sources, including the work of scientists such as Bekhterev, who chaired the First All-Russia Conference on NOT held in Moscow in January 1920, and Nikolai Bernshtein, who joined Gastev's Institute of labor in 1922 to head the Biomechanical Laboratory.[18]

The first public use of the term Biomechanics as applied to actor training appeared in an article Meyerhold wrote, together with Valery Bebutov and Konstantin Derzhavin, entitled "Theatrical Leaflets. I. On Dramaturgy and the Culture of Theatre," published on April 5, 1921.[19] The article, in proposing a culture of physical expressiveness based on the precise laws of biomechanics and kinetics, attacked both the "pseudoscience" of "questionable laws of psychology" [the Moscow Art Theatre] and the "worn-out, decrepit bodies of the intellectual darlings, those 'bath-house attendants' and 'barefoot dancers' making merry in the world of tonal-plastic nonsense [Isadora Duncan and Pletnev]."[20]

It is very likely that Meyerhold was already familiar with the term biomechanics before returning to Moscow at the beginning of September 1920. A report issued by the Student Information Bureau (STINF) at Meyerhold's own Workshop states that Meyerhold's use of the word dates back to 1918.[21] The fact that anatomy and physiology were among the subjects included in the "Courses in the Mastery of Stage Production" Meyerhold and Vivien announced in September of that year would lend credence to the supposition that Meyerhold was by then familiar with the term, all the more since a teacher of anatomy and biomechanics, Dr. A. I. Petrov, was, as already mentioned earlier, included among the faculty members.

The Function of Biomechanics

Meyerhold developed Biomechanics as a standardized but minimal program for the training of the Revolutionary actor. Its goal was to instruct the new actor in all the essentials of scenic movement. But it was expected that each studio and performing group would go beyond it. For instance, in a Ukrainian Proletkult troupe the actors might study, in addition to Biomechanics, medieval Ukrainian military drills, gymnastics, modern dance techniques, choral speech, and diction. In an amateur workers' club theatre, where the actors might be severely restricted in time and training space, only machine movements, verse reading, and Biomechanics might be practiced. Biomechanics was to be the common training link and the basic discipline of actor training in the Proletarian and Constructivist theatres.

When Meyerhold gave his first public demonstration of Biomechanics on June 12, 1922, seated in the audience were some two dozen members of the First Workers Theatre of the Moscow Proletkult. Already dissatisfied with the "Tonal-plastics" system of actor training that had been introduced by Evgeny Prosvetov, the Moscow Proletkult decided shortly afterwards to replace it with Biomechanics. If earlier, movement had occupied only a minor place in the lesson plan of the First Workers Theatre, beginning in the fall of 1922 it assumed primary importance. By the end of the year, Biomechanics was officially adopted as part of the physical culture curriculum for all Proletkult studios and clubs.[22] Other theatres and studios followed suit, and before long Meyerhold and his instructors were teaching Biomechanics at Efraim Loiter's Jewish Studio, at the Bolshoi Theatre, the Theatre of the Revolution, and at other theatres and studios as well.[23] In his memoirs actor Lev Sverdlin also recalls being sent by Meyerhold to teach Biomechanics at the Uzbek Theatre Studio organized in Moscow at the end of 1924.[24] The Department of State Academic Theatres even approached Meyerhold about introducing Biomechanics into their teaching program, though in the end nothing came of it.

In Meyerhold's own Workshops, besides Biomechanics, the actors were trained by professionals in fencing, boxing, Dalcroze Eurhythmics, classical ballet, floor gymnastics, modern dance, "tripod positioning," cabaret dance, juggling, diction, speech, and music. They were also schooled in many other disciplines that Meyerhold felt would be useful to the actor for a particular production or for his general education, such as practice in pre-acting, theatrical history, economics, biology. Clearly, the greater the number of movement skills at the actor's disposal, the more efficiently he could carry out a variety of tasks.

The Magnanimous Cuckold

For the first production with his newly trained actors, Meyerhold chose Crommelynck's *The Magnanimous Cuckold*, which he mounted in 1922 with the assistance of artist Lyubov Popova.[25] Without question, Popova's elegantly abstract and yet kinetic stage construction for *The Cuckold* brought to the theatre a new ideal of beauty based on simplicity

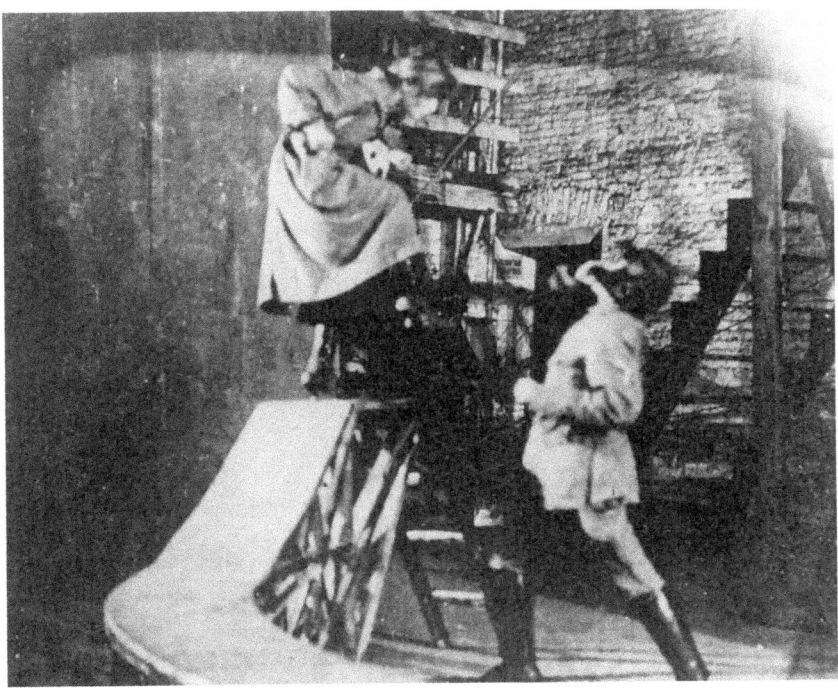

A scene from act 1 of Meyerhold's *The Magnanimous Cuckold*. Stella (Maria Babanova) runs up to the top of the bench. The Count (Maksim Tereshkovich) tries to grab her by the legs. She kicks out at him, saying, "You werewolf!"

and the undisguised use of real materials. But above all, it was as a machine for actors' play ("work" in Constructivist terms) that the construction was most successful. As the critic, Ivan Aksyonov pointed out, the actor "could play with this set like a fan or a cape."[26] By defining and structuring the spatial limits of the performing area, the construction aided the actors in much the same way that a properly designed machine enables a worker to produce more efficiently.

In looking back a number of years later, Meyerhold recalled to Gladkov that, "The *Cuckold* showed everyone that Biomechanics is not the 'arithmetic' of actor training, but already the 'algebra.'"[27] One eyewitness described the production, "The movement of the actors was acrobatic—up the ladders, down the chutes, through the doors and around the constructions with leaps, somersaults, dance, and march steps with a zest, rapidity and vitality that kept the audience in constant tension."[28] In fact, the actors' movements were so tightly choreographed that for every line of dialog in Meyerhold's promptbook there was a precise

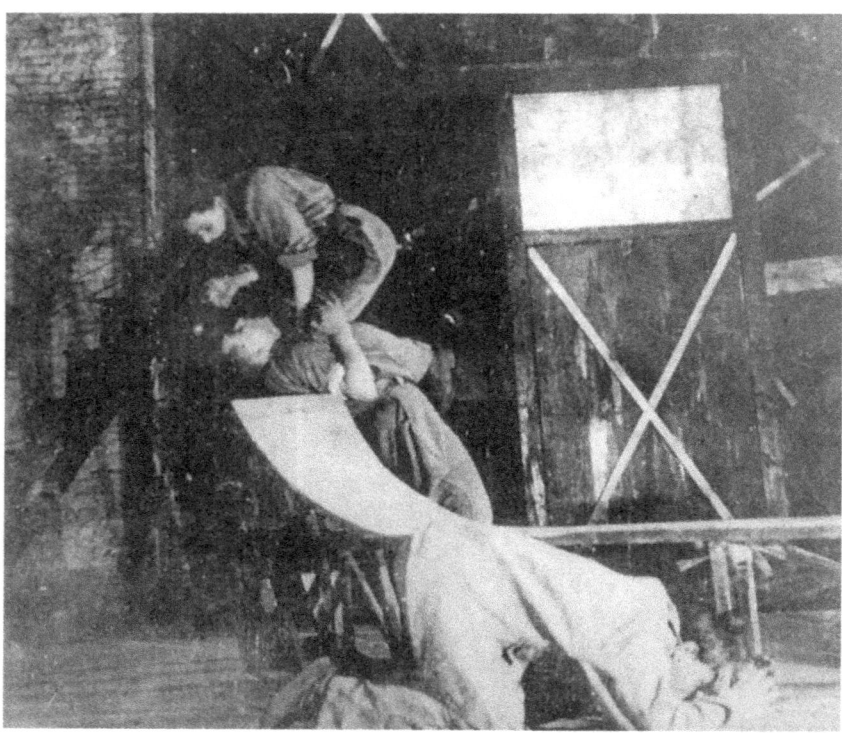

Meyerhold incorporated the biomechanical exercise "Leap on the Chest" into act 2 of his production of *The Magnanimous Cuckold:* The Cooper (Yuri I. Goltsev) comes through the right half of the revolving door. He looks at Bruno (Igor Ilinsky), slowly approaches, and in a flash leaps on his chest, raising his fist as if to strike Bruno on the jaw. Bruno: "Excuse me. It was an attack of lyricism." The Cooper slides to the floor.

description of the action on the stage. And for certain scenes, accompanying diagrams indicated the number of seconds allowed for the actor to move from one point on the stage to another.[29]

Meyerhold himself asserted that he had conceived of his production as "practice, so that the [Workshops] studies would not be merely scholastic, pure gymnastic training or an aesthetic variation of it."[30] *Cuckold* also served as a vehicle for demonstrating the efficacy of the newly-devised biomechanical exercises, and to this end Meyerhold actually incorporated several études into the production. For example, in the "Letter Scene" from act 2, two biomechanical études, "Slap on the Face" and "Leap on the Chest," are demonstrated. Bruno, a village scribe, learns that the Cooper wants him to write a love letter to Stella, Bruno's own wife. He reacts by giving the Cooper a "Slap on the Face." When the Cooper fails

2. Meyerhold: The Triumph of Socialist Realism   45

A scene from act 3 of Meyerhold's *The Magnanimous Cuckold*. The Cowherd (Nikolai Losev) is saved when Bruno (Igor Ilinsky) and Estrugo (Vasily Zaichikov) hide him under a cape at the end of the bench.

to respond with anything but a low moan, Bruno delivers a second, a third, a fourth "Slap," each time eliciting the same reaction. Finally on the fifth "Slap," the Cooper turns and walks slowly to the revolving door. He exits through the left half, and on reappearing through the right half of the door, the Cooper demonstrates a "Leap on the Chest":

> The Cooper pauses and looks at Bruno, then walks slowly towards Bruno and suddenly leaps on his chest. The COOPER raises his fist over Bruno's head. At Bruno's words, "Excuse me. It was an attack of lyricism," the COOPER slides down to the floor.[31]

Over the next two years, Meyerhold continued to incorporate citations from his biomechanical exercises into his productions, most notably in his eccentric staging in 1922 of Sukhovo-Kobylin's *The Death of Tarelkin* (on which Eisenstein worked as a "laboratory assistant"), and in *D.E.* (1924), a political agit-review based on Ilya Ehrenburg's *Trust D.E.* and Bernhard Kellermann's *The Tunnel*. For Meyerhold these citations were included mainly as a way of advertising his new system of actor training. And although in later years Western critics and theatre practitioners

Meyerhold's production of Sukhovo-Kobylin's *The Death of Tarelkin* (1922). Act 3, scene 8. Pakhomov, the yardkeeper (Nikolai Losev, center), is being grilled by Rasplyuev (Dimitrii Orlov, seated at right) with the help of Kachala (Nikolai Okhlopkov, far left) and Shatala (Nikolai Sibiryak), both of whom have their fists raised. In the cooler are Mme. Brandakhlystova (Mikhail Zharov, seated) and the landowner, Chvankin (Nikolai Mologin). Rasplyuev instructs Kachala to strike Shatala on the back of the head at his (Rasplyuev's) signal. Shatala in turn is to strike Pakhomov. Rasplyuev: "Now I can relax. The machinery will operate by itself." This scene typifies the incorporating of biomechanical movements into productions of the 1920s.

have at times referred to Meyerhold's Biomechanics as a "system of acting," nothing could be further from the truth.

Play with Objects

One of the lessons Meyerhold learned from his production of *The Magnanimous Cuckold* was that the most biomechanically effective elements of Popova's construction were those parts such as the revolving door which were dynamic, that is, which gave the actor something to play *with*. Clearly, the next step was to separate these components from the general construction. In effect, this is what Meyerhold did in *The Death of*

Tarelkin (1922), which he staged as a "montage of attractions" featuring special furniture designed by Varvara Stepanova. Each piece was constructed so that it would jump, collapse, or in some way respond to the actor.

In practice, however, the Tarelkin furniture proved so unreliable that it completely lost its effectiveness as an instrument for play. Rather than leading to the kind of precise and spirited acrobatics Meyerhold had envisioned, the furniture too often intimidated the actors, causing them to lose their nerve and physical authority. Mikhail Zharov recalls how Dimitrii Orlov as Tarelkin would sit on the "collapsing chair" as gingerly as if it were an electric chair. Still, there were some unforgettable moments, as when Zharov as Mrs. Brandakhlystova was required to pass through the "meat grinder" into the "cooler."

> I climbed the ladder to the top of the construction and from there dove head first, landing on the "meat grinder" blade, which was made of rigid plywood. Taking the handle of the "meat grinder," Kachala and Shatala cranked me through as I lay on one of the four blades. ...I made a half circle and on reaching the bottom, I crawled into the cage representing the "cooler."[32]

Meyerhold quickly abandoned the idea of building special play constructions, turning instead to the use of real objects having a defined function in everyday life. Thus for his staging in 1923 of *The Earth in Turmoil* (Sergei Tretyakov's reworking of Martinet's *La Nuit*), Meyerhold brought modern technology into the theatre for the first time: machine guns, automobiles, motorcycles, and mobile kitchens. Such documentary authenticity was particularly appropriate for this agitprop production, which on a number of occasions was performed out-of-doors for audiences numbering as many as 25,000.

By 1924, the revolutionary euphoria of Theatrical October was waning and Meyerhold began moving towards a more subtle integration of biomechanical movement and "play" into the fabric of his productions. The transition can already be seen in his production of Aleksandr Ostrovsky's *The Forest* in 1924, where the cascades of physical actions and pantomime play with real and imagined objects alternate with more lyrical scenes, for example, the rendezvous between Aksyusha and Pyotr acted out to the accompaniment of a melancholy tune played on an accordion.

In *The Forest* (1924), Meyerhold achieved for the first time a remarkable synthesis between form in the shape of "play with objects" and idea content. "Objects became" as Boris Alpers so aptly noted, "like a piece of clay in the hands of the actors."[33] The most ordinary chairs served not only as something to sit on, but in a myriad of other ways as well: gymnastic equipment for a mock demonstration of Biomechanics, a defensive barricade, and even weapons.

Meyerhold displayed yet another side of his actors' physical versatility by incorporating a game of basketball into his 1925 production of Aleksei Faiko's *Bubus the Teacher*.

Pre-Acting

When Meyerhold staged Aleksei Faiko's political farce *Bubus the Teacher* in 1925, he introduced into the production "pre-acting," a device borrowed from the Kabuki and popular Chinese theatre. Pre-acting conveys in advance through movement the meaning of the given scenic situation. In his pronouncements explaining pre-acting, Meyerhold emphasized its significance as a means of manipulating the audience's response to a character. As an example of what he meant, Meyerhold cited the Russian actor Aleksandr Lensky's performance in *Much Ado About Nothing* in which the actor's elaborate miming of Benedick's reaction to an overheard conversation about his love for Beatrice causes the audience to burst into applause before the actor has uttered a single word. Meyerhold explained that this was not the same as the embellishment of the text with mime play since it precedes the text rather than accompanying it. "Pre-acting," he said, "prepares the spectator for the perception of the scenic situation by giving him all the details of the scene in such a developed form that he doesn't have to expend any effort in order to understand its underlying meaning."[34]

In a way, as Konstantin Rudnitsky suggests, Meyerhold's pre-acting was his answer to the Moscow Art Theatre's concept of the "subtext" by opposing to it what could be called a "counter-text."[35] That is, in keeping with the principles of reflexology, the Meyerhold actor approached the psychology of a character not internally through "experiencing" his feelings and thoughts, but externally by means of physical actions. "It isn't experiencing that guides us," Meyerhold pointed out to his actors, "but the constant faith in the preciseness of our technical play."[36] Meyerhold believed that pre-acting enabled the actor to achieve maximum expressivity by simultaneously "impersonating" the character he was playing and commenting on that character. However, by obscuring rather than amplifying the text, the abundant use of pre-acting in *Bubus the Teacher* to underscore every significant line of the text and announce each key scene merely confused and bored the audience.

Pre-acting, with its cycle of intention, realization, and reaction, can to a degree also be seen as a slow motion version of Meyerhold's "acting chain," on which Biomechanics is based: intention, equilibrium, and execution. The very fact that in pre-acting the "intention" becomes an end in itself, at times evolving into an entire pantomime, suggests the limitations of using biomechanical principles as a deliberate acting style. From now on, Meyerhold would turn to a more complex use of movement in his productions, one in which Biomechanics is still present, but in much more subtle ways. As Aleksei Levinsky more recently noted,

> For the actor trained in Biomechanics, every movement on the stage should contain a kind of hidden Biomechanics which may not be evident to those around him or to the audience, but which enables him to accomplish the very simplest movements, for example to rise on signal from a sitting position, or to move from one location on the stage to another, easily and naturally.[37]

Rhythm and Movement

For his future work what was perhaps most important in Meyerhold's production of *Bubus the Teacher* wasn't the use of exaggerated pauses for conveying the subtext to the audience. Rather it was, as Edward Braun has pointed out, Meyerhold's "restoration of rhythm as the basis of all dramatic expression ... to the pre-eminence it had enjoyed in such pre–1917 works as *Tristan and Isolde*, *Don Juan,* and *Masquerade.*"[38]

From now on, music would play a far greater role in defining and integrating the actors' movements into the fabric of Meyerhold's productions. Meyerhold, who in his youth had secretly dreamed of becoming a virtuoso violinist, regarded music as a vital tool of communication in the theatre, as important as speech, gesture, and movement. He believed music could convey an emotional tonality or psychological coloration far more effectively than any other means. Meyerhold also liked music for its ability to impose and maintain form in a production. To Meyerhold every word and every movement on stage had to have significance. He told the members of the orchestra prior to the première of *Woe to Wit*, "The use of a rhythmical structure [*ritmizatsiya*] in our productions is fundamental to our theatre."[39] Even in scenes where no music was used, Meyerhold wanted the actor to feel time on the stage the way a musician does. This is why tempo and precise timing are so fundamental to the biomechanical exercises, and why they were done to music. Meyerhold once observed:

> Supported by a rhythmical background of music, the actor's playing acquires precision.... The actor needs a background of music in order to train him to pay attention to the flow of time on the stage. If an actor is used to playing with a musical background, then without it he will sense time completely differently.[40]

As a means of controlling form and tempo, Meyerhold even advocated a return to the ancient system of chronométrage, the exact timing of each performance.[41] He pointed out:

> By slowing down or speeding up an act, we can completely distort a performance. Play Maeterlinck quickly and you get vaudeville. Play *The Neighbor Lady and Her Neighbors* [a one-act French comedy] slowly and it will seem to you that it's Leonid Andreev.[42]

Meyerhold dreamed of one day being able to conduct his theatrical performances in the same way that an orchestra conductor directs a musical performance. As it was, his actors and assistants quickly became accustomed to his use of musical terms during rehearsals: tempo, rhythm, *Luftpause*, staccato, pianissimo, etc.

Meyerhold never completely abandoned the exuberant "play with objects" that characterized his demonstrably biomechanical productions. But with each succeeding production he also began using objects more sparingly and more often for their associative power. In his 1925 production of Nikolai Erdman's *The Warrant*, a piano decorated with fans and paper flowers serves as a powerful metaphor delineating the family's bourgeois background. And in Gogol's *The Inspector General* (1926), as Edward Braun has written, "The pot belly of a wardrobe, the voluptuous curve of a Récamier couch, the deep rose-patterned back of a divan: they were all subtly exaggerated to enhance the poses of the characters and to impinge more firmly on the retina of the spectator."[43]

With *Woe to Wit* (1928) Meyerhold's use of objects underwent a further development. As in preceding productions, there are études, for example "play with a shawl," in which objects are skillfully manipulated to express character; there are also examples of genuine "play," as when

2. Meyerhold: The Triumph of Socialist Realism 51

Meyerhold (at bottom) and Erast Garin rehearsing Gogol's *The Inspector General* (1926). Meyerhold's recoil movement and Garin's expressive physical gestures are another example of the way in which Meyerhold incorporated biomechanical movements into his productions.

Famusov and the maid dart and dodge using various pieces of furniture as part of their game of cat and mouse. But other objects, such as the billiard balls and cues in Episode 7, "The Billiard Room and Library," and the guns in Episode 11, "The Shooting Gallery," go beyond serving solely as instruments for play or even as metaphor. Here it is not so much *what* the characters play *with* as it is the rhythmical structure and sound patterns created by their use of these objects. In the hands of the performers, these objects take on the role of musical instruments for accentuating and accompanying the dialog.

The First Five-Year Plan

With the advent of the First Five-Year Plan in 1928, Meyerhold and his theatre group came under increasing attack for their failure to stage any ideologically suitable Soviet plays. In a cable Meyerhold sent to Mayakovsky on May 4, 1928, he wrote, "For the last time I appeal to your common sense. The theatre is dying. There are no plays. They force me to give up the classics. I do not want to lower the standard of the repertoire. Please tell me seriously: can we count on getting your play this summer?"[44] When Mayakovsky's biting satire of philistinism, *The Bedbug*, finally premièred in January 1929 with Igor Ilinsky, then a popular movie star, in the lead, it was a smashing success with audiences, but it was hardly the kind of contemporary play that Party critics had in mind. The situation was aggravated by Meyerhold's staging a year later of Mayakovsky's *The Bath House* (1930), which was even more strongly condemned by Party critics for its falsification of Soviet reality. Vladimir Ermilov accused Mayakovsky of representing the bureaucrat Pobedonosnikov as a "Party degenerate," and charged Meyerhold with serving up abstractions rather than "living" people.[45]

Meyerhold fared still worse with his staging of Nikolai Erdman's eagerly awaited satire of the unregenerated bourgeoisie, *The Suicide*, which was rehearsed but never premièred at the Vakhtangov Theatre (1929), the Moscow Art Theatre (1931–1932) and Meyerhold's theatre (1931–1932).[46] Meyerhold's failure to get that play before the public in 1932 — it was banned following a closed late-night performance for a small audience of top officials — marked the end of Meyerhold's efforts to stage a contemporary satire.[47]

The Changing Esthetics

With the departure of Maria Babanova in 1927, and the installation of Meyerhold's wife, Zinaida Raikh, as the theatre's leading actress, the aesthetics of Meyerhold's productions began changing significantly. Raikh

2. Meyerhold: The Triumph of Socialist Realism   53

A scene from Meyerhold's 1930 production of Vladimir Mayakovsky's *The Bath House*.

was not a born actress as Babanova was. She had studied in Meyerhold's directing workshops for three years before she made her debut in 1924 as Aksyusha in *The Forest*. Although she was strikingly beautiful and possessed a strong, expressive voice, as Ilinsky noted, "Her helplessness on the stage, her physical unpreparedness, and to put it simply, her awkwardness was only too evident...."[48] One need only compare the original production of *The Magnanimous Cuckold* with Babanova as Stella and the 1928 revival of it, starring Zinaida Raikh, to see what a striking change was taking place. The critic David Talnikov, in reviewing the revival, characterized Raikh's Stella as "moving heavily over the constructions," and as lacking in youthful vitality. "This is an experienced woman who pretends to be naïve and innocent.... One can't help but recall the former, wonderful Stella-Babanova, rhythmic, light, young, using the rapid tempo of farce...."[49] The costumes and setting also underwent a transformation with a softer, more pliant fabric replacing the rough cotton of the *prozodezhda* the actors had worn earlier, and although the basic construction remained, the bare walls of the stage were now curtained over.

Meyerhold's later work was also characterized not so much by the demonstrative physical action called for in his earlier "agit-poster art" productions as by a series of "animated panoramas" and "set pieces" which would display the virtuosity of one or another actor. In part this was the result of the evolution his theatrical troupe underwent as it matured and as his most brilliant biomechanical actors, notably Babanova and Ilinsky, left the theatre.[50] Meyerhold tended to work with the actors he had at hand rather than seeking the ideal performer for a given role. He would develop the physical actions of a character so carefully and in such detail in relation to the production's overall structure that regardless of the degree of an actor's talent, the key moments in the role always remained an unqualified success. In the fourteen years *The Forest* ran in Meyerhold's theatre (performed in all over 1,700 times) a seemingly endless number of beginning actors filled the role of Pyotr. And yet, as one of Meyerhold's assistants recalled, no matter how weak the particular actor's performance might be, Pyotr's "flight on the Giant Strides" and his rendering on the accordion of the old waltz melody "Two Little Dogs" in the courtship scene and again in the finale consistently evoked as if on signal the same wild emotional reaction from the audience.[51]

Meyerhold was a master at taking an actor's particular strengths and turning them into a virtuoso solo. In later productions these set pieces would also be a way of turning a weak play into a memorable performance. This was especially characteristic of Meyerhold's attempts to stage contemporary works in the period from 1929 to 1932. As Aleksandr Matskin has noted, in each of the four productions, Ilya Selvinsky's *The Second Army Commander* (1929), Yury Olesha's *A List of Assets* (1930), Vsevolod Vishnevsky's *The Last, Decisive Battle* (1931) and Yury German's *Prelude* (1933), it is these set pieces that were remembered long after the productions themselves were forgotten.[52]

In the minds of audiences and critics, three memorable scenes from Selvinsky's Civil War verse tragedy, *The Second Army Commander*, stood out: "Rally in the Steppe," in which one speaker after another was driven from the platform by the crowd until it was brought under control by the "iron commander," Chub; the scene in the fifth act in which the Red Army sentry softly sings a song about his brother soldiers, and the intermedia, which Meyerhold staged as the finale of the fifth act. So moving was the singing by the large chorus — the theatre's entire troupe, women included — that when Selvinsky first saw and heard it, he could not hold back tears.[53]

In Meyerhold's production of Vishnevsky's Civil War tragedy, *The Last, Decisive Battle*, it was the final episode set in a school house under enemy siege that left a stunning impression. To the sound of a radio playing a foxtrot and Maurice Chevalier singing, one by one the last twenty-seven sailors die until only Bushuev (Nikolai Bogolyubov) is left. Mortally wounded, he slowly pulls himself up, takes a piece of chalk, and with

The final episode of *The Last, Decisive Battle* (1931). "This was a pantomime without words," Nikolai Bogolyubov recalled, "an entire gamut of physical actions...."

agonizing difficulty he writes on the blackboard like an arithmetic exercise the number 167,000,000 (the country's population) and under it a minus sign and the number 27. Bushuev makes the subtraction, then dropping the chalk, he falls and, with a perplexed smile on his face, dies. "This was a pantomime without words," Bogolyubov recalled, "an entire gamut of physical actions. The struggle [to write out] each letter was built like a musical composition. Various rhythms expressed the power of Bushuev's determination—his struggle: life or death?"[54]

In German's *Prelude* (1933), critics agreed that there were in all three or four episodes in which Meyerhold gave full range to his remarkable craftsmanship in composing a mise en scène. One of the most striking moments in the production was the pantomime scene in the cafe in which Lev Sverdlin as the drunken Hugo Nunbakh, a talented engineer who now sells pornographic postcards, remains behind in the empty room after the other guests have departed. In the flickering candlelight he slowly climbs up on the table and embraces a marble bust of Goethe. Looking into the statue's eyes, he asks, "Why aren't I building houses?" The only answer he receives is silence. So moving were scenes like this that one critic was

56 Meyerhold and Eisenstein

A scene from Meyerhold's production of Yuri German's *Prelude* (1933). In the flickering candlelight, the drunken Hugo Nunbakh slowly climbs up on the table and embraces a marble bust of Goethe. Looking into the statue's eyes, he asks, "Why aren't I building houses?" The only answer he receives is silence.

prompted to speak of Meyerhold's gift for bringing to the foreground some psychological detail and endowing it with enormous significance as evidence that his theatre was not "antipsychological."[55]

The Campaign Against Formalism

By 1931, Meyerhold found himself under siege not only for his choice of plays, but for his entire artistic method as well, which was variously characterized as "schematic," "two-dimensional" and "machine-like." At a meeting held at the State Academy of Art Studies (GAIS) on the tenth anniversary of the Meyerhold Theatre to evaluate its artistic methods, the critic Vladimir A. Pavlov, already notorious for his attack on the Moscow Art Theatre in his book *Theatrical Twilights*, praised the Meyerhold Theatre for being the first to make a decisive break with the "intimate-naturalistic" theatrical traditions of the past. He then went on to note that unfortunately its further development revealed only a "superficial mastery of revolutionary reality," and thus it could not now be considered a Proletarian theatre. "In creating his new system of acting," Pavlov charged, "Meyerhold 'removes' the psychological factor from art and lowers everything to the level of portraying man as a mechanical engine, and art itself to 'a free play of forms.' Such a position is in fundamental contradiction to the Marxist understanding of art, seen primarily as 'a means of spiritual interaction between people' (Plekhanov)."[56]

In responding to Pavlov's charges, Meyerhold objected to being labeled as a "mechanist," arguing that he took the term Biomechanics as the name of his system of actor training in order to make a sharp distinction between it and the system of the "vitalists" as represented by the Moscow Art Theatre and its followers, whose influence on acting had prevailed before the Revolution. Biomechanical training, Meyerhold went on to maintain, was only a preparatory stage for freeing the actor from psychological constraints. "Biomechanics makes no pretense of expressing the internal content of human experience and so forth."[57]

This was only the opening gun in the campaign against Meyerhold and his system of biomechanical training. In a directive adopted by RAPP (Russian Association of Proletarian Writers) at the end of 1931, the attack against Meyerhold continued. Making use of the age-old method of guilt by association, the directive drew a parallel between Meyerhold's use of "mechanical rhythm" as part of his biomechanical system, and

> the idealistic, anthroposophical devices of Mikhail Chekhov and Andrei Bely [rhythm as dialectics]. Technicism, fetishism, constructivism, the reinforcing of leftist rationalism and mechanicalism facilitate the development of the

artistic methodology of Theosophy, and that in turn leads to a peculiar kind of formalism [*Woe to Wit*] and to the search for "pure theatricality," to the mechanical mastery of elements of the so-called "people's theatre" [traditionalism]."[58]

The directive's conclusion was that Meyerhold's theoretical concepts could not serve as the basis for the Soviet theatre, and in fact, worked against its restructuring.

"Everyone speaks of a new stage in GOSTIM's work," Meyerhold said to his actors in October 1931. "I learned of that from the newspapers. Actually, there is no 'new stage,' but when I have to speak or write, I also use that term."[59] While Meyerhold then went on to admit that *The Forest* had turned into "an extremely mechanical production," he at the same time insisted that the solution was not to "burn the old ship and build a new theatre," but rather to strengthen the theatre's earlier principles through reviving the old productions. "Let us probe our entire repertoire," he said to his actors. "Take *The Forest* . . . we must make it genuinely classical in our sense of that word. A classical play in a biomechanical system."[60]

A year and a half later, in June 1933, while the theatre was on tour in Ukraine, Meyerhold set aside four days in Kharkhov for a meeting with his actors on the artistic method of the Meyerhold State Theatre.[61] From the stenographic notes of the conference, it is clear that the principal topic was to be Biomechanics. In his introductory remarks on the first day, Meyerhold spoke of the very practical origins of biomechanical training for actors. Reminding them that acting demands a great deal of stamina and energy, Meyerhold addressed the question of how the actor could prepare himself for a role and for his performance without using some kind of artificial stimuli as actors traditionally had. It was out of this concern, Meyerhold explained, that he turned to a study of the nature of the expressive means available to actors and of the importance of movement. "If you deliver the words and you don't deliver them from head to toe, the line will remain empty, it will not resonate. . . . Some think that a gesture on the stage arises of its own. Nothing of the sort. There are no isolated gestures. . . . The word without movement doesn't exist."[62]

At the same time Meyerhold warned that while Biomechanics was useful as a form of movement training, it mustn't be turned into a dogma leading actors to "mount the exercises like horses" and go all out. What is needed is "a masterful direction of the body" whose objective is precise execution and not machine-like movements.[63]

As important as the need to review with his actors the principles of Biomechanics was the need redefine Biomechanics—which Meyerhold refused to disown—in relation to the ideological debate taking place. In 1932 RAPP had published a booklet entitled *On the Objectives of RAPP* *on the Theatrical Front*⁶⁴ in which it had attacked the "extreme flanks": MXAT and the Stanislavsky system for its "idealism," and Meyerhold and his Biomechanics as "mechanistic." "The biomechanical system leads to the same biologism as the Stanislavsky system," the booklet maintained, "only from the opposite end. Man is regarded as a biological phenomenon, externally organized, which is reduced to muscular and technical sports processes." Thus, it concluded, "external physical action is substituted for the dialectical revelation of the social essence of the image."⁶⁵ In sum, RAPP judged Meyerhold's "theoretical concepts," based on a "mechanistic philosophy" to be not only alien to the reconstruction of the Soviet theatre but to be working against it.⁶⁶

Although RAPP was disbanded shortly after the publication of this booklet, the charges against Meyerhold's theatre remained very much alive. Then, a year later, in response to the concerns of members of his troupe about ideological questions, Meyerhold warned about certain "dangerous words," such as Mikhail Korenev used when he referred to the "naked person" and of how "when we take from him all his coverings we give him a biological nature."⁶⁷ Meyerhold further cautioned, "We must be equally careful when Zlobin says that our exercises borrow a lot from animals."⁶⁸

The fact is, as Korenev pointed out to Meyerhold, some of the actors had become frightened in the course of their discussions over the term "biological." They ask, "Since we are moving toward a classless society, and are living and working in a socialist system that is based on a philosophy of dialectical materialism, how can we say, 'biological?'"⁶⁹

Noting that he had not been afraid at the RAPP conference to distinguish between technology and ideology, Meyerhold went on to say that "only fools could assert that technology and ideology can enter art as equals." He further pointed out, "We who are working in the realm of biomechanical training must know very well the difference between the theories of the vitalists [who] propose a soul, or spirit, which directs certain phenomena in the behavior of a person ... and its exact opposite, those of the extreme biomechanists [who regard] the human organism as a complex chemical-physical laboratory." Meyerhold was very careful not to dismiss what he called "Marxist-Leninist, etc., etc., teachings," but lest there be any misunderstanding, he suggested that the actors speak about Biomechanics only as it concerns actor training and that they not try to talk about it in the context of ideology.⁷⁰

Later that year, as part of a general purge of Communists in Moscow theatres, Meyerhold, "the most prominent representative of Soviet theatrical art" was called upon to answer numerous questions about his role as a Bolshevik in the development of the Soviet theatre.⁷¹ In a lecture lasting several hours, Meyerhold began by reviewing his entire career in detail. He next turned to a defense of Biomechanics. Denying that he assigned to it any kind of "universal meaning," Meyerhold explained that Biomechanics was "not a theoretical dogma, but a codex of technological laws, based on a materialistic study of the actor's art."[72] He also rejected the charge that he and his theatre were heading in the direction of either the biomechanicists or the vitalists. And once again, as he would many times during the next several years, Meyerhold argued the need for a laboratory where the materials on the art of acting he and his assistants had accumulated over the years in the course of rehearsals, could be studied, adding that "the physiologist Ivan Pavlov is deeply interested in my scientific material."[73]

The Lady of the Camellias

Among Meyerhold's productions in the 1930s only one, *The Lady of the Camellias*, stands out as a masterpiece. Staged in 1934, it synthesized the exquisite visual richness of such pre-Revolutionary productions as *Don Juan* and *The Masquerade* and the "higher mathematics" of his biomechanical system that he once spoke of hoping to achieve. While Meyerhold was sharply criticized for choosing a work with so little social significance, *The Lady of the Camellias* proved to be highly popular with audiences, bringing the first full houses to the Meyerhold Theatre in a long time.

Many saw *The Lady of the Camellias* as the beginning of a new period in Meyerhold's work, a movement toward the more profound psychological development of character that the Stanislavsky System typified. Meyerhold himself acknowledged to the actor, Lev Snezhnitsky, that

> It's difficult to say what work on a role should begin with. A lot depends on the actor's personality. Some are helped by physical factors, others by psychological ones. Our system is often juxtaposed to the Moscow Art Theatre's, but that's not correct.... One can start with the psychological factors that will prompt the correct physical position. Or one can begin with the physical factors that will allow one to find the correct inner life.[74]

Nevertheless, as the rehearsal notes for *The Lady of the Camellias* testify, for Meyerhold, physical actions continued to be the starting point in his directing a production, just as they had twenty years earlier. "Superfluous words and lines should be thrown out," he said in justifying his cuts in the text, "the action alone will reveal the essence."[75] For his interpretation of Dumas' melodrama, Meyerhold choreographed a complex score of brilliant group compositions, lovers' duets and highly dramatic

The Party scene from act 4 of Meyerhold's 1934 production of *The Lady of the Camellias*.

solos by Zinaida Raikh as Marguerite, in which every movement was worked out with extreme precision.

Leonid Varpakhovsky recalls Meyerhold stating that the death scene in *The Lady of the Camellias* was built entirely on the biomechanical principle of the recoil.[76] In Meyerhold's words, "In order to shoot an arrow, one must first draw the bowstring." Thus, rather than present Marguerite's dying directly, Meyerhold begins with the reverse (i.e., the recoil): Marguerite's denial, her forced cheerfulness, and the sun streaming through the window, all of these only serving to heighten the impact of her death, which can then be depicted as Meyerhold did with only the most minimal gesture. In economy of means for maximum expressiveness, this scene is generally acknowledged as one of Meyerhold's masterpieces of stagecraft.

In Meyerhold's edited version of the text, Marguerite's final words are, "I'm not suffering! ... You see, I'm smiling, I'm strong...." Marguerite suddenly rises from her armchair (which is placed half-turned away from the audience), she straightens, and with her two hands she reaches out, grabs the shutters and opens them, letting in the bright sunlight. Still grasping the edge of the shutter with her left hand, Marguerite drops back into the armchair. Only her left arm is visible on the arm of the chair. She stiffens ever so slightly. An extended pause. Her left hand drops from the armrest, hanging limply. This is the only sign of her death.[77]

The Lady of the Camellias also stood out for the elegance of the set Meyerhold designed, with its sweeping staircase and beautiful furnishings, many of them antiques. Nevertheless, Meyerhold remained true to the principles he had established in his earliest biomechanical productions that there be nothing superfluous on the stage. "Everything, including the furniture," he said in working out the mise en scène for the death scene, "is an object for play. There is nothing superfluous. Everything is placed and is illuminated in such a way that one can predict the future action."[78]

Socialist Realism

Although RAPP was dissolved in 1932, the criticism against Meyerhold for the ideological shortcomings of his production methods continued. Meyerhold vigorously defended himself against these and similar charges, but in the end the fate of both his system of Biomechanics and his theatre were doomed. The imposition of Socialist Realism in 1934 meant that there could be only one correct system of actor training and only one style of theatrical presentation. That the Moscow Art Theatre fitted the model of Socialist Realism more closely than Meyerhold's should probably not come as a surprise. It too had been subjected to serious criticism for its "idealism" and "conservatism." The Moscow Art Theatre, however, proved itself far more adept in adjusting its philosophy of "truthfulness to life" to the requirements called for by the new Communist aesthetics.

While Meyerhold attempted to accommodate publicly to the new ideological demands of Socialist Realism, much of his creative energy in the 1930s went into reviving or restaging earlier productions, including several that he had directed prior to the Revolution. Of his Soviet productions, in addition to *The Cuckold*, revived in 1928, Meyerhold also refurbished *The Forest* (including removing Bulanov's green wig—a sop to those who had used it as an example of Meyerhold's formalist tendencies—and reducing the number of episodes) and *The Inspector General*. In 1936 Meyerhold staged an updated version of his *Woe to Wit*, this time under its original title of *Woe from Wit*. In speaking of his new, "Moscow Version" of Griboedov's classic, Meyerhold tacitly acknowledged the attacks against him and his artistic methods by stating that while the earlier version had traces of his pre-Revolutionary work, the new one would be "stylized, but at the same time deeply realistic."[79]

As he had throughout his directing career, Meyerhold insisted on retaining sole leadership of his theatre's artistic program, and in this, too, he increasingly found himself at odds with prevailing cultural policies. Ilinsky was undoubtedly right when he observed

> Instead of uniting with the collective—theatre art, and especially Soviet theatre art, is a genuinely collective art—Meyerhold "preserved" himself as an unquestioned "leader," in spite of his many mistakes and controversial assertions. ...Among his actors and assistant directors, his pupils, were many talented people. He could have trusted them completely and relied on many of them, but he continued to be a dictator standing above all the rest.[80]

Furthermore, Meyerhold seemed incapable of staging the kind of Soviet dramaturgy that the Party program had called for in launching the second Five-Year Plan in 1933: "We need the vivid portrayal of the heroes of the U.S.S.R., the great enthusiasm of the work of socialist construction. Towards the Magnito-construction [a reference to construction of the city of Magnitogorsk during the first Five-Year Plan] of theatrical art—that's the direction the Meyerhold Theatre must take."[81]

By 1934 Meyerhold had gained international renown. In recalling his visit to Moscow in 1934, Lee Strasberg noted, "The great experience in the Moscow Theatre was the discovery of Meyerhold, who to me is the greatest director of all times."[82] It was a view shared by many theatre practitioners. Meyerhold's theatre became a mecca through whose portals in the next few years a steady stream of prominent visitors poured.

In honor of his sixtieth birthday on February 10, 1934, the prestigious Russian theatre journal *Theatre and Dramaturgy* dedicated a good part of its February issue to "the master of the revolutionary theatre." As the prominent critic Pavel Markov noted in his "Letter about Meyerhold" in this issue, "More has been written about Meyerhold, especially in the last few years, than about any other figure in the theatre."[83] That these words were written to honor Meyerhold and his theatre could not help but have enraged Stalin, whose preference and support were solidly behind the Moscow Art Theatre. But for the moment Stalin needed artists and scientists like Meyerhold, Eisenstein, Gorky, and Pavlov as window dressing to impress the Western world. And so, like many of the other mannequins in Stalin's display window, Meyerhold would be spared for awhile, but not indefinitely.

Gradually the signs of official disfavor began to accumulate against him. In 1934, Meyerhold was refused permission to mark his sixtieth birthday at his theatre.[84] Eleven years earlier Meyerhold's twenty-fifth anniversary as a director had been celebrated at the Bolshoi Theatre and he had been awarded the prestigious title of "Peoples' Artist of the Republic." But when the new and even more distinguished award of

Honored Artist of the U.S.S.R. was established on September 6, 1936, "for the most eminent figures in the art of the peoples of the U.S.S.R., particularly those who distinguished themselves in the development of Soviet theatre, music, and film," Meyerhold's name was noticeably absent.[85]

Pressure increased for Meyerhold to stage a Soviet play. Premier Molotov even had a talk with him on the subject, but Meyerhold argued that there were not any suitable ones worth staging. Instead he retreated to the past by staging three of Chekhov's one-act plays under the title *33 Swoons*; and at the Marinsky Theatre in Leningrad, he directed his own edited version of Tchaikovsky's opera *The Queen of Spades*. Meyerhold also began rehearsals of Pushkin's *Boris Godunov*, which he would rehearse on and off for the next year and a half.

In January 1936, when Dmitri Shostakovich was attacked in *Pravda* and his opera *Lady Macbeth of Mtsensk District* was banned, Meyerhold refused to join in the campaign against his close friend and one-time collaborator, an act at the time of great courage.[86] Shortly afterwards the possibility of a meeting between Meyerhold and Stalin arose as a means of improving the situation of Meyerhold and his theatre, but the idea was dropped when Boris Pasternak advised against it. Recalling how Stalin had hung up on him when he had telephoned on Osip Mandelshtam's behalf, Pasternak argued that it would be unworthy of Meyerhold to appeal to Stalin as a petitioner, and he couldn't be in any other position at that time. "People like Stalin and Meyerhold must either speak as equals," Pasternak said, "or not at all."[87]

As the campaign against formalism in the arts (the code word for "bourgeois ideology hostile to the Soviet people") took on a new stridency, criticism against Meyerhold in the press grew increasingly harsh. When the term "Meyerholditis" as denoting formalism in the theatre, began appearing, Meyerhold was quick to respond. In a speech in Leningrad on March 14, 1936, while allowing that he had made many mistakes in his productions, Meyerhold nevertheless justified these experiments in terms of the scope of his efforts to convey the content of a given work. Meyerhold then went on to charge his former disciples, including Sergei Radlov and Nikolai Okhlopkov, of debasing his artistic methods by stealing his formal devices and using them out of context. In Meyerhold's view, here was the real Meyerholditis that warranted attack.[88]

At a conference of workers in the arts in Moscow held at the same time to discuss the charges against Shostakovich and to assess the implications of formalism in the arts, Meyerhold came under heavy attack for trying to shift the blame for his own shortcomings to others.[89] Once more Meyerhold responded, again refusing to concede anything to his critics. He rejected the idea of devoting his speech to self-criticism, stating that he had spent his entire career in just that. He then went on to defend his experimental work as part of his constant search for new means of dramatic expression.

Meyerhold also spoke of the influence of his productions on the work of other theatres. "The Maly production of [Trenev's] *Lyubov Yarovaya* would never have been staged as it was had we not previously put on *The Magnanimous Cuckold*." And if it failed, Meyerhold pointed out, it was "because the director could not see that the 'constructvist setting' (so-called) demanded a new style of makeup, new costumes and a new acting method to help the actors to break away from the slavish portrayal of real life." He went on to remind his accusers, "Without our *Forest*, Konstantin Sergeevich Stanislavsky would never have produced his splendid *A Fervent Heart* at the Moscow Art Theatre."[90]

Meyerhold denied that he was trying to escape from reality by staging the classics instead of contemporary Soviet plays. He charged Soviet playwrights with trying to hide their mediocrity "behind the smoke screen of Soviet themes." Finally he warned of "throwing out the baby with the bath" in the campaign against formalism, maintaining that experimentation is vital to the theatre.[91]

At the beginning of 1937, Meyerhold put aside *Boris* and attempted to stage Lidiya Seifullina's *Natasha*. But its everyday picture of rural life was so painfully alien to his aesthetic vocabulary that the production only brought new charges against the director as having deliberately staged it in such a way as to "desecrate realism."[92] The conclusion was that Meyerhold was incapable of staging a realistic play, and the production was never shown to the public.

In his quest for a suitable Soviet play, Meyerhold next considered and then abandoned a new version of Mayakovsky's *The Bedbug*. Finally he turned to an adaptation by Evgeny Gabrilovich of Nikolai Ostrovsky's *How the Steel Was Tempered*, entitled *One Day*. From all accounts it was a powerful production, especially Pavel Korchagin's final monolog, delivered directly to the audience. Eisenstein was stunned by it, and he rushed backstage after the performance to tell Evgeny Samoilov, who played Korchagin, "I just saw on the stage a real revolutionary outburst and a true revolutionary!"[93] But Platon Kerzhentsev and his Committee on the Arts felt otherwise. Planned for the twentieth anniversary of the October Revolution, the production's tragic tone could hardly have been less appropriate. It was banned without being shown to the public, leaving the Meyerhold Theatre the only one of the 700 professional Soviet theatres without a production to celebrate this important holiday.

In the August 1937 issue of *Teatr* there had appeared an article by A. Nefedov entitled, "Teach [Us] How to Live!"[94] In it, the author, a metal worker–Komsomol member from the Stalin Factory, reviewed the kinds of productions his fellow factory workers wanted to see. Listing as their favorite theatres the Moscow Art, the Maly, and the Bolshoi, the metal worker next asked, "When is [Meyerhold] at last going to break his enigmatic silence; when is he going to stage without any incomprehensible trickery, a Soviet play from our life or a play about the struggle of our peoples with the past?" The metal worker, clearly an official mouthpiece, concluded by stating the basic program that was to govern all theatres in the coming decades: "The theatre must show in its full scale the heroes of the Stalin epoch who can serve for us as models of the new people, who could become our ideals, [so that] in striving to be like them we might grow and perfect ourselves."[95]

Other articles followed. Then on December 17, 1937, an article entitled "An Alien Theatre" appeared in *Pravda*.[96] Seven years earlier, the author of the article, Kerzhentsev, had defended Meyerhold as the director who had "delivered the heaviest blow to the old theatre and was *the first one* to find the way to show on the stage our revolution and our epoch in general."[97] Now, as head of the Committee on the Arts, Kerzhentsev would deliver a similar blow to Meyerhold by attacking him for having consistently "shunned real life" throughout his entire career as a director. There could be only one conclusion, Kerzhentsev maintained, after cataloging the shortcomings of Meyerhold's productions in the Soviet period:

> It has become absolutely clear that Meyerhold cannot (and, apparently, will not) comprehend Soviet reality or depict the problems which concern every Soviet citizen.... Do Soviet art and the Soviet public really need such a theatre?[98]

The answer came less than a month later. On January 7, 1938, the Committee passed a resolution liquidating Meyerhold's theatre as "alien to Soviet art."[99]

"Meyerholditis Has No Place in Soviet Art," a follow-up article in *Soviet Art* headlined in endorsing the liquidation of the Meyerhold Theatre as "expressing the will of the Soviet theatre-goer."[100] In reviewing Meyerhold's career, the unsigned article maintained that while "proclaiming himself an enemy of empty bourgeois aesthetics, in actuality he had established his system on those very same bourgeois aesthetics, merely masking them with flashy, pseudo-revolutionary phraseology." And lest there be any misunderstanding, the article further warned that the closing of Meyerhold's theatre "should force many artists to stop and think, [especially] the group of directors who proudly called themselves Meyerhold's pupils."[101]

The Prodigal Son Returns

On January 8, 1938, the Meyerhold Theatre gave its final performance, a matinee of *The Inspector General*.[102] The resolution liquidating the Meyerhold Theatre noted that "The question of the possibility of further work by Vs. Meyerhold in the theatre would be considered separately."[103] Shortly after the theatre's closing Meyerhold and Zinaida Raikh were offered positions at the regional Lensoviet Theatre. Zinaida Nikolaevna, who was in a state of near collapse, turned down the offer. But Meyerhold didn't hesitate for a moment. To him any theatre at all would be better than none. According to Gladkov there were also some vague offers from Leningrad.[104] But before Meyerhold could act on any of them, one morning a few weeks later he received a telephone call from Stanislavsky inviting him to come to his home on Leontyev Lane. The result of their many hours of conversation at this meeting and others over the next few weeks was an invitation for Meyerhold to work with him at the Opera Studio.[105]

Stanislavsky had always followed Meyerhold's work as a director closely and with keen interest. He saw only a few of his post–Revolutionary productions, but he knew in detail about all of them from detailed reports by trusted "spies." Stanislavsky didn't always like what Meyerhold was doing, but he never lost his respect for his former pupil as an innovator. With his growing interest, following his return from France in 1930, in finding a way to speed up the rehearsal process, Stanislavsky began experimenting with what would ultimately become known as the "Method of Physical Action." With this rehearsal technique, the actors would begin not with a detailed analysis of the text while sitting passively around the table, but on their feet by means of études with an improvised text.[106]

In July 1935 Stanislavsky formed a new Opera-Dramatic Studio, and it was here that he hoped to explore and develop his new Method of Physical Action. As testimony to his growing interest in movement, over the course of three years during the 1930s Zosima Zlobin visited Stanislavsky in order to demonstrate and explain the principles of Biomechanics to him.[107] It was also during this period that Stanislavsky gave serious thought to the reorganization of the Art and Opera theatres. As part of this plan, Stanislavsky proposed turning the Moscow Art Theatre Filial into a "purely experimental stage for contemporary work with Meyerhold" where Stanislavsky would create one group based on his method of "experiencing" the role and for Meyerhold a second one based on his Biomechanics.[108]

Stanislavsky had already wanted to invite Meyerhold to direct at the Moscow Art Theatre earlier in the thirties, but at that time Nemirovich-

Danchenko vetoed the idea.[109] Nemirovich-Danchenko and Meyerhold were barely on speaking terms, and it was clear that as long as Nemirovich-Danchenko was alive Meyerhold would never be allowed to work at the MXAT. Now that he had his own opera-drama studio separate from the Art Theatre, Stanislavsky could at last realize his desire to work again with Meyerhold as they had back in 1905 at the Theatre-Studio on Povarskaya Street in St. Petersburg. Even so, Stanislavsky went about it very quietly. Toward the end of 1936 Stanislavsky and Meyerhold began meeting regularly to discuss "various matters connected with the theatre."[110] In a visit to Stanislavsky in August 1937 while the latter was at the sanitorium in Barvikha, the two men talked of "wide-ranging reforms both in the theatre and in training."[111]

When Stanislavsky spoke of inviting Meyerhold to direct at his Opera Theatre, his sister, Zinaida Sokolova, one of the directors and teachers there, dismissed the notion as "one of Kostya's whims," and another member of the Theatre objected that, "Meyerhold is alien for us, he's hostile to our traditions." But Stanislavsky simply answered, "We need Meyerhold." He was also forced to overcome the opposition of Kerzhensev and the Committee on the Arts, stating that he would take full responsibility for the decision, and they too humored the old man's "whim."[112]

But this was more than another of Stanislavsky's "whims." As Boris Vershilov, then chief director of the Stanislavsky Opera Theatre, told Meyerhold at a general meeting of the Opera Theatre's workers on August 27, 1938, "Konstantin Sergeevich said that we should study physical actions with you."[113] Stanislavsky was well aware that opera singers like Chaliapin who had perfect mastery of their bodies were rare. "In our opera," he commented to Yury Bakhrushin, head of the Literary Department at the Opera Theatre, "the singers sing very well, and often they don't perform too badly, but they don't know how to handle their bodies." Stanislavsky went on to add, "I'm counting a great deal on Meyerhold. He's a master of that. If emotions influence the physical actions of a person, then physical actions must to an equal degree influence the emotions...."[114]

Stanislavsky had initially been forced to compromise by bringing Meyerhold into the Opera-Drama Studio as a teacher. Then in May 1938 an announcement appeared stating that Meyerhold had been appointed a director at the Stanislavsky Opera Theatre.[115] During the weeks remaining before Stanislavsky's death in August 1938, Meyerhold provided the firm hand that the dying Stanislavsky needed to conduct the rehearsals of *Rigoletto* at the Opera Theatre. They also met frequently to discuss plans to stage Mozart's opera *Don Giovanni*. As Jean Benedetti notes in his biography of Stanislavsky, "There was a creative excitement in their talk which Stanislavski had not experienced for many years."[116] Stanislavsky now saw Meyerhold as the only one who could take his place. One of his final instructions to Yury Bakhrushin was, "Look after Meyerhold, he is my sole heir in the theatre, not only in ours, but in the theatre as a whole."[117]

The Curtain Comes Down

Following Stanislavsky's death in August 1938, Meyerhold continued on at the Stanislavsky Opera Theatre, completing the production of *Rigoletto*. In October 1938, he was named chief director. In a feverish burst of activity during the 1938-1939 season, in addition to *Rigoletto* (which premièred on March 14, 1939), Meyerhold also took part in the completion of several other productions at the Opera Theatre. Working with the artist, Pavel Konchalovsky, he began preparations for staging Mozart's *Don Giovanni*. Also, his new position allowed Meyerhold to invite Sergei Prokofiev to stage his new opera *Semyon Kotko* based on Valentin Kataev's *I Am a Son of the Working People* at the Opera Theatre.[118] In addition, Meyerhold held discussions in Leningrad about a revival of his production of Lermontov's *The Masquerade* which he had originally staged at the Alexandrinsky Theatre on the eve of the Revolution.

Time was running out for Meyerhold when in May 1939 he was approached by Nikolai Sery, a star athlete from the Lesgaft Institute in Leningrad, about directing the Leningrad contribution to the Day of Physical Culture held each July in Red Square.[119] It was one of the major festivals of the year, and for it each of the Republics as well as major cities such as Moscow, Leningrad, and Minsk organized their own presentations. Sery had been working on the Leningrad contribution to the festival for three years, and by 1939 he decided that he would invite a theatre director to work with him in order to learn how he could make the performance more theatrical.

"I first approached another director by the name of Aleksandrov, but he turned me down. I then decided to ask Meyerhold. He so readily accepted my invitation when I went to see him at his apartment that I was really surprised." (What the twenty-six year old Sery did not know at the time was that Meyerhold was desperate to earn money, as he had no steady income except for his position as head of the Stanislavsky Opera Studio.)

"The one thing Meyerhold asked, though," Sery recalled, "was that we use his choice of composers. Up to then I had been using Dunaevsky, but Meyerhold wanted Prokofiev, and I agreed." Prokofiev did write some music for the spectacle, including a march. "I didn't think the music was at all suitable, but when I mentioned it to Meyerhold he said, 'Nonsense, it's not the music, it's the pianist you're using. She doesn't know how to play it. Wait until you hear Prokofiev play it!'"

Sery recalls that he met with Meyerhold several times at the apartment on Bryusov Lane, and Meyerhold also went to see him at his apartment before going up to Leningrad to begin rehearsals. But before leaving for Leningrad, Meyerhold, as one of the major Soviet directors and a member of the Department of Directing at VTO (All-Russia Theatre Society), was scheduled to take part in the First All-Union Conference of Theatre Directors, to be held in the auditorium at the Central House of Actors on Gorky Street scheduled for June 13 through June 20.

Chairing the Conference was Andrei Vishinsky. Already famous as Stalin's prosecutor-general, he was now making his debut as the new deputy chairman of the Soviet People's Commissariat. In his opening speech entitled "The Objectives of the Soviet Theatre," Vishinsky called on all artists of the theatre to carry on the struggle to eradicate all remains of the old bourgeois consciousness.[120] Reminding his audience what a "powerful weapon" the theatre is, he urged them to fight against the last remnants of formalism and naturalism "hindering the search for new, rich, clear, brilliant forms of new, socialist art."[121]

Vishinsky's opening remarks were followed by five days of speeches by the delegates, among them many leading figures in the Soviet theatre: Solomon Mikhoels, Nikolai Akimov, Sergei Radlov, Andrei D. Popov, and Serafima Birman. Even at a distance of more than fifty years it is a sad experience to read the groveling praise accorded that "great master of human happiness, the inspirer of the artistic growth of Soviet artists—our own, beloved comrade STALIN!" to whom the conference was dedicated.[122] Even the "wise and magical" Mikhoels, who spoke several times, couldn't refrain from proclaiming that, "The only thing that can enlighten and renew art, the only thing that can inspire genuine enthusiasm is the genuine desire to . . . turn art into a weapon in the struggle for the happiness of man . . . is what the Party and comrade Stalin teach us."[123]

On June 15, the third day of the conference, a weary-looking grayhaired man rose from a chair in the auditorium. The delegates burst into wild applause as Meyerhold approached the podium. Meyerhold stood awkwardly on the podium waiting for the applause to die down.

"Comrades," Meyerhold began, "we are gathered here in order that the theatre art of our country, appreciated by our people, by our government, our party, an art of the highest level—we are gathered here in order to make it, that art, an art worthy of the mighty Stalinist epoch.

"We are gathered here, comrades, in order to reveal the fundamental mistakes of the formalists and the naturalists, and to say over and over again to the people, the government, and the party that we will not in the future repeat those mistakes. Life has taught us to work in the conditions of a constant analysis of our mistakes, and comrade STALIN has given us the wisest instructions: learn to catch your mistakes, learn to reveal their roots, learn to show that you were in error, learn never to repeat your mistakes. Our leader, our teacher, the friend of workers of the entire world serves as a model to us of the greatest caution in relation to all and any mistakes on our remarkable path leading to the greatest happiness of mankind...."[124]

If anyone expected the once proud Meyerhold to deliver the kind of speech Juri Jelagin describes in his book on Meyerhold, they were doomed to disappointment.[125] The defiant words Jelagin cites from the notes he claims to have made at the conference simply are not there. Acknowledging that he as well as other artists had made mistakes, Meyerhold went on to express his appreciation that "we—myself, and Shostakovich, and Sergei Eisenstein—that all of us have been given the full possibility to continue our work, and only through our work to correct our mistakes. Comrades, tell me, where, in what other country on the globe, would such a phenomenon be possible."

Meyerhold next asked that "the applause, so stormy, which had filled the auditorium on the first and second day at each mention of my name—I ask you to say together with me that this, your applause was directed not at me, but at our government, our party, and above all at the one who inspires us, we artists, to great deeds in our construction, to great deeds in creating the first communist society, at the creator of that constitution which could create the conditions for us who have made mistakes to correct them through hard work."

In the long speech that followed Meyerhold went into detail about the mistakes he had made, expressing the hope that those in the the auditorium would never make the same ones. Once hailed as the "Father of Constructivism," Meyerhold now acknowledged that he should never have shown his "laboratory experiments" to the public. While Constructivism had its usefulness in liberating the actor, it shouldn't have been "foisted" on audiences, Meyerhold allowed. He further admitted that in being carried away by the classics he had ignored Soviet plays and as a result many playwrights weren't given a helping hand. And in acknowledgement of his free adaptations of the classics, Meyerhold confessed that, "The experimentation I did with *The Forest* and *The Inspector General* should not have been shown to the public but only to a small circle of actors, directors, and so forth." And finally, Meyerhold acknowledged that "As sad as it is for me personally to have lost my theatre, I must consider that the order by the Central Committee and our government that that theatre be closed was right."

Meyerhold ended his litany of mistakes by stating that he hoped that what he had done could serve as a good lesson to all those who want to "smuggle" formalism into their work. The remainder of his speech Meyerhold devoted to a wide-ranging discussion of what he called "certain weak spots on our theatrical front," from repertory problems to building new theatres, worker safety, and the sad quality of actor education, in particular its failure to include any form of physical training for actors.

Finally, in his concluding remarks Meyerhold spoke of the need for a "heroic theatre" of the kind that "the government, the party, and the people are awaiting." He pointed out, "We often talk about the creation of a heroic theatre ... but why drag onto the stage some Hippolytuses, Oedipuses, Antigones, when heroes are walking among us. We even have a title, 'Hero of the Soviet Union.' We must, comrades, urge dramatists to write these kinds of plays."

Looking into the future, Meyerhold asserted:

> We living in the Country of Soviets, we living in the magnificent Stalinist epoch can with certainty say that in the Union of Soviet Socialist Republics, with the grandiose third Stalinist Five-Year Plan, art begins to become what in our epoch could be called the epoch of a new Renaissance.... In educating us, comrade Stalin, together with our party, wants to make people in the arts worthy so that their names go down in history together with the names of the leading builders of communist society.

It is difficult to make a fair comparison between the stenographic report of Meyerhold's address, which did not appear in the published report of the conference (all other references to him by other speakers were also removed), and the published speeches by other directors and critics. In reading over the latter, however, one message does seem clear from the constant references to Stanislavsky and his teachings, and that is the overwhelming affirmation of those teachings for actor training and as a system of staging a production. This emphasis is all the more curious because, while he did touch upon actor training, Meyerhold never once mentioned the name of his former teacher. It is difficult to escape the conclusion that the selectivity in the speeches to be published, as well as in their editing was intended to strengthen the position of Stanislavsky's teachings as the sole model for the Soviet theatre, as indeed, was to be the case right up until the Gorbachev reforms. Even after the thaw, if Meyerhold's name was mentioned, it always had to be in tandem with Stanislavsky's.

Meyerhold returned home after his speech feeling very depressed. He was afraid Vishinsky would think that Meyerhold himself had organized the demonstrative support for him, the wild applause that had greeted the director when he approached the podium. Other directors, including Popov and Mikhoels, had also spoken warmly of Meyerhold in their speeches, Popov noting that, "They were indebted to him for everything new in the theatre." That night Meyerhold left by train for Leningrad, where he spent the next several days working with Nikolai Sery and his former teacher of Biomechanics, Zosima Zlobin, on staging the sports spectacle. According to Sery, "Meyerhold's main concern was to somehow wake up the audience, the Politburo members and all the guests who would have already been watching for hours. One of his ideas, and it proved quite an innovation, was to have the sports performers come into Red Square from both sides and swoop up toward the reviewing stand rather than simply passing by in the manner of a traditional parade."

Meyerhold spent the evening of June 19 at the apartment of his friends, Erast Garin, his wife Khesia, and their mutual friend, also a former member of the Meyerhold Theatre, Elena Tyapkina. About seven the next morning Meyerhold left for his own apartment on Karpov Embankment, where members of the NKVD were waiting to arrest him. On June 22, Meyerhold was returned by night train to Moscow, where he was incarcerated in Lubyanka Prison. Three weeks later, on the night of July 14, Meyerhold's wife, Zinaida Raikh, was brutally murdered in their apartment on Bryusov Lane. After seven months of grueling interrogation and torture, Meyerhold, who was accused of being a Trotskyist since 1923 as well as a British and Japanese spy, confessed.[126] He was executed in Moscow on February 2, 1940. For the next fifteen years, until his rehabilitation in 1955, Meyerhold's name could not be spoken aloud in public. All references to him were eliminated from writings and teachings on the Soviet theatre. It was as though Meyerhold, one of the greatest theatre directors of the twentieth century, had never existed.

Chapter 3

Eisenstein: From Engineer to Revolutionary Filmmaker

> *The alpha and omega of theoretical baggage on Expressive Movement taken from the studies in Biomechanics is completely contained in Thesis No. 1: All of Biomechanics is based on the premise that if the tip of the nose works, so does the entire body. . . . All the rest of my teachings on Expressive Movement are Mine.*[1]
>
> Sergei Eisenstein

Without question, Meyerhold's must brilliant student was Sergei Eisenstein, the *enfant terrible* of the 1920s silent motion picture era. From his startling international success with the epic film *The Battleship Potemkin* in 1926 until his death in 1948, Eisenstein and his writings dominated the intellectual discourse on cinematic art in every artistic capital. Eisenstein's trips to Western Europe and North America in the twenties and thirties galvanized members of the film community and left-leaning artists everywhere. Like Mayakovsky, El Lissitzky, and Meyerhold himself, Eisenstein came to symbolize the revolutionary art of the Soviet Union during the interwar years.

The importance of Meyerhold and Eisenstein's personal relationship has been suggested in the vast literature on the two men, but it has never been fully explored.[2] For both artists, young Eisenstein's phenomenal and sudden rise — first in the theatre, then in the cinema — initiated a twenty-five-year psychological struggle. Love, hate, deep affection, envy, guilt were only a few of the emotions that the master teacher and loyal pupil experienced when they had to respond to the other's exalted reputation.

Curiously, Biomechanics and the scientific analysis of the actor's expressiveness became one of the chief battlegrounds between these two extraordinary giants of twentieth-century performing arts. Despite his renown for theatrical inventiveness throughout his career, Meyerhold was never much interested in theory. He left that to others. In fact, one of Eisenstein's chief functions during his year and a half in Meyerhold's Directors Workshops was to create a scientific-theoretical framework for Biomechanics. Eisenstein's empirical and scholarly research led him to rebel against Meyerhold as the former engineer-*cum*-director developed his own system of Expressive Movement. In a way, Eisenstein, through his super-rational means, was the only avant-garde artist who fully explored the aesthetic and scientific principles of Biomechanics. Today, we owe much of our understanding of Meyerhold's ideas on acting and movement to Eisenstein's critical appraisal and elaborations.

Eisenstein's Early Years

The son of Mikhail Osipovich Eisenstein, a Riga architect and engineer, Sergei Mikhailovich was born into a well-to-do Russian bourgeois household in 1898. A child prodigy who was encouraged in his studies of foreign languages, art, and mathematics, Eisenstein suffered emotionally under the weight of his family's adopted Victorian mores. In 1906 his parents took their only child to Paris to escape the aftermath of the 1905 revolution, and it was there that the young Eisenstein saw his first film. By the time he was ten, he was already organizing a children's theatre group in Riga with his childhood friend, Maksim Shtraukh. Throughout his adolescence, Eisenstein's passion for drawing, as well as for popular entertainment and cinema, developed unceasingly.

In 1909 Eisenstein's parents were divorced. His mother, Julia Ivanovna, moved to St. Petersburg, leaving Eisenstein with his father in Riga. It had long since been decided that he would follow in his father's footsteps, and in 1915 the seventeen-year-old Eisenstein entered the Institute of Civil Engineering in Petrograd. It was there in Petrograd that in early 1917 Eisenstein received a "thunderbolt."[3] Meyerhold's productions of Molière's *Don Juan* and Lermontov's *Masquerade* at the Alexandrinsky Theatre changed him forever. Like a master engineer, Meyerhold directed these difficult classic dramas with absolute precision and originality. A virtuoso of stage tricks, "Doctor Dapertutto" planted the seed for Eisenstein's ultimate calling.

In the spring of 1917 Eisenstein was transferred to the Ensigns Engineering School in Petrograd where he remained until January 1918 when the school was disbanded. Shortly afterwards Eisenstein volunteered for active service in the Red Army. Thus the nineteen-year-old Eisenstein completely broke with his background in the most striking way imaginable, since his father was with the opposing White Army. Like others of his generation and class, Eisenstein found in the Bolshevik Revolution a political, artistic, and personal liberation.

When the defeated counter-revolutionary armies dissolved after the Civil War, the elder Eisenstein fled to Berlin, where he died of a heart attack in 1920 at the age of fifty-three.[4] Whether Eisenstein visited his father's grave during his 1926 stay in Berlin is not known. For all his ironic detachment and self-deprecating humor, this was not a subject Eisenstein could easily talk about. In time, as he recognized toward the end of his life, he would acquire a second emotionally distant father figure: Meyerhold.

Between 1918 and 1920, Eisenstein served the Red Army in two capacities: first as a draftsman and military engineer on the Western front and later as a scenic designer for a mobile unit of agitprop performers. In August 1920, the agit train to which Eisenstein was assigned arrived in newly-liberated Minsk. It was here that he, along with the poet and playwright Pavel Arensky and the artist Leonid Nikitin (Eisentein's future collaborator on the first version of *The Mexican*) decided to study Japanese in order to be posted to the General Staff Academy in Moscow. At the time all three were working together at the headquarters of the Western Front. Eisenstein's ultimate goal, as he wrote in a letter to his mother, was to travel to Japan to study the Japanese theatre. By mid-September the trio had successfully passed the entrance examination, and at the end of September Eisenstein moved to Moscow.

Shortly after Eisenstein arrived in Moscow to learn Japanese, he was appointed head of the Scenic Design Department of the Central Workers' Theatre of the All-Russia Proletkult. "It's just the job I've been dreaming of," he wrote his mother. "I'm in charge of a whole group of workshops (scenery, props, maquettes, carpentry), and I'll probably have my own costume shop."[5] Within a few months, Eisenstein was devoting himself fully to the newly-formed Moscow Proletkult, eventually dropping his Japanese language studies.

In February 1921, Eisenstein began attending evening classes in Émile Jaques-Dalcroze's Eurhythmics and Evgeny Prosvetov's Tonal-Plastics at the Proletkult dramatic studios. In a letter to his mother, he described his enthusiasm for this movement work:

> What an enormous delight! I never thought earlier that some galloping to music or high kicking, rhythmical running, etc. could give such pleasure and have such a beneficial effect on one's mood. It would seem that everything is fine, but I want very much to study. I feel, on the one hand, that I can

accomplish a lot, but on the other, that I lack knowledge and experience. But where shall I go? Where can I study?"[6]

During this expansive period in his life, Eisenstein designed and codirected an adaptation of Jack London's melodramatic short story "The Mexican," in collaboration with Valentin Smyshlyaev, a student of Stanislavsky. Although the production was well received when it opened on the Proletkult stage on March 10, 1921, Eisenstein felt frustrated and even cheated by Smyshlyaev's traditional Moscow Art Theatre approach. (Two years later, Eisenstein radically redirected the play in an environmental presentation.) Eisenstein quickly began seeking other venues for his unbridled energy and scenic talents both inside and outside the Proletkult Theatre.

On April 20, 1921, Eisenstein managed to sneak into a final dress rehearsal of Mayakovsky's *Mystery-Bouffe* at the R.S.F.S.R. Theatre No. 1. At the conclusion of the preparatory work, Eisenstein met briefly with the celebrated playwright and the equally legendary director, Vsevolod Meyerhold. Four months later, in August, Eisenstein and his then partner, Yutkevich, auditioned for Meyerhold's new directing workshop at GVRM (State Higher Directors Workshops). For their audition, the two Sergeis had to demonstrate their skill in shooting an imaginary arrow from an imaginary bow — the rudiments of a basic biomechanical étude. They were also asked to sketch a theatrical solution for a chase scene involving "six in pursuit of one." As Sergei Yutkevich later recalled, Eisenstein quickly produced a Constructivist-looking stage set with six hinged doors, a design concept that Meyerhold himself would use in *The Inspector General* some five years later.[7] Both Eisenstein and Yutkevich found themselves in a schoolboy's euphoria when they were notified that each had satisfied Meyerhold's seemingly unrealizable entrance requirements.

A Student at Meyerhold's Workshops

On September 15, 1921, the two Sergeis formally enrolled in Meyerhold's Directors Workshops on Novinsky Boulevard. For three days, Eisenstein observed Meyerhold's directorial work on Ibsen's *A Doll's House*. Twenty-five years later, writing in his autobiography, Eisenstein remembered that truncated rehearsal period as an artistic epiphany. After listing forty of the greatest experiences and personal introductions in his life — among them, watching Charlie Chaplin shoot a film and George Gershwin perform, attending the Ziegfeld Follies and a New Orleans Mardi Gras, observing Lloyd George in the English Parliament and Tsar Nikolai II in Riga, lunching with Marlene Dietrich and Douglas Fairbanks —

Eisenstein concluded, "But not a single one of these impressions will ever erase from my memory the impressions left on me by those three days. ...I remember shivering continuously. I was not cold; it was excitement, it was nerves stretched to their limit."[8]

From Meyerhold, Eisenstein learned to see the director's role as that of the omniscient figure who totally understands (and utilizes) the invisible efficacy of the theatre's ability to communicate. Watching the "theatrical magician and wizard" teach, Eisenstein fell into a kind of trance. Again from Eisenstein's memoirs: "His lectures were mirages and dreams. The listener would jot down something feverishly. ...But one cannot remember what Meyerhold *said*. Aromas, colors, sounds. A golden haze over everything."[9]

Throughout the fall and winter of 1921, Eisenstein and Yutkevich worked with exceptional vigor in the Directors Workshops. It became evident that there was something unusual about the clownish-looking engineer from Riga, with his bushy hair and open-soled shoes. Aleksandr Fevralsky later recalled, "Eisenstein stood out among the students, even though their numbers included many very talented people."[10] And despite his unathletic appearance, Eisenstein excelled in the Biomechanics and movement sessions. In fact, Eisenstein was appointed to teach Biomechanics to the younger students. Meyerhold himself recognized Eisenstein's special talents and assigned him to research and write entries on theatrical movement and expressive behavior for a planned (but uncompleted) theatrical encyclopedia, a project which Eisenstein took on with considerable enthusiasm.[11]

Outside Meyerhold's theatre, Eisenstein's reputation as a leading innovative theatrical designer grew significantly in the years 1921 and 1922. At the Proletkult and at Nikolai Foregger's independent MASTFOR Theatre, Eisenstein's costume and set designs with their eccentric and risqué details evoked strong interest among the theatregoing intelligentsia. Moreover, stage designers at the large professional theatres like Aleksandr Tairov's Kamerny began imitating Eisenstein's eccentric style almost immediately. But Eisenstein's aesthetic heart lay elsewhere: he wanted to direct.

In December 1921, as part of his GVTM examination, Meyerhold set Eisenstein to work designing an arena stage for a production of Ludwig Tieck's *Puss in Boots*. Drawing on the training he'd received at the Institute of Civil Engineering, Eisenstein was able to complete the student project in just two days. A week later he delivered another scenic design for *The Count of Monte Cristo*. All of this made a suitable impression on the master. At the beginning of 1922, Eisenstein was invited by Meyerhold to work as designer-constructor on his production of George Bernard

Shaw's *Heartbreak House* at the Theatre of the Actor, a collective formed at the beginning of 1922 from the actors of the R.S.F.S.R. Theatre No. 1 and the former Nezlobin Theatre.[12] While the production was rehearsed for several months, it was never mounted. For Eisenstein, who had put so much energy into the planning and designing of the sets and costumes, Meyerhold's abandonment of the production proved a bitter blow. Other disappointments followed.

Eisenstein's initial dispute with Meyerhold was rather basic: Meyerhold seemed to deliberately withhold essential operational information from his young directors. That is, Meyerhold gladly demonstrated his extraordinary ability to reinterpret a play text and block out teams of performers on his vast proscenium stage, but discussion of his inner technique—the creative essence of Meyerhold's thinking—was denied to the members of the Directors Workshops. When Eisenstein insisted that Meyerhold reveal to them "the secrets of his stage direction," Meyerhold became coy and evasive. Then the loyal disciple was shockingly rebuffed. In a flash, Eisenstein was reminded of a traumatic childhood episode when his father refused to explain to him the biological facts of life. Rather than enlighten his naturally curious and sensitive son, Eisenstein's father ridiculed the boy's ignorance. Both of these events remained forever imprinted in Eisenstein's consciousness, to be replayed endlessly in the future. The suddenly withdrawn, then mocking expression that registered on his father's moustached face almost two decades before seemed to reappear vividly on Meyerhold's long and aquiline countenance.[13]

Outwardly Eisenstein showed little response, repeating his adolescent behavior, as he continued to study and design projects for Meyerhold. On April 25, 1922, Eisenstein witnessed the legendary opening night of Meyerhold's Constructivist *The Magnanimous Cuckold*. The next day he departed for Petrograd. Under the influence of Foregger and the youthful Petrograd group, FEKS (the Factory of the Eccentric Actor), Eisenstein and Yutkevich wrote an eccentric pantomime, *Columbine's Garter*. They dedicated it to Meyerhold, who had directed a more traditional version of Arthur Schnitzler's text, *The Veil of Pierrette*, in 1910.

Shortly before the *Cuckold* première, Eisenstein was appointed head of the Moscow Proletkult's theatre department, fulfilling one of his earliest ambitions. He wrote his mother immediately of his joy at now having "full freedom as a director."[14] All summer long in Petrograd Eisenstein worked on his own actor-training program for the Proletkult, which incorporated eccentric movement, acrobatics, boxing, fencing, Biomechanics, sports, diction and speech. When it was put in place in early October, Eisenstein's regimen received much public notice.

In November 1922, Eisenstein began working as an apprentice

director on Meyerhold's staging of Sukhovo-Kobylin's *The Death of Tarelkin*. A landmark of "Eccentricism" in the theatre, the production was planned around a collection of white-painted constructions by artist Varvara Stepanova, all of which were designed to respond in some manner to the actors' "play." Eisenstein eagerly took on the challenge, going even further than Meyerhold in transforming every turn of the text's action into a circus "attraction," a fact which, according to Mikhail Zharov (who played the role of the washerwoman, Mrs. Brandakhlystova), led to considerable friction between Eisenstein and Meyerhold. (Zharov tells how at rehearsal Eisenstein would look around to make certain Meyerhold was nowhere in sight and then call to the actors to "go out and clown it up!"[15])

At the same time Eisenstein was rehearsing *Tarelkin* he was also busy staging circus numbers in Meyerhold's workshop as well as rehearsing his first independent production—Ostrovsky's *Enough Stupidity in Every Wiseman*—at the Proletkult Theatre. In a letter to his mother dated November 11, 1922, Eisenstein outlined his schedule as follows: "Yesterday from 11-3:00 Proletkult—two lectures, 3-6:30—rehearsal of *Tarelkin*, 7-11:30—technical meeting and work on the production at Proletkult."[16]

By the time *Tarelkin* premièred in November 1922, it had become increasingly clear that Eisenstein had outgrown his role of apprentice to Meyerhold. Then in mid-December he received a note during one of his classes from Zinaida Raikh, Meyerhold's wife and one of the professors in the Workshops, saying, "I consider it essential for you to leave Meyerhold, just as Meyerhold once left Stanislavsky. You have matured. I would suggest that you yourself terminate your studies here. When the pupil is not merely the equal to his teacher, but superior, then it is best for the pupil to leave."[17]

This note precipitated a decision that was undoubtedly already growing in Eisenstein's mind. He ended his studies at the Meyerhold Workshops that very day.

Eisenstein's "Wiseman" and "The Montage of Attractions"

On April 2, 1923, for Meyerhold's twenty-fifth anniversary of working in theatre, both Foregger's MASTFOR dance unit and Eisenstein's Proletkult troupe performed work-in-progress scenes for the master. When Eisenstein's *Wiseman* premièred one month later, there was a comic citation of Meyerhold's biomechanical dactyl in an interpolated film clip of

Glumov's diary. (A similar movement quote of Foregger's 1922 mechanized acting grid, Tefiztrenage — an acronym for *telo-fizicheskii-trenazh*, or physical training of the body — would later appear in Eisenstein's epic film *Ivan the Terrible* in 1944.) The jester in Eisenstein would not let him forget his teachers or childhood oppressors.

Eisenstein's departure from Meyerhold's Workshops left him free to concentrate full-time on his production of *The Wiseman* at the Proletkult Theatre. It was during this period of intensive artistic creativity that Eisenstein began developing many of his most lasting aesthetic ideas. Looking at the theatre from a materialist — even an industrial — point of view, Eisenstein began to justify many of the most illogical, eccentric, and possibly ridiculous aspects of the new Constructivist theatre. If the theatre, like a factory, were reduced to its essential, productive elements, what would be left? For Eisenstein, only those features that cause emotional or ideological reactions in the spectator. Those shocks, or "attractions" — not the plot, language, dramatic interactions, etc. — held the key to the new ideological art. For example, the political, social, emotional imprints that are registered in the spectator's mind during a four-hour performance of *Hamlet* could be created in a fraction of that time with the proper sequence of "attractions." Among these "attractions," a great many could be discovered in popular entertainments. Constructivist theatre now had a scientific and cogent performance theory, "The Montage of Attractions."

Reworking Ostrovsky's nineteenth-century comedy *Enough Stupidity in Every Wiseman* into a contemporary, zany circus production, called *The Wiseman* for short, Eisenstein and his Proletkult actors transformed the "Montage" theory into an hysterical and startling evening of topical jokes, melodramatic film clips, tightrope walking, tap dancing, vaudeville stunts, scatological and political puns, clowning, and more. The immediate success of *The Wiseman*, which opened on May 8, 1923, and the publication of his "Montage of Attractions" in *Lef*[18] did much to enhance Eisenstein's reputation — he became almost a celebrity.

But now much of the criticism leveled against other Constructivist directors also applied to Eisenstein. The "mathematically calculated" shocks were for the most part arbitrarily or intuitively placed in the play. Left-wing critics found the entire production, supposedly for a proletarian audience, unintelligible to anyone. Even the acting in *The Wiseman*, largely improvisational and Commedia-like, ran counter to the efficient, streamlined actions called for by the Constructivists. Eisenstein now set off on a new path, one more in line with current avant-garde concerns and his own theories.

Director and Teacher at the Proletkult

Just as soon as Eisenstein took over as head of the Proletkult's Touring Theatre (Pere Tru, short for Peredvizhnaya truppa) in autumn 1922, he began to expand and redesign the Proletkult workshop's basic training program. Under the leadership of Valentin Smyshlyaev, an actor from the First Studio of the Moscow Art Theatre, Proletkult students had formerly been schooled in Prosvetov's tonal-plastic techniques, a kind of musical acrobatics which, according to Aleksandr Levshin, Eisenstein dubbed "Plastitution."[19] Now, under Eisenstein's guidance they concentrated on a wide range of physical training activities, including boxing, fencing, team sports, tumbling, acrobatics, circus techniques and Biomechanics.

In his search for additional material on movement, Eisenstein turned to a number of texts just coming out of Central Europe, many of which Sergei Tretyakov had brought back from Germany in 1922. The most important of these was Rudolf Bode's *Expressive Gymnastics*,[20] a book that would provide a basis for much of Eisenstein's work with the actor in both theatre and film. Not only did Bode's theories resolve certain internal conflicts between Constructivist doctrine and scenic practice for Eisenstein, they answered many criticisms directed at Constructivist performance per se. Now the creative role of the actor was clear.

In 1911, Rudolf Bode had established a studio for the study of human movement in Munich. Once a pupil of Dalcroze and his Eurhythmics, Bode vehemently rejected the popular movement philosophy that linked music to human rhythms. According to Bode, recent French, Italian, and German findings proved the folly of exercising the body in artificial, dissociated ways. Only full, natural movements allowed the body to function properly. This "organic-rhythmic" training, Expressive Gymnastics, had gained many adherents in Germany by the early twenties.

For Eisenstein, Bode's book furnished a veritable gold mine of new movement ideas, scientific terminology, and even a set number of exercises and tables. Some of Meyerhold's chief acting concerns—the primacy of balance, the muscular release between gestures, and so forth—were discussed by Bode, but along more modern, anatomical lines. Exactly how much Bode's gymnastics figured directly in the Proletkult training sessions is not clear. However, the lectures on Biomechanics dating from that period which Eisenstein gave at the Proletkult Theatre clearly reflect the influence of Bode's writing on expressive movement.

In his new training program at the Proletkult, Eisenstein divided each performer's stage actions into expressive movements and *raccourcis*. For Eisenstein an expressive movement was one that was executed with animal- or machine-like efficiency, but was bound up with human psychology—a dialectic of instinctive and rationalized reaction. If a Proletkult performer was requested to commit a strangulation on the stage, his behavior and action would more closely resemble the rhythm and pacing of a mindful cobra attacking a rabbit than the stagy indications of a proscenium actor. Eisenstein took certain common expressive gestures like the unfolding of a fist, the arching of an eyebrow, and the chattering of teeth, and isolated and enlarged them. Then, finely choreographing all his stage performers according to specific, "attractive" sculptural groupings (*raccourcis*), he was able to guide the eye of the spectator toward these expressive details. In this way, Eisenstein developed the theatrical equivalent of a cinematic close-up.

By alternating between expressive movements and *raccourcis* devised according to strict mathematical formulas, a visual rhythm could be created on the stage that Eisenstein claimed would powerfully affect the psyche of the spectator. Together with the automatically shocking attractions, this "montage of movements" would effect an emotional and intellectual change in the audience. In practice, these experiments proved more successful than anyone from the Proletkult had suspected.

Using the various Communist revolts in Germany and Hungary after World War I as its inspiration, Tretyakov's new play, *Do You Hear, Moscow?!, An Agit-Guignol*,[21] owed as much to the Grand Guignol and traditional melodrama as to the historical documentation. Filled with stock characters, the play detailed the struggle between a decadent aristocrat and his reactionary cronies against the leaders of a subdued working class. Unlike *The Wiseman*, the language and plotting were so simple as to resemble a children's story.

The many dozens of attractions with which Eisenstein overburdened *The Wiseman* were reduced in *Do You Hear, Moscow?!* to approximately twenty. Each of the four acts was given its own mood and pacing, filled with long pauses that reminded many critics of the work of the Moscow Art Theatre. The first act, for example, was organized around the themes of sexual struggle and class betrayal. In other acts, the attractions revolved around themes of violence, pathos, and mystery: the sound of a gunshot (act 4); the unmasking of Shtumm (act 2); his stabbing (act 2); the secret plan (act 2); the kicking and beating of the critically-wounded Kurt (act 3); the pairing of the hammer and sickle (act 4); the unveiling of Lenin's portrait in the place of the reactionary statue (act 4); and finally, the workers' revolt (act 4).

The première of *Do You Hear, Moscow?!* was reserved for November 7, the anniversary of the Bolshevik Revolution. This was also supposed to be the actual time that the play's last act was to take place. Interestingly, a number of critics who were commissioned to review the performance wrote very little about the production itself.[22] Nevertheless, Eisenstein and Tretyakov were both very pleased with the results. At one performance, Tretyakov noted, someone in the audience shouted at the actors that the Count was escaping in the fourth act.[23] Members of the audience applauded with the killing of each reactionary. In a back row, a soldier with a handgun became so excited that he started to move toward the stage in order to assist the actors playing the revolutionaries. Eventually someone grabbed him and brought the soldier to his senses.

Tretyakov wrote that the performers themselves were affected by these audience reactions.[24] At one performance, the student actors who were hired to construct the Count's festival platform in a rhythmic fashion during each night's intermission rushed the stage when the uprising occurred in the last act. Like *The Wiseman*, *Do You Hear, Moscow?!* remained in the Proletkult's repertoire until the end of spring 1925. It played a total of sixty-three performances.

The Proletkult's announcement that its next production, Tretyakov's *Gas Masks*,[25] would be presented in the Moscow Gas Works on the outskirts of the city caused quite a stir. Based on an actual newspaper report, *Gas Masks* recorded the heroic struggle of Soviet workers to seal a gas leak without the aid of any protective garments or masks. Eisenstein set the production in the center of the factory amidst turbines and catwalks, seating the audience on wooden benches in a cleared area. The acrid, gassy smell, the peculiar lighting, the enormous gas tanks and slowly revolving machinery manned by actual workers, all produced a strange and novel effect on the audience. Although years later Eisenstein in a credit-debit accounting of his professional career listed this as one of his failures,[26] others who saw the production thought otherwise.

Clearly, *Gas Masks* encountered serious production problems that no one had considered. Few Moscow spectators wanted to take the long tram ride into the dreary gray suburbs. Even the Moscow Gas Works administrators found the performances something of a nuisance. The inclusion of a real environment in performance, while novel, just made too many demands on a theatre-jaded public. In all, *Gas Masks* was performed only six times in March and April of 1924 and six times the following fall.

Film Acting

Eisenstein's radical transformation from theatre to film director following his production of *Gas Masks* in 1924 has often been overstated. In fact, his work with film actors on the set and in the classroom bears many resemblances to his directing in the theatre. In one of his first statements as a filmmaker, written for Aleksandr Belenson's *Cinema Today* (Moscow, 1925), but edited in an unacceptable form, Eisenstein made frequent references to the overlapping elements of the revolutionary theatre and cinema.

For his first film, *Strike*, in 1924, Eisenstein reworked the theatrical modes of his earlier Proletkult productions into a cinematic anthology of acting styles. The professional Proletkult actors and circus performers in *Strike* enacted the parts of labor villains, spies, cabaret entertainers, and ridiculous lowlifes according to Eisenstein's own trademark comic-grotesque from the *Wiseman*. These characters, with their clownish make-up and somersaulting antics, created a sharp contrast to the naturalistic, slow-moving proletariat, who were drawn from a pool of real workers and their families. Cast according to realistic appearance only, there was virtually nothing theatrical or artistic about this mass protagonist. The dramatic use of nonactors had its origins in Eisenstein's environmental *Gas Masks*, where factory workers manipulated machinery and gas jets at intervals during the productions. Finally, Expressive Movement as he developed it in *Do You Hear, Moscow?!* formed a basis of acting behavior during the moments of physical struggle and sexual seduction in *Strike*. On the street, in the private cabaret rooms, and across the generator booth, Proletkult performers executed Bode's exercises under Eisenstein's exacting direction to show the maximum amount of expressiveness in human conflict. Never again would Eisenstein's acting ideas appear so theatrically classifiable within a film.

Expressive Movement

There is a section in Eisenstein's 1924 essay "The Montage of Film Attractions"[27] that discusses Bode and other movement philosophers. In addition there is a citation referring the reader to Eisenstein's own brochure on *Expressive Movement*. Although never published, the brochure Eisenstein had in mind was the manuscript on Expressive Movement he wrote jointly with Tretyakov in 1923. Meyerhold's invitation to write on movement for the proposed theatrical encyclopedia at his State Higher Theatre Workshops had been just the excuse Eisenstein needed to set to work on his favorite theme of expressive movement. He wanted his study to be scientific, and considering himself a poor writer, he asked Tretyakov, a brilliant stylist, to help him. Tretyakov, who at the time was working with Eisenstein on *The Wiseman*, also became interested in the question of expressive movement, and together they completed the manuscript.[28]

In the first section of "Expressive Movement" Eisenstein reviews and restates Bode's basic axioms. Essentially, Eisenstein uncritically accepted Bode's assertions:

1. Movements are caused by willed conscious impulses or natural reflexive actions.
2. The development of the body must be based on full, natural movements that involve the entire musculature, as opposed to isolated, artifical exercises.
3. Inner rhythms of movements are fixed in the body—they can only be consciously retarded or quickened.
4. Relaxation is based on the natural release of muscles, or rhythm.

According to Bode, Expressive Movement involves the dialectic between goal-oriented, willed activity (sports) and pure, instinctive movement (dance). Correctly executed, an Expressive Movement would utilize the total—internal/external, muscular/nervous—aspects of our being. To Eisenstein, the difference between nonexpressive and expressive action would roughly be the difference between a chorus girl's smile and a peasant girl's: the former uses only her facial muscles; the latter, her entire body.

About the same time, Eisenstein also made notes for a study of "Biomechanics in the Representational Aspects of Honoré Daumier's Lithographs." Eisenstein's objective in doing such an analysis was to determine how, through the depiction of a *raccourci* (a fixed moment of movement), the impression of expressive movement could be conveyed. One of the key points Eisenstein makes in his notes is that "the object of the actor's *raccourci* is not the reproduction of something, but through himself (i.e., through excitation by him of the spectator) to evoke in another person something determined in advance." This evocation of emotion in the spectator (i.e., "attraction-ness"), Eisenstein goes on to point out, is impossible unless the movement is organically, that is, biomechanically, constructed.

These unpublished works detail Eisenstein's key concepts of Expressive Movement, aspects of which can clearly be seen in the stills for his last two theatre productions and in certain sections of *Strike* (1925), especially in the third part. They are also very much present in segments of *Ivan the Terrible* (1944–1946), and in a sense Eisenstein's final film was, as Naum Kleiman hypothesizes, a prolog to the major work on Expressive Movement which Eisenstein had long planned to write.[29] In a curious way Eisenstein was so schooled in Biomechanics that consciously or unconsciously its principles also went into his drawings, many of which could easily serve as illustrations for certain of the biomechanical exercises and études.

Eisenstein could never quite forgive Meyerhold for not creating a theoretical basis for his work with actors. In his diary (February 22, 1929) Eisenstein called "the pitiful rags of biomechanical theory, in comparison to the graceful teachings of the Bode Schule, pure impressionistic empiricism."[30] In the same diary entry Eisenstein maintains that what Meyerhold taught was not a system but simply the accumulation of his own wealth of acting experience. Eisenstein was also very sensitive to any suggestion that his theories on Expressive Movement had come from Meyerhold.

Still, in talking to his students Eisenstein frequently referred to Meyerhold's Biomechanics, and biomechanical exercises were included in the courses on movement that were taught at the State Institute of Cinematography beginning in the late 1920s. Although in many respects flawed as a training system for the actor, Eisenstein regarded Biomechanics as "the best there is," adding that "from it, you can get some kind of basic positions." His main criticism of other forms of physical training, especially those relying on gymnastic equipment, were that they developed the upper torso, rather than the musculature man needs in his activities today. As Eisenstein reminded his students, "People long ago stopped swinging from branch to branch."[31]

Eisenstein believed it was just as important for directors as for actors to know, not in the abstract, but through actual training, all of the principles of Expressive Movement. As he stated in his first lecture on film directing:

> Supposing you need to show someone a gesture, or not even show it, but think one up. Keep in mind that if you can't even embryonically, even "in an atom" make some movement, you can't think up that movement either. That may seem unbelievable to you, but that's the way it is. It doesn't mean that if you know what a somersault is, you must be able to make one. But you must know how *in a motor sense to experience* a somersault, to have the feeling of how it is done.
>
> It is almost impossible to remember a movement just by seeing it, it is remembered only by means of movements by the entire body. And there are a whole series of things you can't put into words because they won't fit into words. When you have to find the best of all the variant movements, you must know how to demonstrate it with your own body since you cannot describe it in words.[32]

Eisenstein and Meyerhold, Artistic Rivals

The saga of Eisenstein and Meyerhold did not end with Eisenstein's departure from GVRM. In the spring of 1925, when Eisenstein broke with the Proletkult Theatre over the increasingly reactionary policies of its leaders, a break that was precipitated by the dispute over the authorship of the script of *The Strike*, it was Meyerhold who came to his former pupil's defense.[33] In a long discussion with Eisenstein, Meyerhold tried to persuade him not to abandon the theatre entirely in favor of film. He even offered him a choice of productions—*Hamlet*, *The Inspector General*, or *Woe from Wit*—to direct independently at the Meyerhold Theatre. On July 7, 1925, an announcement appeared in *Pravda* stating that Eisenstein would be directing Crommelynck's *Golden Guts* at the Meyerhold Theatre. But by then, Eisenstein was already immersed in filming *The Battleship Potemkin*, and nothing further was heard of this project.[34]

Even as Eisenstein's star as a film director continued to rise, thoughts of Meyerhold never left his mind. Eisenstein never publicly criticized his former teacher, preferring instead to confide all his feelings of resentment and jealousy to his diary.[35] "Meier's 'Saturnism,' devouring his children—his way of throwing out [his pupils] the moment they reveal the least sign of independence or talent...." he wrote in an entry dated February 22, 1927.[36] The theme of Saturn devouring his offspring came up again that same year in a discussion with the Austrian writer Stefan Zweig of Sigmund Freud's jealousy and suspicion. The German psychiatrist's ruthless treatment of his disciples when they sought to go their own way again led Eisenstein to draw disturbing parallels with his own separation from Meyerhold.[37] And so obsessed was Eisenstein with the haunting specter of his tutor that in the middle of shooting in Mexico four years later, when falsely informed that the old man had died, he immediately dashed off an obituary for Meyerhold. Praising Meyerhold the individual genius, not the teacher or director, Eisenstein wrote, "The last bearer of true theatre has died.... The most complete exponent of the Theatre. ...And the most brilliant of Theatres."[38]

Eisenstein and Meyerhold's paths again crossed following the film director's return from Mexico in May 1932. This was a period of great personal crisis for Eisenstein, not only because of his devastating failure to complete *Que Viva Mexico!*, but also because he came back to a completely different political-cultural situation from the one he had left in August 1929.

On October 1, Eisenstein was confirmed as chairman of the Department of Film Directing at the State Institute of Cinematography (GIK), and the following year he immersed himself in teaching directing at the Institute. Among the courses included was one on Biomechanics conducted by one of Meyerhold's teachers, Zosima Zlobin. It was at this time that Eisenstein also began exploring in greater detail certain aspects of Biomechanics, for example, the theoretical basis of the recoil (*otkaz*) not only in relation to physical movement, but also as a psychological process.

While there is little specific information presently available documenting Meyerhold and Eisenstein's relationship during the 1930s, it is clear that in the period between his return from Mexico and the start of work on *Bezhin Meadow* in 1935, Eisenstein attended Meyerhold's rehearsals, including *The Prelude*, where in one photograph taken at rehearsal Eisenstein is seen seated at a table with Meyerhold. And as indicated by his lecture, "*Katerina Izmailova* and *The Lady of the Camellias*," Eisenstein was far more familiar with Meyerhold's 1934 production of Dumas *fils*' classic than would have been possible from merely having attended a performance.[39]

On August 20, 1934, an announcement appeared in the newspaper *Evening Moscow* stating that Eisenstein would be directing in collaboration with Ilya Shlepyanov (also a former pupil of Meyerhold's), Natan A. Zarkhi's *Moscow Two* at Meyerhold's former Theatre of the Revolution.[40] But following the announcement nothing more was heard of the project.

Two years later, in early 1936, a group of young actors from Nikolai Khmelev's studio asked Eisenstein to organize a theatre under his leadership. Eisenstein met with the artist Pyotr Vilyams and the composer Vissarion Shebalin (both friends and colleagues of Meyerhold's) along with Aleksandr Gladkov, representing the actors, to discuss the project. As Gladkov recalled, "Eisenstein treated the [proposal] enigmatically — both ironically and with interest. He didn't say no, more accurately, he agreed, but put off his participation in the work of the young theatre until the completion of his film, *Bezhin Meadow*."[41]

But once again, Eisenstein backed away from coming into direct competition with Meyerhold in the theatre, preferring to continue his covert polemic with his former teacher through film. Not until after Meyerhold was arrested in June 1939 did Eisenstein return to the theatre, this time to direct a production of Wagner's *Die Walküre* which premièred at the Bolshoi Theatre on November 21, 1940.

According to Aleksandr Fevralsky, it was during this same period that Eisenstein received several proposals to take part in projects connected with the theory of theatre. As secretary of the directing sector of the All-Russia Theatre Society (VTO) Leonid Varpakhovsky announced that at the behest of Stanislavsky, Meyerhold (chairman of the theatre sector), and Eisenstein, a proposal was made to Ivan Pavlov to collaborate on a project for the study of the nervous system at the moment of elevated artistic arousal, and that Pavlov had agreed. However, nothing came of this project. In 1936, Eisenstein's name was also listed as one of the staff of the Scientific-Research Laboratory at Meyerhold's Theatre, although, as Fevralsky notes, Eisenstein took no part in the Laboratory's work.[42]

Meyerhold, too, could not get Eisenstein out of his mind. In a lecture on June 13, 1936, comparing the "astonishing resemblance between the work of Chaplin and Eisenstein," Meyerhold maintained that "All Eisenstein's work has its origins in the laboratory where we once worked together as a teacher and pupil. But our relationship was not so much the relationship of teacher and pupil as of two artists in revolt...."[43] One month later, he sent Eisenstein a photograph inscribed, "I am proud of the pupil who is already a master. I love the master who has already created a school. To this pupil, this master—Sergei Eisenstein—my admiration."[44]

During this period of reconciliation when both artists were under attack by the increasingly repressive cultural apparatus, Eisenstein sat in on the rehearsals of Meyerhold's unrealized production of Pushkin's *Boris Godunov*, as well as of Meyerhold's final production, *One Life*.[45] Mikhail Sadovsky, who joined Meyerhold's theatre in 1934, also recalls Eisenstein's presence at a gathering at the Meyerhold apartment on Bryusov Lane to celebrate Zinaida Raikh's birthday.[46] And during the summer of 1937, Eisenstein served as an intermediary in effecting a reconciliation between playwright Vsevolod Vishnevsky and Meyerhold.[47]

Although Eisenstein was himself under a cloud following the banning of his film *Bezhin Meadow*, when word reached him that the Meyerhold Theatre was to be closed following the performance of *The Lady of the Camellias* on Saturday evening, January 7, 1938, he immediately began calling around to his friends urging them to attend, and at least one of them, Aleksandr Dovzhenko, did.[48]

Following the closing of the Meyerhold Theatre, a group of leading actors from that theatre met several times at Fevralsky's apartment to discuss how they could continue to work together to preserve the best traditions of Meyerhold's Theatre. As Fevralsky reports, they decided to form a new theatre to be called the Mayakovsky Theatre. And as its head all agreed on one person, Sergei Eisenstein. "He didn't immediately give his answer—he needed time to think over the proposal," Fevralsky recalls. "I renewed talks with him several times, and finally Sergei Mikhailovich said that he could not take on the leadership of the theatre."[49]

Eisenstein and Meyerhold met for the last time, most probably, in early 1939. From the very poignant description of this final meeting in Eisenstein's memoirs entitled, "Farewell," it is possible to hypothesize that since the taller figure (Meyerhold) was wearing a topcoat and galoshes, the encounter took place in either late winter or early spring of that year.[50] The square Eisenstein describes "in the heart of Moscow," his references to the cupolas of Russian cathedrals and to the bell tower of Ivan the Terrible point to the fact that this final meeting took place in the Kremlin. As Naum Kleiman speculates, it is not coincidental that Eisenstein chose as a backdrop the decor Golovin had painted for the coronation scene in Meyerhold's 1911 production of the opera, *Boris Godunov*, which, in fact, Eisenstein had seen as a student in St. Petersburg.[51] Or that he was at the time working on a project for a film about Pushkin, perhaps inspired by the rehearsals he had witnessed of Meyerhold's *Boris*.[52]

And here in this scene out of Russian history, like a faithful page, Eisenstein at great risk remains with his master, handing him his topcoat.[53] As for the date of this final meeting, on February 1, Eisenstein, by order of the Presidium of the Supreme Soviet of the U.S.S.R., had been awarded the Order of Lenin for his film *Alexander Nevsky*. Eisenstein, who did not like attending official receptions, would however, have been obliged to be present for the presentation of the awards at the Kremlin on February 17.[54] And Meyerhold, as head of the Stanislavsky Opera Theatre, would also have received an invitation. Very likely it was this occasion that brought the two men together for the last time.

To the end of his life, Eisenstein remained true to his former teacher. On the eve of World War II, at the request of Meyerhold's stepdaughter, Tatiana Esenina, Eisenstein agreed to secrete Meyerhold's personal archive at his dacha on the outskirts of Moscow.[55] This act of loyalty was done at great personal risk for a man who had suffered more than once at the hands of the Kremlin censors and anxious apparatchiks. With his arrest in June 1939, Meyerhold had suddenly become a nonentity, never to be referred to or spoken of, in the Stalinist attempt to reedit Soviet history and culture. But Eisenstein was psychologically compelled to rescue the memory of his teacher. Their relationship had yet to be resolved.

In his premature obituary of Meyerhold written in 1931, Eisenstein wrote, "I think that the highest tribute of respect to the teacher from the student-surgeon would be to ... examine him after his death ... in no way [as] an insult to the dead, but [as] a tribute of the highest respect and admiration."[56] With Meyerhold's papers now in his possession, Eisenstein at last had the opportunity to delve into the "methodological treasure-house" that Meyerhold had always refused to reveal to him. And indeed, Eisenstein did just that in the remaining years of his life, even carrying a part of the archive with him to Alma Alta to pore over as he worked on his final film project, *Ivan the Terrible*.[57]

In September 1940, Eisenstein started writing the scenario for the three-part epic *Ivan the Terrible*. Although American and European critics saw direct resemblances between the brutal and persecuted figure of the sixteenth-century Tsar, as envisaged by Eisenstein, and the contemporary Stalin, more personal factors manifested themselves in this difficult, complex art piece. For one, a scene showing the adolescent Tsar sitting on the throne with his feet dangling over the edge, short of the floor,

A scene from Sergei Eisenstein's film, *Ivan the Terrible*. Ivan (Nikolai Cherkasov) grabs the dagger from the hand of the messenger with a classic biomechanical gesture.

paralleled the comic image of the diminutive Eisenstein doing the same in the Tsar's palace many years before.

More significantly, *Ivan* reflects for the last time that complex relationship between pupil and teacher that more than once had motivated Eisenstein's film work. With this film, Eisenstein completes the tragic history of Russia begun by Meyerhold in *Boris Godunov*. And at the same time, in Nikolai Cherkasov's portrayal Ivan was made to look and even behave like Meyerhold, who back in his Moscow Art Theatre days had played the role of Ivan for Stanislavsky in 1899. Cherkasov, who came close to suffering a complete nervous breakdown from Eisenstein's manic and exacting direction, thought the film director was totally obsessed with the character of Ivan. Delays brought about by Eisenstein's constant tinkering with the script and editing almost doomed the entire film.[58]

While recuperating from a heart attack in 1946, Eisenstein wrote in his posthumously-published memoirs, "I never loved, idolized, worshipped anyone as I did my teacher. ...The divine! The incomparable! Meyerhold. ...I was to worship him all my life."[59] This was Eisenstein's last statement on Vsevolod Meyerhold. Fourteen months later, Eisenstein, having just turned fifty, like his father died of a heart attack.

Part II
Biomechanics

Eisenstein:	What basic principles of movement are found in Biomechanics, what are its basic tenets?
Tryaskin:	Movement with a minimal expenditure of energy.
Ivanov:	Everything is from the big toe.
Gakel:	Springs.
Tokmasib:	The working out of precision in movement.
Tryaskin:	Coordination of all movements.
Eisenstein:	According to what principle?
Volodarsky:	In Biomechanics there is maximum efficiency. It is like a worker's lathe: without taking emotion and experiencing into account.
Kustov:	According to the simplest route.
Eisenstein:	And what is that simplest route?
Kustov:	The most economical, the most expressive.
Eisenstein:	What else?
Goltsov:	Probably with the least expenditure of energy.
Eisenstein:	I must say that your information, to put it mildly, is superficial.

Sergei Eisenstein and his students
Institute of Cinematography
March 29, 1935

Chapter 4

Introduction

> *In creating Biomechanics, I tried to shield the young actor from a passion for the saccharine barefoot dancing à la Duncan, or the plastic affectation in the spirit of Goleizovsky.* [1]
> V. E. Meyerhold

The Three-Dimensional Actor

To Meyerhold, technique was just as important for the actor as for the pianist or ballet dancer. He deplored the fact that so little attention was devoted to teaching the art of form and movement as a means of dramatic expression. During a rehearsal in 1935 he observed:

> You could chop off both hands of any Russian actor and nothing would change because the Russian actor has not cultivated the language of gesture. He has no language of the hands. [He moves his hands about] but that has nothing to do with the expressive language of gesture. It's only filling the air, often for no known purpose.[2]

If physical action on the stage and psychological state were interrelated, Meyerhold did not belabor the point as Stanislavsky did. Instead, he concentrated on the outward manifestation of whatever inner emotion might be involved. Citing Constant-Benoît Coquelin, he pointed out that "the talented actor always deeply experiences his role, the untalented only presents it."[3]

But to "experience" the role was not the same in Meyerhold's lexicon as that total infusion of the actor with his role that Stanislavsky had in mind when he talked about the "magical, creative *if*" which would enable the actor to pass "from the plane of actual reality into the plane of another life, created and imagined by himself."[4] Like Coquelin, Meyerhold argued that the actor "should not forget for a single moment that there is an audience before him, under his feet a stage, and around him, a stage setting."[5]

Furthermore, Meyerhold said, the actor must always bear in mind the duality of his position: that he is at the same time both the artist and the object of his art. The actor must deliberately cultivate the ability to do what Meyerhold called "mirrorizing" one's self. By this, Meyerhold meant not only to act, but simultaneously to observe one's self from the outside as if in a mirror. The objective of such observation was not to find some "pretty" or "interesting" gesture or movement. But, as in the Kabuki theatre, when the actor studies his role in front of the mirror, it was to achieve an elegance of line and form, free of all extraneous elements.

When Meyerhold did speak to his actors about "feeling," he often had in mind something quite different from Stanislavsky's "expression of emotion." For Meyerhold, "feeling" was strictly a technical term having to do with helping the actor to find positions and movements that were not only expressive, but also ones he could live with. Meyerhold always knew exactly what effect he wanted his actors to achieve. Hence his reputation for being something of a dictator. This was true of Stanislavsky as well, but his use of psychological techniques and "guided" improvisation as part of his actor training tended to mask this fact.

Meyerhold was very aware that the actor had to *feel* physically right in the performance of his role. As he said to the actress who played Liza in his 1928 production of Griboyedov's classic *Woe from Wit* (which Meyerhold retitled *Woe to Wit*):

> I'm not saying that you have to do exactly that.... I could suggest something, of course, but it would be better if you fixed [the movements] yourself. I could suggest something that wasn't at all right, and it would be uncomfortable for you to carry it out.... I can only say that [a given movement] will be grasped by the spectators well, and [another] poorly.[6]

Meyerhold never forgot for a moment what the effect of a performer's action would be on the audience. And for him this was always the ultimate test. During rehearsal he once called to an actor, "Stop, change your position! Sit more firmly, more comfortably." And when the actor objected that he was quite comfortable, Meyerhold replied:

> I don't care so much if you're comfortable. I care much more that the spectator doesn't fear for you, that he doesn't worry about your being uncomfortable. This pointless worry distracts him from the scene we are playing....[7]

In rehearsing a scene, Meyerhold functioned like a super mirror, constantly "reflecting back" to the actors the effect on the audience of their movements and pauses. At the same time, he was the master artist making certain that at each instant every individual actor was properly placed in the overall composition. Boris Alpers wrote:

> The acting image lost its independent significance. It became one of the many equal elements in the general landscape of the production. The performer's acting in large measure took on a decorative, pictorial quality. The actor had to know how, at any given moment, to incorporate himself into the ensemble of the *decor* as an essential and deliberate part of it, as a detail in it.[8]

Throughout his career as a director, Meyerhold always formulated a production in terms of very concrete pictorial images. Meyerhold knew and loved art. An inveterate collector of art reproductions, he frequently used specific paintings in determining a mise en scène. For example, when staging *Sister Beatrice* in 1906, he brought pictures of altar paintings by Hans Memling to the theatre to show his actors the kind of compositional arrangements he was trying to achieve. His staging of Episode 14, "The Dining Room," for his 1928 production of *Woe to Wit* drew upon works by such diverse artists as Leonardo da Vinci, George Grosz, and Diego Rivera to create one of the most extraordinary scenic compositions of his career. His 1934 production of Dumas' *The Lady of the Camellias*, on the other hand, was inspired by the paintings and drawings of Degas, Manet, and especially Renoir.

In one of his last lectures in 1938, Meyerhold told a class of future directors:

> In the pictures of great artists you will find interesting compositions, original rhythmical solutions. Then when you have to find a compositional solution for a scene in a production, your imagination, trained on works by great artists, will indicate the correct way to you.[9]

For Meyerhold, patterns of movement on the stage were always a key element of these visual compositions. He had an exceptional gift for seeing action on the stage with the eye of an artist composing a painting. He frequently advised his actors to "look at good pictures more often, and you'll never have to think about what to do with your hands and feet. They will find the right position by themselves."[10] Meyerhold would develop even the most insignificant moment in a production with painstaking care to make it as visually expressive as possible. And always in his mind was the creation of an effective *raccourci*, or "instantaneous, expressive moment of repose."

The *raccourci*, an art term borrowed from the French, and meaning "foreshortening," is a key concept for understanding Meyerhold's work with actors. Related to the *mie* of the Kabuki theatre, it is what Alpers refers to when he speaks of the replacement of the acrobatic principle, "movement as a uninterrupted chain of changes in the actor's position,"

position," which characterized Meyerhold's earliest productions, by the principle of "distinct segments of movement always ending with a static position, a pose, a frozen moment of mime."[11]

Speaking to pupils at the Proletkult Theatre on Meyerhold's Biomechanics, Eisenstein made a crucial distinction between the "pose," which he characterized as "an arrangement of the body in a harmonious whole, pleasant for observation, without a utilitarian objective," and the *raccourci*, which, he said, is "an arrangement for maximum expressiveness, the essentiality of the movement, mechanically made acute."

One of the main reasons why Meyerhold's productions have remained so vivid in the memories of those who saw them is precisely because of his awareness of the importance of the *raccourci*, the significant moment, in staging a production. In effect, it is these moments, what dance photographer Barbara Morgan has called, "the crystallization of . . . essential gestures," imprinted in the memory of the spectator, that are later recalled like so many photographs to once again bring the production back to life.[12]

Chapter 5

Biomechanical Exercises

Biomechanics is an actor training system made up of a series of physical exercises and études. These psycho-physical routines range in complexity from simple movements (raising the body on tiptoe, balancing on one foot) to the most complex, coordinated actions for individuals ("Shooting with Bow and Arrow"), pairs ("Slap on the Face," "Stab with a Dagger") or groups ("Horse," "Fool"). All of the exercises are based on natural, organic movements and require no special gymnastic equipment.

Each of the exercises was designed with the following objectives in mind:

1. To enable the actor to feel the balance and center of gravity within himself, that is, to develop complete control over one's own body.

2. To enable the actor to position and coordinate himself three-dimensionally in relation to the stage space, one's partner, and the stage properties. In other words, to facilitate the development of a "good eye" so that the actor becomes a moving part of a harmonious whole.

3. To develop in the actor physical or reflexive arousal for instantaneous and non-conscious reaction.

Meyerhold liked to compare the Biomechanical exercises to the Hannon scales and the Czerny études a pianist uses to learn technique. With a mastery of the principles of Biomechanics, the actor is equipped to break up movements into their basic components and to arrange particular movements to form *raccourcis*. As Eisenstein stated in his 1923 lecture on Biomechanics, it is the ability to "analyze, synthesize, and construct a movement, consciously to develop and use the *raccourci*" that is achieved through Biomechanics.

Occasionally assisted by Meyerhold, the Biomechanics instructors Valery Inkizhinov, Mikhail Korenev, and later Nikolai Kustov, and Meyerhold's daughter, Irina, each designed their own daily one-hour sessions for each class of actors, which varied from eight to approximately thirty

100 Biomechanics

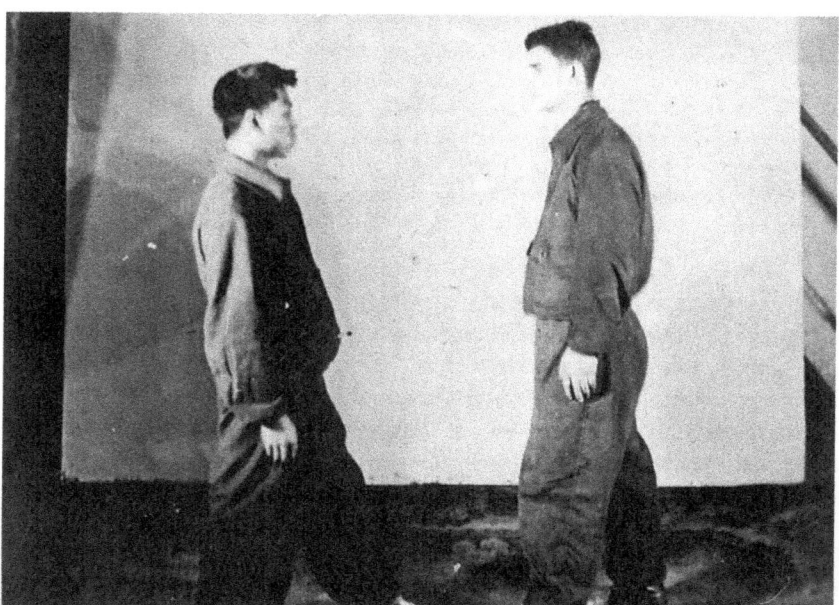

This and facing pages: Parade and preliminary positioning of partners for the exercise "Slap on the Face."

5. *Biomechanical Exercises* 101

Note: All of the photographs of Meyerhold's actors performing biomechanical exercises were taken between 1922 and 1924.

members. Typically, a single session consisted of practice in supplementary biomechanical exercises, which were keyed to the physical execution of the exercises, and two biomechanical études separated by one fifteen-minute rest period.

Meyerhold recommended that the actors wear lightweight practice clothes—shirts and skirts for the women, trousers for the men—rather than tights of the type used by ballet dancers. In this way the students learned to get a feel for the lines and folds of a costume. It was only in demonstrations that the actors wore shorts to enable the audience to observe their movements more closely.

All of the exercises are initially conducted to commands given by the instructor. The command can be simply a snapping of the fingers, but most generally the word "Hup!" is used to designate the shift from one stage of the exercise to the next. Once the exercises and études are mastered, they can then be performed without a verbal command.

Piano music is also used to guide the actor in setting an emotional tempo that sometimes conflicts with the natural rhythmic organization of the étude. The music itself, which may vary from classical and romantic melodies such as Chopin études to a vaudevillian tune, functions differently in each étude, frequently correlating body rhythms to melody; at other times, notes and tempos are played against rests and breathing spans. The objective is to develop in the actor the ability to translate rhythm and tempo into the language of movement. The biomechanical exercises, unlike the études—since their purpose is a purely physical adjunct for the psycho-physical études—are performed without music.

There are in Biomechanics many elements of general physical training. But whereas gymnastics relies mainly on developing the shoulders and upper torso and leads to mechanized, unnatural movement, Biomechanics is focused on the waist and the springiness of the legs. Although tension or muscular strength is often called for, there must never be any suggestion of military rigidity or robot-like movements. "Remember," Meyerhold frequently noted to his actors, "you don't have two feet, but four: the right forward and the right rear, the left forward and the left rear." The actor must always strive for loose, relaxed movements, as if on "springs," as Korenev characterized it in his "Principles," or in the spirit of what Meyerhold called "dancingness [*dantsantnost'*]."

In contrast to pantomime, in which the movements are highly refined (the fingers, the hands), biomechanical movements are much larger and broader (the torso, the shoulders, legs, and arms). When the hands and fingers are not called into play (making a fist, pulling out an imaginary bow, pointing), they always remain completely relaxed, wrists loose. For the beginner, this "looseness" is one of the most difficult things to achieve, especially for anyone trained in ballet, in which the hands and fingers play an entirely different role.

Also, unlike fencing or boxing études, all of which depend on the central idea of aggression and force, attack and defense, the premise in Biomechanics is an entirely different one: "Strike me! I will gladly receive your attack, and then we will trade places." It is a completely different internal approach having nothing to do with whether the movements are realistic or stylized, but having very much to do with the development of completely natural movements.

In executing the exercises, one must constantly keep in mind the fundamental rule of Biomechanics that "The entire body takes part in the work of the most insignificant organ of the body." Thus, as Meyerhold frequently observed, "If the tip of the nose works, the whole body works." Also, there must be no superfluous movements in executing the exercises. Each movement must be done precisely, without any secondary movements such as adjusting the hand or shifting the foot to get it into the proper position. It goes without saying that one must also refrain from such distractions as touching one's hair or face while executing the exercises. It is important that in learning the exercises they be done to a verbal command, until they are mastered to the point where this "command" becomes internalized and the movements become reflexes. Finally, in working on the exercises, especially those that are complex, it is helpful to practice certain of the key movements separately so that they become second nature.

The first movement the actor learns is the dactyl, a signaling exercise to indicate both the precise moment of initiation of the biomechanical exercise, and the withdrawal from play at the completion of the exercise. The objectives of the dactyl are first, concentration—to focus the attention of the performer; and second, balance—to establish coordination of the body in space and in relation to the other participants before the execution of the exercise.

The dactyl is executed as follows:

    a. The actor stands in a state of full muscular relaxation, feet parallel and slightly apart. (The stance, reminiscent of a boxer's, is the opposite of the turned-out position for exercises at the barre.) The knees are slightly flexed, the arms hang loose at the sides.

    b. On a signal, the actor sweeps his hands swiftly upward, his body following until he is on the balls of his feet. The palms of the hands face each other near the forehead.

    c. The hands are then brought swiftly and sharply downward to execute in rapid succession two short claps (parallel to the chest and stomach), the momentum of the claps causes the knees to flex and the hands to be thrown back as they separate after the second clap.

104 *Biomechanics*

The Dactyl, a signaling exercise to indicate the initiation and completion of a given exercise (see the text for an explication of what is portrayed here).

d. This abrupt movement is transferred to the actor's entire body in a forward and downward motion as the energy is conveyed to his calves and feet. The actor is now prepared to perform the exercise.

List of Biomechanical Exercises

The following "List of Exercises" was prepared by one of Meyerhold's student assistants. It is an enumeration of all the biomechanical exercises that were taught in the first two years at the Meyerhold Workshops.

1. Shooting with Bow and Arrow (M, N)
2. **Leap on Partner's Back and Transfer of Weight** (C, D)
3. **Falling and Catching [of Partner] and Lifting One's Weight** (K: Falling and Catching)
4. **Blow on the Nose** (B)
5. **Slap on the Face** (J)
6. **Pushing Down a Kneeling Figure with the Foot** (F)
7. **Play with a Stick and Juggling** (L: Exercises with sticks)
8. **Bouncing a Ball in the Air**
9. **Throwing a Stone** (A)
10. **Leap on the Chest of Opponent** (E)
11. **Play with a (Short) Dagger** (G: Stab with a Dagger)
12. **Quadrille**
13. **Rope**
14. **Horse** (O: Horses)
15. **Four Skaters**
16. **Stumbling**
17. **Bridge**
18. **Sawing**
19. **Scythe**
20. **Funeral**
21. **Fool** (H, I: Throwing a Figure into the Sea)
22. **Leapfrog**

Note: The letters following the Biomechanical exercises indicate those which are described in Chapter 6.

Chapter 6

Description of the Exercises

As part of the Workshops program, various students were assigned to write down descriptions of a number of the exercises. These descriptions (published here for the first time), were apparently intended to serve more as an outline of the key movements than as instruction on how the exercises should be done. As an aid in understanding the exercises, we have offered annotations in brackets, based on our own teaching of Biomechanics.

A. Throwing a Stone

It is important to know how to run, not only "facing forward," but also sideways. (The position of the figure is caused by the weight of the stone — the weight is on the tensed, right arm, the left hangs easy and free, like a lash.)

1. Walk in a circle.
2. Slow movement.
3. *Run* [in a circle].
4. Accelerated run.
5. Lift the stone.
6. Run with the stone in the right hand. [The stone, actually more like a heavy rock, is an imaginary object.]
7. Accelerated run with the weight in the right hand (during accelerated running, the leaps are stronger, more elevated), count one, two.
8. Stop.
9. The throw: (a) quick steps backwards; (b) choice of leap; (c) swinging of the arm; (d) final swing; (e) body is motionless and concentrated; (f) pause; (g) the hit and the shout of "*Popal*! [Bull's-eye!]"
10. Run.

Note: This exercise may begin directly with Number 6 and proceed as follows:

1. Walk in a circle.
2. *Run.*

3. Bend down.
4. Rise, lifting stone.
5. Run with the stone.
6. Stop.
7. Quick steps backward.
8. Choice of target.
9. Recoil for throw.
10. Throw.
11. Run.

[For another account of this exercise, see Van Gyseghem's description in Chapter 10.]

B. **Blow on the Nose**

The Figures are arranged in two ranks of Active Figures (Attackers) and Passive Figures, facing each other.

1. Run in place.
2. Active Figures (Attackers) take quick steps backward.
3. Active Figures advance for attack.
4. Attackers break ranks and Passive Figures retreat.
5. Stop.
6. Recoil for blow by Attackers, and recoil by Passive Figures for receiving it.
7. Blow and stepping back by Attackers.
8. Fall by Passive Figures.
9. Recoil for somersault.
10. First somersault.
11. Second somersault.
12. Squatting by both ranks.
13. Leap upwards.
14. Stand firmly in place.

C. **Leap on Partner's Back**

All of the participants are divided into Light and Heavy Figures. The Heavy Figures stand in a separate group at a certain distance from the Light ones, who are also separated into a group. Each Light Figure has its own partner in the Heavy group whom he faces on a diagonal line. Both groups are in a checkerboard arrangement.

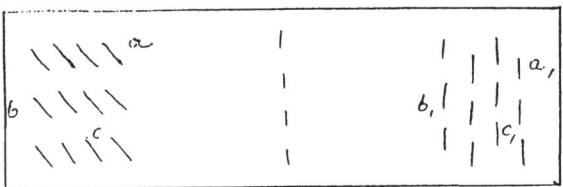

"Throwing a Stone"

6. *Description of the Exercises* 109

110 *Biomechanics*

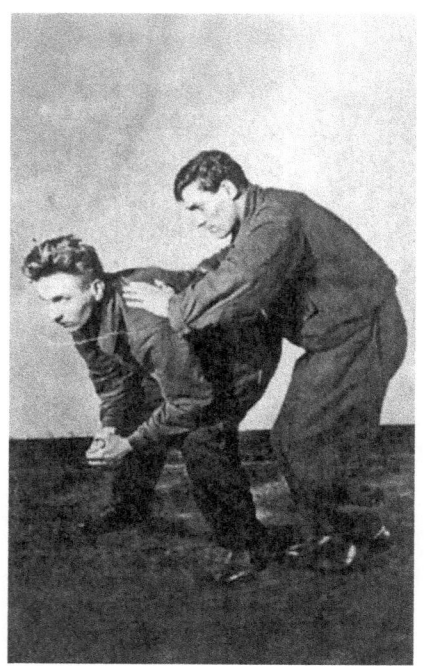

"Leap on Partner's Back and Transfer of Weight"

6. Description of the Exercises   111

Those of the Light group whose Heavy partners stand at the back of their group, place themselves at the front of the Light group. Those of the Light group whose Heavy Figures are at the front, stand at the back:

Fig. 2: a + a, b + b, c + c in pairs.

First command [Hup!]. Both groups raise their arms upward and simultaneously clap their hands two times as the point of departure for the beginning of work [dactyl]. The Light Figures step back with one foot in preparation for the position of running; the Heavy Figures place their feet a shoulder's width apart, taking a steady position. (The music begins to play).

Second command. The Light Figures recoil, taking several steps back. (The number of steps depends on each individual.) In the process, the Light Figures place themselves in position for fighting.

Third command. The Light Figures run in a group toward the Heavy Figures and stand before them to the side, each near his partner.

Fourth command. The Heavy Figures bend over half squatting so the torso is parallel to the ground. The shoulder blades are turned upward, elbows braced on the knees. Thus, a bench is formed for the Light Figures.

Fifth command. The Light Figures place their hands on the Heavy Figures, one hand on the nearer shoulder of the Heavy partner, the other on the far side near the shoulder.

Sixth command. The Light Figures squat and, leaning on their hands, leap onto the backs of the Heavy Figures, landing so that their knees are together, and between the shoulder blades of the Heavy Figures. Their legs are bent at an angle and are braced by the upper part of the sole on the derrière of the partner. The hand on the far side near the shoulder of the Heavy Figure is transferred to the shoulder itself as the Light Figure seeks a steady position. The Heavy Figures accept the leap by the Lights (at the moment the knees touch the back), slightly tensing downward.

Seventh command. The Light Figures remove their hands from the shoulders and raise them upward. They straighten out their torsos.

Eighth command. The Light Figures lower their hands to the shoulders of their partners. They are in the position of the sixth command.

Ninth command. The Light Figures carefully make a small twist-jump and sit down on the partner from the side (from which they originally jumped). Their legs hang down independently. The hands don't leave the shoulders of the partner.

Tenth command. The Light Figures, bracing their hands on the shoulders of their partners, jump off and stand next to them, so that they are side by side. The Heavy Figures straighten up.

Eleventh command. The Heavy Figures take a step back; the Light Figures take two steps forward.

Eleventh command. The Heavy Figures take a step back; the Light Figures take two steps forward.

Twelfth command. Placing their left foot forward, the Light Figures lean the torso back as far as possible, taking a falling position. Their hands hang down at the back. The Heavy Figures run back several steps in a diagonal from the Light Figures and take the position of a steady run. (The left foot forward, the torso bent and shifted to the right foot. The arms are forward for seizing.) [Notation by Pavel Urbanovich]

D. Leap on Partner's Back and Transfer of Weight

Initial position: placement of Heavy and Light Figures. A clap of the hands (accentuation). Initial situation—positioning of the body.
Tasks:

1. Recoil by Light Figures.
2. Light Figures run up to the Heavy Figures.
3. Heavy Figures [simultaneously] position themselves for receiving the Light Figures on their backs.
4. Preparation of Light Figures for the leap onto backs of the Heavy Figures.
5. Light Figures execute the leap onto the back.
6. Light Figures raise their arms and straighten their torsos.
7. Light Figures lower their hands to shoulders of Heavy Figures.
8. Light Figures sit down sideways.
9. Light Figures jump down from Heavy Figures.
10. Heavy and Light Figures position themselves for picking up the Light Ones.
11. The Light Figures fall, the Heavy Figures recoil.
12. Heavy Figures run up and prepare to lift up the Light Figures.
13. The Light Figures are lifted.
14. Heavy Figures position themselves in a circle.
15. Movement in a circle.
16. Stop.
17. Turning toward the center of the circle.
18. Dropping (of the Light Figures).
19. *Circle*.
20. Movement in a circle.

E. Leap on Opponent's Chest

[Meyerhold himself acknowledged that he had based this exercise on his observations of the Sicilian actor Giovanni Grasso, who visited Russia in 1908. See Chapter 8 for Erast Garin's description of Meyerhold demonstrating this exercise.]

The Figures range themselves in two ranks facing each other.

6. *Description of the Exercises* 113

"Pushing Down a Kneeling Figure with the Foot"

114 Biomechanics

"Stab with a Dagger"

1. Recoil by the Attacker.
2. The Attacker takes quick steps backward and Passive Figure recoils.
3. Attacker *leaps* onto the chest of the Passive Figure.
4. Attacker pulls out the [imaginary] dagger.
5. *Killing* of the Passive Figure by the Attacker.
6. The Attacker slides down the Passive Figure who then falls.

F. Pushing Down a Kneeling Figure with the Foot

1. *Placement of the Figures*: Figures place themselves in a circle, Heavy and Light Figures facing each other, with a space between the pairs.
2. *Initial position*: outer circle on its knees, facing the line of the circle; the inner circle preparing to run in the same direction.
3. Accentuation—a clap of the hands [Dactyl].
4. Run by the inner circle of Figures.
5. Stop.
6. Find one's balance.
7. *Stance*.
8. *Aim* with the [right] foot.
9. Push down with the foot.
10. Return to preparatory position for running.
11. *Run*.

G. Stab with a Dagger

Placement of the Figures: In pairs, facing each other on the playing area in checkerboard arrangement.

Initial position: The pairs stand opposite each other (face to face about a half-step apart). One foot is placed symmetrically forward parallel to the second foot.

The Figure delivering the blow [the First Figure] has its weight on the forward foot, the body inclined forward, the hand on the hilt of the [imaginary] dagger. The Figure receiving the blow [the Second Figure] has its weight on the back foot and the torso inclined backwards. The eyes of the two Figures are fixed on each other. (They hypnotize each other according to the hypnotic method of K. R. Lig. and K-v.)

1. The First Figure pulls out the dagger.
2. The Second Figure steps backward [with right foot], as the First Figure leans forward.
3. The First Figure straightens up and raises the dagger.
4. The First Figure advances; leaning back and defense of the Second Figure.
5. First Figure stops.
6. First Figure raises the dagger.

116 *Biomechanics*

    7. Recoil by First Figure for delivery of the blow and delivery of the blow.
    8. First Figure steps back; recoil for fall by Second Figure (placement of the hands).
    9. Second Figure falls forward   } legato
   10. Then backward to prone position

In the film demonstration of this exercise, at this point the First Figure steps around behind the Second Figure. At a command, the Second Figure straightens out in a rigid position with arms at side. The First Figure lifts the Second Figure up by the back of the neck, then turns so that the Second Figure is resting on the First's back, arms dangling. The First Figure pivots in a half circle and exits.

H. **The Fool**
    [For five persons]
    Initial position.
    1. Fall by the Fool.
    2. First Moor runs out and falls.
    3. The other three Moors run out, First Moor jumps up.
    4. Moors recoil for lifting up the Fool.
    5. Moors lift him and position themselves.
    6. The Moors swing the Fool.
    7. They throw the Fool.
    8. Blows by the Fool.
    9. The Moors throw down the Fool.
  10. Recoil and kick by the fourth Moor, somersault.
  11. Fool runs around.

I. **The Fool (Throwing a Figure into the Sea)**
    [This dramatized version of the preceding exercise is a good example of how one of the exercises might be developed into an étude.]

A group of five persons takes part. They stand on a diagonal all facing in one direction.
    1. Recoil and fall of the Fool; the four Active Figures turn to face the prone Figure.
    2. Recoil of the Active Figures for running.
    3. Active Figures run up, Fool recoils in preparation for being lifted.
    4. Fool is lifted, positioning.
    5. Swinging of the Fool.
    6. *Throwing*.
    7. Blows by the Fool; slap, fall and somersault by the Active Figures.
    8. Throwing down of the Fool.

9. Recoil and blow by the Holding Figure; somersault by the Holding Figure.

10. Running of the Fool.

> Dramatic Script for the Exercise "The Fool,"
> from Calderón's
> *The Constant Prince*
> Scene 14

(*Brito, alone*)
Brito: We can't get out of this tight spot
Two armies joined against one.
A terribly vile joke, I'm telling you.
Oh, for a key to open up the skies.

Give me at least a chink,
That this poor wretch may evade death,
Who wandered into battle,
Knowing neither why nor wherefore.

Let me pretend to be dead,
I swear I won't be a fool.
This time I'll persuade myself I am a corpse.
And death will pass me by.
(*He throws himself on the ground.*)

> Scene 20

(*Moors, Brito*)
First Moor: Another dead Christian.
Second Moor: Today we had a good fight.
Third Moor: Let's throw the corpses in the sea.
Fourth Moor: To avoid the plague.
(*Comically*)
Brito (*jumping up*): But first let me open wide your skulls. Even when dead we Portuguese are pretty fast on the draw.
(*He pursues them with his [imaginary] sword.*)

J. **Slap on the Face**

Placement: The Figures stand in two ranks at a distance of a half-step from each other, face to face on a diagonal, the feet placed symmetrically along the line of the toe, the weight of the body equally on both feet (boxer's stance).

1. Full recoil by the Hitting Figure (as Receiver leans forward).
2. False [practice] blow, Receiver leans backward.

118 Biomechanics

"Falling and Catching of Partner"

    3. A slight recoil by Hitting Figure, delivery of blow, receiving of blow by Receiver.

    4. Figures reposition for blow by the other hand [or reverse action with other partner].

K. Falling and Catching

    1. Light Figures recoil for running [up to Heavy Figures].

    2. Running approach by Light Figures toward Heavy Figures and positioning.

    3. Large [forward] recoil by Light Figures for the falling.

    4. Light Figures fall in parallel with recoil by Heavy Figures for running up and seizing.

    5. Heavy Figures run up and seize Light Figures.

    6. Fall by Light Figures (landing, lowering, lying down).

    7. Recoil of Heavy Figures for crossover [i.e., for stepping over the Light Figures.]

    8. Heavy Figures cross over the Light Figures.

    9. Recoil by Heavy and Light Figures for the accentuation.

    10. (Accentuation). Thrust by Heavy Figures and grouping by Light Figures.

    11. Recoil of Heavy Figures for leap by Light Figures [onto chest of Heavy Figures].

    12. Recoil by Light Figures.

    13. Leap.

6. *Description of the Exercises* 119

Note: The training exercise for the leap by the Lights is as follows: The Heavy and Light Figures stand face to face. The Light Figures place their hands on the shoulders of the Heavy ones, and flexing their knees, they lift their bodies upward.

L. Exercises with Sticks

[The exercises with sticks are fundamental for the development of balance. Walking along an imaginary tightrope or railing can also be used to develop balance.]

1. Place the stick on two fingers of the right hand and balance it as long as possible without moving from one's place.
2. Place the stick on the palm of the right hand and gently toss it upward.
3. Toss the stick upward and receive it alternately on the palm (second exercise) and on the back of the wrist.
4. Place the stick on two fingers (the index and middle fingers) of the right hand; transfer the stick to the thumb, gradually raising the hand upward.
5. Place the stick on the forearm, transferring it with a flick of the palm.
6. Balance the stick (in succession): on the chin, on the nose, and on the forehead, as long as possible without moving the feet.
7. Transfer the stick from the index and the middle finger to the thumb, holding it for awhile on the thumb (fourth exercise), and then gradually raise the hand upward, transferring the stick to the nose, forehead, chin, etc.
8. Balance the stick on the shoulder, on the knee, on the toe, if possible without moving the feet.
9. Transfer the stick with a throw from the toe and the knee to the palm.
10. Toss the stick on the palm, taking it on the palm by one and then by the other end of the stick. The stick describes a circle in the air.
11. Walk along a definite, predetermined line with the stick balanced on the nose.
12. Balance the stick on the nose while kneeling.
13. With the stick balanced on the nose, lower oneself to one's knees and rise up from the knees.

(Note: The order of numbers, aside from its usual meaning, also serves as an indication of the difficulty of execution.)

General rules for exercises with a stick:
1. The basic position for the exercise with the sticks is: legs slightly

apart and slightly bent at the knees. Arms relaxed and extended to the sides. This position gives maximum steadiness and resiliency.

2. During all of the exercises, the eyes are fixed on the upper end of the stick.

3. In holding the stick on the nose or the chin, the head leans back for better balance.

4. In holding the stick on the toe or the knee, the leg resting on the ground is bent at the knee no more than it is when in the basic position.

5. For preserving balance in the kneeling position, the knees must be shifted just as the feet are shifted when standing.

6. All of the exercises, when it is not necessary for their execution, must be done as much as possible without moving from one's place.

7. In walking with the stick, it is necessary to avoid swinging the body downward, upward, and to the sides. [Notation by Ivan Savelev]

M. Shooting with Bow and Arrow

[Meyerhold once commented that this exercise called to mind an Egyptian or Assyrian fresco.]

Parade. Entrance in single file, formation in a row. First Actor gravitates to the right. (Sokol placement on a diagonal by fives.)

After the parade there is always a preparation for work—a transition to taking up the starting position. In straightening up the line, it is essential to look at the partner's feet. The location on the stage is defined by the positions of the feet. The correct placement of the feet is: toes parallel to each other. The most desirable position for the hands is to have them together at the back.

1. Initially there is concern only with the body without the arms—a torso on springs in repose. Above all, one must place the torso on "tested springs" (to check how they spring).

2. The diagonal is a section crosswise to the direction of the perpendicular.

3. The basic requirements are balance, precision, absence of wobbling.

4. The starting point: an imaginary object, the bow, is lying on the stage. The bow is indicated by pointing: "I will now take this." In indicating, a simple gesture is used. The task of indicating by pointing with the finger is a difficult one. A preliminary recoil is necessary.

5. The body weight is on the left foot, the left hand is on the hip. In order to make the gesture of indication, shift the body weight to the right foot, place the right hand on the hip; the left hand makes the sign of recoil and the gesture of indication, the right and left hands are lowered, and the exercise begins.

In this exercise, the body is organized on the principle of a boat: the fist gripping the bow, the toe, and the head are in one plane — the plane of the keel. The head is the stern, the fist is the prow of the boat.

6. The complete lowering of the body to pick up the bow does not occur immediately. At first a half-squat, only after that, a full lowering. There remains a reserve of energy.

7. To show what has been taken, grab the imaginary bow with the hand.

8. Check the position to the right and to the left. The "aligning of the line" takes place at the interval points. The alignment is a constant goal of every exercise, alignment of the line, the organization of the exercise to the end.

9. The entire body in this exercise is like the skeleton of a small boat. Each boat is a genuine fish in its construction: a spine with parallel ribs, and an extremely strong pivot. The only difference is that the fish has the ability to bend.

10. In this exercise the head must be kept in a straight line, and with the fist serve as points of extremity. There is a colossal tension, an enormous strength in the clenching of the fist.

11. The checking may be as slow as one desires. There must be no military rigidity.

The shoulder is steady. The right hand is on the hip. The head is the stern; the fist is the prow of the boat. The fist is the gunsight. In running, the sight [fist] is always at head level. This defines the position of the head. The hand is in the direction of the toe.

12. In pulling out the arrow from the imaginary quiver, the extended left hand holding the bow in tension keeps the entire body rigid. The body doesn't bend, the torso is straight, the shoulders are not pulled back. The hand with the bow is on the plane of the horizon, in the field of vision and at eye level. In the recoil, the torso is precise and tense. So that the arm will not move it from its place, everything is activated. The body is perpendicular to the floor. At the thrust of the left arm, the body doesn't change position: first a push by the hand, then the thrust.

In pulling out the arrow, the actor stands in a postion that enables him to show the audience the precise work of pulling out, with the fingertips clutching one thin twig from the sheaf of twigs. Enormous steadiness, enormous tension are required for greater vividness and seeming ease of work. In performance, the finer the work with the fingertips and wrists, the more tension there is in the torso.

In the thrust of the arms, the tendency is for vertical arm movements perpendicular to the plane of the floor. The body straightens up and then settles [knees bent], but doesn't sway. The hand is under the right shoulder blade, lowering the body on its feet, the weight is on both feet.

13. The legs send the arm upward without completely straightening, the body looks at the target, the palm upward.

14. The hand turns upward, the weight shifts to the left foot, the right is on the toe, the leg slightly bent. The arms are extended at an angle to each other.

15. In placing the arrow, the body weight shifts to the left foot.

16. With great tension of the fist, the left shoulder is constant, the right is spring-like.

17. The right arm swings back from the shoulder. The elbow of the right arm shows the movement of pulling straight back. The arrow and the bowstring are held by the thumb and index finger. The torso and legs accompany the checking of the bowstring; they are resilient, springy, there is a light shifting of the feet.

18. The arms and shoulders shift to the left, the body leans forward without bending, the shoulder rotates to the center of the torso in a tight screwing movement, the arms and shoulders move back.

19. A sharp turn to the right, the arms horizontal, parallel to the ground. Any unsteadiness is inadmissible.

20. A minimal jump. The right foot steps forward, the left back practically cutting the ground (*raser la terre*).

21. Checking as in No. 17.

22. A sharp shift to the right foot with recoil, the torso bends to the side, the arms are raised upward, without straightening them, the arrow is pulled back; the head in the same plane shifts backward.

23. The hands meet: The right hand is brought to the left, the position of the torso remains the same.

24. A leap upward with both feet.

25. The body weight is on the left foot, the torso and the head are thrust between the arms; the left arm moves sharply upward, the right sharply downward in the plane of the thrust, with a shake of the wrists.

26. After the shot, the body weight is on the left foot, the body follows the line of the left arm. A stamp of the feet: ta-ta (I) stronger and sharper. "*Ecotav* in the feet," to reach the height.

27. Stand in the position of the finished exercise, end of the story line.

The left arm drops, the right hand goes to the hip, the weight is on both feet. Admiration.

M. **Shooting with Bow and Arrow**

[This is another description of the preceding exercise by a different student, P. Urbanovich.]

Music: Grieg: "Solveig's Wedding;" Parade: "In the Trolls' Castle."
The exercise:

1. Chopin, "Étude in C Minor."
2. Bach, "Prelude to the First Fugue."
3. Schloesser, "Étude in A-Sharp Major."

Tasks:

1. Parade.
2. Stance.
3. Dactyl.
4. Shift of the torso.
5. Gesture—indicating the location of the [imaginary] bow.
6. Lowering of the body to pick up the bow.
7. Taking of the bow.
8. Straightening up.
9. Rising.
10. Placement of the torso.
11. Checking
12. Recoil for the pulling out of the [imaginary] arrow.
13. Thrust of the arm to take the arrow.
14. Holding of the arrow.
15. Turning of the arm.
16. Placement of the arrow in the bow.
17. Checking of the bowstring.
18. Recoil for the turn.
19. Turn.
20. Shifting of the feet.
21. Checking of the bowstring.
22. Aim upward.
23. Contraction of the arm. (Pulling back the arrow).
24. Leap upward (with both feet).
25. Stance on the right foot.
26. Stamp of the left foot and the breaking apart of the arms.
27. Shout.
28. Finale.
29. Exit parade.

S
H
O
T

O. Horses [for three]
Starting position.

1. Arms on the shoulders. [To form the Horse, the First Figure (rear of Horse) leans forward and places his hands on the shoulders of Second Figure (head of Horse) to form a saddle for the Rider.]
2. Rider moves backward.
3. Horse (two Figures) and Rider run.
4. Rider runs up to the Horse.
5. Placement of the hands.
6. Stopping.
7. Positioning of the Horse.
8. Leap onto the Horse.
9. Rider takes a sitting position.
10. Running.
11. Recoil by Rider for leap from the Horse.
12. Leap by Rider from the Horse.

[This exercise was sometimes expanded to demonstrate variations in balance by the Riders.]

Chapter 7

Program of Studies

The "Program of Studies" devised for the students in Meyerhold's Workshops is of particular interest for revealing the broad range of subject matter, both theoretical and practical, which Meyerhold included in his actor training program. Not only were the students schooled in the biomechanical exercises, they were also expected to study the physiological foundations for them. Other subjects included a study of different systems of acting and the organization by the actor of his own work.

The Workshops' "Examination in Biomechanics" follows the "Program of Studies."

Program for First Year

1. Training in various types of sports and gymnastics. The actor must know and study all types of movement, without dwelling on any of them too long, in order not to develop heavy muscles which hinder ease and freedom in movement (example: the Japanese actor).

2. Biomechanical gymnastics sets as its objective the development in the actor of:

    a. Smooth and flowing movements (legato);
    b. Sharp, quick, and distinct movements (staccato).

It strives to make possible a larger range of movement.

3. Biomechanical exercises have as their objective to train the actor for:

    a. Feeling the balance and center of gravity in oneself and in the area situated outside of oneself.
    b. Coordination with the stage area, with one's partner, and with the stage properties.

c. Physical (reflexive) arousal (quick reaction to the director's demands), thus preserving the healthy psyche and nervous system of the actor.

4. To develop in the trainee a director (a control over one's material) in coordination with the playing area, one's partner, one's costume and the stage properties.

Biomechanical Gymnastics

Positioning of the body and of the extremities.
   a. *Positioning* of the body.
      1. Bending, rising swiftly or slowly in all directions.
      2. Squatting with the rear tucked under.
      3. Work on the abdomen and diaphragm.
      4. Work on the shoulders.
   b. *Positioning* of the head, arms and legs.
      1. Work on the neck. Balancing with a ball. Fast and slow turns.
      2. Hands and fingers. Juggling with sticks.
      3. Legs: extending the legs. Rapid arrangement in a group, running, squatting. The Charleston; the foot. Balancing a ball on the foot, balancing with a stick on the foot.

The Elements of Biomechanical Exercises

Individual training in exercises:
   1. Standing.
   2. Walking.
   3. Running.
   4. Falling.
   5. Arrangement (in a group).
   6. Throwing the discus, spear, shot put.
   7. Touching the hands and head to the feet.
   8. Positioning in a *raccourci*.

Biomechanical Exercises

The development of attention, coordination, and reflexive arousal.
   1. Shooting with Bow and Arrow.
   2. Throwing a Stone.
   3. Falling and Catching.
   4. Stab with a Dagger.
   5. Pushing Down a Kneeling Figure.

6. Slap on the Face.
7. From *D.E.* (the production).

The Actor

A. Material (A_2)
   1. The Body
      a. The torso as a mass.
      b. The extremities (arms, legs).
      c. The head (face: eyes, mouth).
   2. Voice and diction (see the special course on the word).

B. Biomechanics
   1. The nature of expressive movements and actions is determined by the biological construction of the organism.
      a. The human organism as an auto motor.
      b. Repeated automatic actions.
      c. Mimeticism and its biological significance (Bekhterev).
      d. Motor actions of a person: movements of individual organs (tremor or enervation of the muscles, shifting of the eyes, mime movements of the head, arms, legs, separate groups of muscles.)
   2. The complex of movements of the entire organism or a chain of actions (shifting of the entire organism), walking, running, acts such as reading, writing, carrying weights, the most complex movements which make up one or another kind of work (acts of doing).
   3. Acts of restraint (inactivity) externally devoid of motor character or conveying a motor effect in a barely noticeable degree (patient tolerance of blows, acts of refraining from active repulsion and so forth).
      e. Play as a release of excessive energy.
      f. Receptors, conductors, effectors.
      g. A study of the reactive mechanism of the nervous system.
      h. Psychic reactions as an objective of natural science.
      i. Psychic phenomena—simple physical and mimetic reactions in the form of: tropisms, taxis, or purely physiological reflexes.
      j. Instinctive reflex.
      k. Reflexes, their connections, linking, interdependence.
      l. Mechanization (unconscious habitual acts).
      m. Physical and reflexive normalization.
      n. Influence of sound stimuli (role of a shout at the moment of tense action).
      o. Movement and musical background (construction of a score of movements in relation to a given musical score according to the laws of counterpoint, or the construction of a musical score in relation to a given movement score according to the same laws).
      p. Meter and rhythm.

7. *Program of Studies* 127

C. Mimeticism

    1. Study by the actor of muscle movements (direction, force, pressure or pull produced by a movement, extension — the length of the trajectory, speed).
    2. Movement of the torso, arms, legs, head (center of gravity, *raccourci*).
    3. Rationalization of movements.
    4. Sign of recoil.
    5. Tempos of movements.
    6. Legato, staccato.
    7. Gesture as a result of movement.
    8. Large and small gestures.
    9. Laws of coordination of the body and of objects outside it, of the body and objects in the hands of the actors (juggling), of the body and the costume clothing it.
    10. Laws of coordination in time and space.
    11. Geometrizing.
    12. Laws of odd and even numbers.
    13. Laws of construction.
    14. Dance.
    16. Acrobatics.
    17. Tricks peculiar to the theatre.
    18. Eccentricism.
    19. *Concept manuals*.
    20. Word-movement.

D. Acting

    1. Three systems of acting: emotive, living the role, motorization.
    2. $N = A_1 \underset{o}{} A_2$.
    3. $A_1 = N \underset{r}{/\backslash/\backslash/\backslash}$ or $A_1 = N \overset{o\ o}{/\backslash'/\backslash'/\backslash}$ *
    4. Emploi (inherent traits, scenic function).
    5. Grotesque.
    6. Improvisation.
    7. Actor and spectator.
    8. Ensemble.
    9. Diary.

---

* N = *namerenie* (intention); o = *osushchestvlenie* (execution, fulfillment of intention); r = *reaktsiya* (reaction to the initial position).

E. Taking into Account Experience, Study

    1. A study of themes according to their sources.
    2. A study of schools and trends (of style).
    3. A study of acting techniques of various schools.

F. Organization of Work

    1. Actor workshop.
    2. Work clothes [*prozodezhda*].

3. Equipment.
   4. Actor's score.
      a. Initial idea.
      b. Final idea.
   5. Diary.
   6. Regimen (rehearsals, performances).
   7. Work on one's role.

Examination in Biomechanics

Exercises:
   1. Shooting With Bow and Arrow
   2. Throwing a Stone
   3. Leap on Partner's Back and Transfer of Weight
   4. Falling, Catching, and Lifting One's Weight
   5. Blow on the Nose (for two persons)
   6. Slap on the Face
   7. Pushing Down a Kneeling Figure with the Foot
   8. Leap on the Chest of Opponent
   9. Play with a Dagger
   10. Horses (for three)
   11. Fool (for five)

The first group is tested on eleven exercises. Each must do the work for its Figure (Light or Heavy) and know the work of the partner. All must correct the mistakes of the other performers.

The second group is tested on seven exercises (1, 2, 3, 4, 5, 6, 11). Each does the work for its Figure (Light or Heavy). Two of the exercises (with the exception of 1, 2, and 11) may be replaced by two others from the eleven (7, 8, 9).

The third group is tested on the same exercises as the second.

In addition to the exercise test, balance, and balancing and walking along a bridge are also tested.

Professor
Chairman of the Department

Part III
Documents

Chapter 8

Meyerhold Documents on Biomechanics

> *The basic law of Biomechanics is very simple: the whole body takes part in each of our movements. The rest is elaboration, exercises, études. Tell me, what is there in this that could disturb people, provoke protests, seem heretical, unacceptable?*
>
> V. E. Meyerhold

Introduction

Meyerhold wrote virtually nothing of substance on Biomechanics. When asked about Biomechanics at a conference in December 1933, Meyerhold answered that in his 1922 review of Aleksandr Tairov's *Notes of a Director* could be found "the basic tenets of Biomechanics."[1] But in his attack on Tairov's balletic theatre, Meyerhold only reiterated what he had already stated that same year in *The Emploi of the Actor*. Written in collaboration with Valery Bebutov and Ivan Aksyonov, it pointed out the two-fold function of the actor as both instrument and material of his art ($N = A_1 + A_2$), an equation borrowed from Coquelin. Yet none of this led to an analytical or practical understanding of Biomechanics.

Meyerhold frequently spoke of the book on actor and director training he would someday write. "We won't call it a system, as Konstantin Sergeevich usually does," he told a group of graduates in 1936. "We're more modest; we'll call that document a manual essential for the actor and director. We want to establish a series of rules, a series of axioms, to show a series of exercises which are essential in order to master that subject."[2] Such a manual was never completed, in part because time ran out, but also

132 *Documents*

because Meyerhold much preferred to present his ideas on actor training and movement through actual work on a production rather than through writing about it.

It was left for Meyerhold's students and director-assistants to formulate most of the basic documents on Biomechanics. Among them were Mikhail Korenev, who along with Sergei Eisenstein was part of the group of students assigned to prepare material for a planned theatrical encyclopedia. Included in the Meyerhold documents on Biomechanics are a brief but concise definition of Biomechanics, a description of the Workshops' Biomechanical Laboratory, and the forty-four "Principles of Biomechanics," all worked out by Korenev at Meyerhold's request.

Another valuable source of information on Biomechanics can be found in memoirs by Meyerhold's actors. Of these, we have selected Erast Garin's account of an exercise class at the Meyerhold Directors Workshops on Novinsky Boulevard in 1921. It offers a lively description of Meyerhold demonstrating the exercise "Leap on the Chest" for his young students.

On June 12, 1922, Meyerhold gave his first public demonstration of Biomechanics in the Little Auditorium of the Moscow Conservatory. A report of the demonstration entitled "The Actor of the Future and Biomechanics" vividly conveys the excitement surrounding this important event.

But not everyone enthusiastically accepted either Meyerhold's program of actor training or the sweeping claims he made for Biomechanics. Principal among Meyerhold's opponents was Ippolit Sokolov, who wrote an article, "Biomechanics According to Meyerhold," attacking Meyerhold's understanding of Biomechanics as "extremely general, amorphous, and hazy."

Arkady Pozdnev, a Meyerhold student at the time, responded to Sokolov's attack with an article, "Taylorism on the Stage." Here he differentiated between the Biomechanics of the factory worker (as Gastev defined them) and the Biomechanics of the theatre, where the "product" was the reaction produced in the spectator. But in the end it was left to Sergei Eisenstein to establish the theoretical framework for Biomechanics and to refute Sokolov's charges that Biomechanics could cause physical harm.

In response to criticism from a commission of the NARKOMPROS, which investigated the Meyerhold State Theatre School in March 1935, Meyerhold announced that he himself would "energetically" set to work reforming the school's program. Toward this end, he selected a group of his director-laboratory assistants to examine the school's program and come up with new proposals. One of the results was the "Profile of the Actor Graduating from the Meyerhold State Theatre School" prepared by

Nikolai A. Basilov, which we have included as the penultimate document.

The director's promptbook, prepared by one of Meyerhold's student-directors, Stefan V. Kozikov, for his 1922 production of *The Magnanimous Cuckold*, offers an extraordinarily detailed description of the movement score for every line of the play text. As the final document we present a scene from this promptbook—The Letter Scene from act 2—illustrating how Meyerhold incorporated two biomechanical exercises, "The Slap on the Face," and "Leap on the Chest" into his production.

THE BIOMECHANICS OF VSEVOLOD MEYERHOLD
by Mikhail Korenev

In 1922, Meyerhold organized a Biomechanical Laboratory to explore and develop the scientific foundations for Biomechanics. As part of the laboratory's work, Meyerhold assigned to Mikhail Korenev the task of formulating a definition of Biomechanics, outlining the laboratory's program and enumerating the basic principles of Biomechanics.

The laboratory, in one form or another, continued to operate until Meyerhold's theatre was closed in 1939. In the 1930s, Meyerhold frequently complained that he did not have adequate laboratory facilities to study the principles of acting. "If only they would give us a lab like Pavlov's instead of sending us congratulatory telegrams for our anniversary," he commented at one meeting with his company.[3]

Mikhail Korenev joined Meyerhold's Directors Workshops in 1922 and stayed on to serve Meyerhold in a variety of capacities from assistant director to unofficial secretary. We are indebted to him for many of the carefully preserved documents of Meyerhold's theatre work in the 1920s and 1930s. All three of the following documents by Korenev come from private archives and are published here for the first time.

"Biomechanics" is the term created by Vsevolod Meyerhold for a special course of study in which the actor, on the basis of the study of the natural movements of man and animals, works out in himself the specific abilities and habits essential for professional work on the stage.

The "Biomechanics of Vsevolod Meyerhold" seeks to establish the laws of movement by the actor in stage space, the working out by experimental means of a program of training exercises and acting devices based on exact calculation and regulation of the actor's behavior on the stage.

The well-trained body, a good state of the nervous system, the regulation of arousal, speed and exactness of reaction, the awareness of one's own body and of its position on the stage platform, coordination with one's partners, a feeling for time, a good eye judgment, and the exact calculation of all the means for affecting the spectator, in short, a complete mastery of one's own body and full control over the exact carrying out of the objectives which have been set—these are the results of a mastery of Biomechanics and a mastery at the same time of those basic demands which together with musicality and an essential broad cultural development are presented to the actor by the biomechanical system of Vsevolod Meyerhold.

The Biomechanical Laboratory
by Mikhail Korenev

The purpose of the biomechanical laboratory is the working out by experimental means of the biomechanical system of acting and of actor training. The work of the laboratory is carried out on two levels: (a) theoretical; (b) practical.

The theoretical area covers the study of the biological and social bases of acting mastery:

1. a study of the animal organism,
2. a study of individual and collective reflexology,
3. the establishing of laws of actor movement in the stage space.

In the area of the practical is the construction of a series of exercises from the simplest task of individual movement to the most complex, coordinated group movements. The training of a *"new accelerated man"* (A. Gastev's formula) with his quick reactions, with his facility for always being on the watch for the idea of socialist construction, with his ability to spare himself, expending a minimum of nervous energy. The training of a passion for construction. Caring for the body and the nerves. The proper position of the torso. The establishing of *raccourcis*. In all areas of this complex system, there should be constant, persistent practice.

"Biomechanics" or the "Biomechanical" system of Meyerhold strives to establish the laws of actor movement in stage space, the working out by experimental means of a scheme of training exercises and acting devices based on exact calculation and regulation of actor behavior on the stage.

Principles of Biomechanics
by Mikhail Korenev

1. All of Biomechanics is based on the premise that if the tip of the nose works, so does the entire body. The entire body takes part in the work of the most insignificant organ of the body. One must, first of all, establish the equilibrium of the entire body. Under the least tension, the entire body works.

2. A story line in the exercise is a necessity difficult to escape. Play by the body is made much easier with a story line. However one must never be carried away by the story line, and one must avoid "making too much" of the story.

One must pay strict attention to each element of the exercise and give it meaning. Only in this manner is precision achieved.

3. In the work process, each participant in the exercise must show that he has mastered the method and consciously grasps the instructions.

4. Each worker must perceive when he can move from one position to another.

A caesura is obligatory after each element of the task.

5. In Biomechanics, each movement is formed of three factors: (a) intention, (b) equilibrium, (c) execution.

6. Orientation in space in the presence of a large number of persons is an extremely important matter. The task of each one is to find his separate way in the complex movement of the group.

7. During a group exercise, each one must occupy his own place, planning it in relation to all of the partners and to that space within whose limits he is working. The precision of the orientation, the exactness of the calculation, a quick sight estimation, must be carried to the *maximum*. (Such an adaptability, a good eye — even unconsciously — is developed by inhabitants of large cities.)

8. Coordination in space and on the stage platform, the ability to control oneself in mass movement, adaptability, the calculation of exact sight estimation — these are the basic demands of Biomechanics.

9. Exclamation — the mark of the degree of excitation — must always have a technical basis. Exclamation can be permitted only when everything is tense, when the whole of the technical material is organized.

10. Complete calm and exactly-found equilibrium are the primary conditions in good and precise work.

11. In an exercise which is being performed together with a partner, each participant, when sure of himself, must signal to the partner with a recoil or by other means imperceptible to the spectator his readiness to carry out the next task.

12. The necessary filling up of the stage platform, the preservation of the required intervals, are the objective and concern of each participant.

13. During an exercise, one must forbid to oneself any manifestation of "playfulness" and "temperament." One must not hurry or take up too much space. Restraint, calm, and a methodical approach come first.

14. Each participant must be in the convincing state of a man in equilibrium; he must have a reserve of movements and poses, of various *raccourcis* of the body for the observance of equilibrium (Hokusai). Each must find for himself the the equilibrium needed at a given moment.

15. Each participant must understand and be aware of which leg he is standing on, the right, the left, or on both together. Each change in the position of the body and of its separate parts must be immediately perceived by him.

16. A gesture is the result of the work of the entire body. A gesture is always the result of what is in the technical reserve of the actor who is demonstrating the acting.

17. Excitation arises in the process of work as a result of the successful use of well-trained material.

18. Any art is the organization of material. In order to organize this material, the actor must have a colossal reserve of technical means. The difficulty and peculiarity of the art of acting consists in the fact that the actor is at one and the same time the material and the organizer of it. Acting is a tricky matter. At each moment the actor is a composer.

19. The difficulty of the actor's art lies in the extremely strict coordination of all the elements of his work. All of the actor's well-being lies in his good physical state.

20. The physical condition of the well-trained material is the fulcrum of our system of acting. Each task in its performing is precisely planned on various parts of the stage platform; then all the movements of the actor, even reflexive ones, will always be strictly organized.

21. The spectator must always have a certain feeling of tension. Watching the exercise, he follows the process of the setting and turning of levers.

22. Each movement must have a strong basis. Each element of the task must have its own point of support: the beginning and end of the execution of every task must be distinctly accentuated. The point of departure must always be indicated. Each exercise is a series of such points.

23. In each collective exercise, every participant must give up forever the constant desire of the actor to be a soloist.

24. The biomechanical movement of an actor on the stage platform is a half-run, half-walk, and always on springs.

25. It is important to perform each exercise with precision, not only in the sense of correct work, but with precision in the sense of parade, the use of the stage platform, affect, and so forth.

26. For each movement the actor must have his parade.

27. The line of direction of the general movement is obligatory for each participant in a collective exercise.

28. All art is built on self-limitation. Art is always, and above all, a struggle with the material.

29. One must not give free rein to movement. One must observe a great economy of movement—on this the apparatus of the director and actor is tested.

30. Piano and forte are always relative.

In the auditorium, there must always remain the impression of an unused reserve. Never and nowhere should the actor use up all of his reserves. Even the broadest gesture must leave the possibility of some even broader gesture.

31. Upon receiving a command, one must come to the appointed place, on the way making a predetermined number of steps, so that it is done economically. This is the best test of a good eye.

32. Biomechanics doesn't tolerate anything accidental. Everything must be done consciously, with prior calculation. Each movement must be precisely established by the worker who must know in what position his body is in and freely use each part of it for the execution of the purpose.

33. It is a general law of the theatre that he who allows himself to give free rein to his emotions at the beginning of his work, inevitably spends it earlier than the completion of the work and spoils the entire execution.

34. No superficiality on the technical level is permissible. Comfort and well-being must emerge when the material is well-equipped technically, is prepared for by sound training. Only then can what is called excitation be put into play. Otherwise the work will be ruined.

35. At preliminary exercises, at rehearsal, all emotions must be designated lightly by a dotted line, only noting exactly where and when the explosion must take place. Shouts which are unjustified technically, inevitably break the balance; it has to be sought again, that is, one must begin the whole work anew.

36. In separate elements of the work, a state of concentration is necessary in expectation of the future transition and change of movement. From here come the points of departure and of arrival at the final station.

37. The most important thing for the actor is the checking of the

body. In our minds we hold not an image but a reserve of technical material. The actor is always in the position of a person who is organizing his material. He must know exactly his range and all the devices which he has technically at his disposal for the fulfillment of a given purpose. The qualifications of an actor are always proportional to the number of combinations he has in his reserve of devices.

38. Each exercise is preceded by a parade which is followed by tensing up for work. Only with well-tensed material can one embark on execution of the task.

39. Just as music is always an exact sequence of measures which do not break up the musical whole, so our exercises are a sequence of mathematically exact shifts, which must be exactly observed, and which will in no way interfere with the preciseness of the general pattern of exercises. In the purely theatrical biomechanical exercises, illustrative, imitative exercises are introduced instead of exercises based on physical strength. Everything disparaging Meyerhold ever said about Duncan's plastics can be applied to Biomechanics. Why are Duncan's illustrative gestures imitating a breeze or a sea wave bad, and the illustrative movements of shooting the arrow (!) or play with daggers (!) in Biomechanics good? Why? The principle of imitative movements is one and the same in plastics and in Biomechanics. The only expedient circus stunts—a blow on the nose, a slap on the face—are, of course, in no way biomechanical.

40. When an exercise is broken up into small elements it must be done staccato; the legato will appear when the exercise is executed as an unbroken flowing whole.

41. In the playing with the wrists and the fingers, an enormous tension and an enormous stability of the entire body is needed.

42. In work, an absolute economy is essential, a total Taylorism. All the tasks must be fulfilled with a minimum number of devices, with the utmost expediency.

43. Coordination, attention, precision—these are the elements of our system. Concentration of attention on the physical level comes first of all. The loose condition of a physically uncontrolled person (Duncanism) is inadmissible. With us, everything is organized, each step, each slightest movement is included in the count. Sight estimation is always in operation.

44. The first principle of Biomechanics: the body is a machine, the actor is the machinist.

(Note that this numerical sequence is not in any special systematic order. M. K.).

MEYERHOLD DEMONSTRATES A BIOMECHANICAL EXERCISE
by Erast Garin

One of Meyerhold's most biomechanical actors, Erast Garin, joined Meyerhold's Directors Workshops in 1921. Among his major roles were Gulyachkin in Nikolai Erdman's The Warrant *(1925) and Khlestakov in Gogol's* The Inspector General. *Although, like many of Meyerhold's actors, Garin left the theatre in the 1930s, he and his wife, Khesia Lokshina, remained close to Meyerhold. In fact, it was in their apartment in Leningrad that Meyerhold spent his final evening before his arrest in the early morning hours of June 20, 1939. Garin's description of Meyerhold demonstrating the "Leap on the Chest," offers one of the most vivid pictures of the Master at work with his students.*

Often during our exercise classes in rhythmic gymnastics, dancing, or acrobatics Meyerhold would appear in the room.

He would come in the door with a green military greatcoat over his shoulders (one of our allies furnished Russia with greatcoats like that before the Revolution). The temperature in the room was never very high. It didn't bother us young people, especially since we were moving so vigorously. Meyerhold would sit near the potbellied tile stove puffing at a rolled cigarette of shag tobacco (he was the only one permitted to smoke), and watch as if he were studying each one of us.

That's how I remember him, sitting alone by the Dutch tile stove from the former house of the former honey-tongued lawyer, Plevako.

He was observing his fledglings.

He resembled a kindly gray wolf with his grey eyes, grey hair, grey jacket. His eyes, kind and cool, studied us intently.

But now he throws off his coat. He interrupts our class. It's time to switch to Biomechanics. He puts a table in the middle of the room. He chooses one of the more powerfully-built students, Khrisanf Khersonsky. He leads him to the table. He places Khersonsky so that he is leaning back, supporting himself with his hands on the edge of the table. He tests his aptitude for resiliency and steps back, asking the students to pay attention. Now intention arises in him. He, as they say in boxing, crouches and stealthily approaches the person who is leaning back with his hands on the table. A leap and Meyerhold is on Khersonsky's shoulders. The maestro's right knee is resting on the student's left shoulder, the left knee is pressing against his chest, keeping the entire body in balance.

Next he puts his right hand behind his back and pulls out an imaginary knife. In one movement he delivers a blow to the neck, slides down to the floor and runs off to one side.

That exercise seemed to us like some magic trick. Meyerhold was about the same age as our fathers. His adeptness and youthful coordination amazed us. To this day I don't know whether Khersonsky was prepared, or whether that étude was as much a surprise to him as it was to us.

Within a month all of the students were doing that exercise.

Meyerhold had shown us one of the most complicated exercises. But our regular studies began with simpler ones: running, developing in the students an "electric" reaction, as he called the instant response to an external command.

Walking and running train the student to move smoothly. It makes it possible to walk or run without spilling any water if a vessel is placed on the head or is carried in the hands. Once the student can make these movements freely he is allowed to do an étude.

The first position of a student for executing an étude is the signal to begin: two hand claps. These blows are made in a downward direction and the movement is conveyed to the entire body, giving a springiness to the entire figure, after which the soles of the feet receive the movement begun by the hands. The soles are placed almost parallel, the heels a little apart and the toes turned slightly inward. The stance is reminiscent of a boxer's in contrast to the turned-out position of the classical barre.

The étude, "Shooting with Bow and Arrow" is executed by the student without actual objects. The left hand "carries" the bow. In walking and running the left shoulder leads. When the student spots the target, he stops, balancing his weight equally on both feet. His right hand makes a broad sweep in order to pull out the imaginary arrow attached at his back to an imaginary belt. The movement by the hand is conveyed to the entire body, shifting the weight to the rear foot.

The hand takes the arrow and places it in the bow. The weight is shifted to the forward foot. The aiming. The imaginary bow is stretched with the simultaneous transfer of the weight to the rear foot. The shot — and a culminating leap and exclamation.

This exercise, one of the first, already accustoms the student to be aware of himself in space, to focus his energy. It develops springiness, balance, and an understanding that the least gesture of the hand, for example, has an effect on the student's entire body. This étude acquaints the student with "acting links." "Acting links" consist of, as we see from the étude: intention, realization and reaction by the actor, which in this case is one of joy.

This sequence, the chain of acting links, of segments, will make up the role and constitute the actor's performance.

The beginning exercises in Biomechanics placed before the student the complex task of complete mastery of the acting material, that is, of his body. Meyerhold demanded clarity from us, preciseness in being aware of our body in space, movement with a conscious center of gravity, awareness of the gesture as a result of movement even when in a static position.

[Erast Garin, *S Meierkhol'dom* (Moscow: Iskusstvo, 1974), pp. 34–35.]

THE ACTOR OF THE FUTURE AND BIOMECHANICS
by V. Es.

Meyerhold's lecture is revealing for the grandiose program he set forth in which he stated that "art-amusement" would give way to "art-work" so that rest would be, in fact, a work process. Meyerhold went on to call for a reexamination of all the canons of the actor's art, which he said must be based on a firm physical foundation. "We," he said, "that is I, and all who are with me, are not concerned with the psychic world, but with the physical.... We don't need ecstasy, we need arousal based on a firm physical foundation."

According to Aleksandr Fevralsky, this account of the evening was written by Meyerhold or by one of his assistants. For another report of the same evening, see "The Actor of the Future" ["Akter budushchego," Ermitazh, no. 6 (1922) pp. 10–11], translated in Braun, Meyerhold on Theatre, pp. 199–200. This translation is based on a typescript given to Alma Law by the late Aleksandr Fevralsky.

Last Monday in the Little Auditorium of the Conservatory, V. E. Meyerhold "conversed" on that important, timely, and exciting subject. Actually, it was more of a passionate, friendly conversation than the usual smooth "official" lecture.

The lecturer "perched" on the stage somewhere near the piano. To the horror of the ushers, in the auditorium there was a mix-up on the tickets (there were three people trying to occupy a single seat), and the aisles were jammed with an excited mass of people. Members of the countless Moscow studios named after great actors and playwrights were sprawled in front of the first row as though posing for a group picture. In a word, everyone had decided: let's listen, and "never mind the seats."

"The acting craft of the past," Meyerhold said, "which used to be called art, was always closely connected with public life, with the structure of the state. The actor of the future will be even more dependent on the general principles of a working society.

"I would like for a moment to shift your attention to a somewhat utopian level.... Let's approach it gradually. Worker fatigue, the reduction of work to allow for rest periods, the rational organization of the work day—these are the main questions that concern and interest us today. Rest is essential, but what kind of rest? ... Many scholars, especially in America, are now striving to insure that the hours free from labor are not *absolute rest*. Formerly, art was born mainly in those hours when man was totally free from labor; to the man at rest were given the products of art, he was presented with art-amusement.

"Today, this is not the case. Now each year is equal to ten—and so we must hurry. We must *organize our labor so that rest will be, in fact, a work process*. Edison, for example, rested by working ... when work is constant, we must, of course, reject definitively art as art-amusement. This is the basic difference between the art of the past and the art of the future.

"The foundations on which the art of the past was built and the foundations on which the art of the future is being built are different. This difference must be reflected also in the actor-worker. *All the canons of the actor's art must be reexamined; the entire actor's workshop must be reorganized*. For example, an actor ordinarily comes to the theatre one hour before the beginning of a performance in order to put on his makeup and costume and so forth. (This is in accordance with the so-called regular contract.) But when work becomes a religion, when it is constant, that becomes impossible. The new actor will need to abolish makeup and create a work outfit. The actor will himself labor as a worker, and in his free time he will show his art, his artistic craft to his fellow workers. The result will be a *wonderously constant work process*, the realization of that plan to which I called your attention when I referred to it as *thus far* utopian...."

"In our day," Meyerhold continued, "all of the basic principles of art are being reexamined. Sculptors, architects and painters are also reexamining their artistic concepts. Constructivism, for example, has appeared. *Art-amusement* is turning into *art-labor*. It is clear that the art of the actor must also be reexamined. Who is the actor of the future? What is his art like? The actor of the future must first of all be *well-formed*, *rhythmical*, able to organize his body in space.

"The reexamination of the actor's 'physical condition' and the abolition of his arhythmicality are the 'ABCs' without which it will be impossible to approach labor in the theatre of the future.

"When Jaques-Dalcroze invented his rhythmical gymnastics [Eurhythmics], he had in mind mainly helping musicians. But it turned out that *the problem of rhythm* is equally important FOR *everyone*.

"Whether we use a saw poorly, whether we handle a knife and fork clumsily, whether we walk awkwardly on the stage, we can all learn from Dalcroze. Every master-blacksmith, foundry worker, actor must have a sense of rhythm; he must know the laws of balance. The actor who doesn't know the laws of Biomechanics is not even an apprentice. For example, a lack of knowledge of Biomechanics by the leaders of the Kamerny Theatre has brought the most dismal results. Neither fencing nor acrobatics helped. We had instead a cult of elegance created by tailors and shoemakers.

"How, then, do we approach the formation of the new actor?

"I think it is very simple.... When we observe the movements of a child, we are enjoying his biomechanical ability. If we place this child in conditions where gymnastics and all types of sports are both accessible and required, we will get a new man capable of any kind of work. *Only by means of the sports arena can we approach the theatrical arena.*"

"Each movement," Meyerhold said further, "is a hieroglyph which has its own meaning. On the stage there must be only those movements which can be deciphered instantly, otherwise they are superfluous. I must point out that we, that is I, and all who are with me, are not concerned with the *psychic* world, but with the *physical* world. The work of the new actor on the stage will consist of the grouping of his movements and his technical achievements. That does not mean, of course, that the actor turns into an automaton without a psyche. No. In the actor-acrobat there is always a duality. In order to master a difficult piece of music, the pianist *divides it into segments*, and having mastered them, he stops making mistakes and gives a perfect rendering. The same thing applies to the work of the actor. Only after mastering the role *technically*, mathematically, can we *allow* ourselves *the ecstasy of inspiration*. Let us turn to Pushkin: '*inspiration is needed*, both in *geometry* and in *poetry*; *ecstasy is not required*.' Ecstasy is that notorious emoting, that 'emotional experiencing;' it is the system of my teacher, Konstantin Stanislavsky, which incidentally, he will probably soon reject. We don't need *ecstasy*, we need *arousal*, based on a firm physical foundation."

The main part of Meyerhold's talk was over. He next read a *Statement of the Principles of Biomechanics* worked out in GVTM, and then there was a demonstration.

"The students of GVTM," Meyerhold warned, "have been studying for only a few months; they will be master craftsman only after three years, and therefore we must not make too large or too strict demands." This "request for leniency" turned out to be completely unnecessary—the audience wildly applauded the GVTM students in admiration for the precision of their work and ... envied them loudly.

Indeed, if the actors in our model academic and "better" theatres were to do one one-hundredth of this program, it would soon be necessary to call the ambulances in order to load them with the meat of those masters of "pure and sacred" art.

Among the examples of Biomechanics that were demonstrated, "Play with the Dagger" and "Leap on the Chest" stand out. When the Sicilian tragedian Giovanni Grasso came to Russia, he used that device in one of the plays in his repertory. At the time, everyone said it was temperament, expressiveness, and deep emotion. "Nonsense," Meyerhold stated, "It is work and work alone. Without question, Grasso spent many hours preparing and working out that device. He didn't do it suddenly under the stress of an outburst of emotion."

The demonstration was already long over, but the audience was still applauding Meyerhold, surrounded by his students in their blue work clothes. In three years they will be master craftsmen. The slogans of the old Russian acting profession—"I'll manage somehow;" "emoting will help," "I can get by on temperament"—will all be alien to them.

On their workshop banner will be written in capital letters: THE ART OF THE ACTOR IS THE ORGANIZATION OF HIS LABOR.

Biomechanics According to Meyerhold
by Ippolit Sokolov

One of Meyerhold's leftist opponents, the critic Ippolit Sokolov, founded his own short-lived studio, the Laboratory of Theatrical Expressionism, in 1922. In denouncing the exercises Meyerhold's pupils demonstrated as a mishmash of circus acrobatics, plastics, movement play, and pyramids from Sokol Gymnastics, Sokolov was probably motivated by a desire to establish the credibility of his own rather strange system combining (according to one witness) Expressionism, Taylorism, and Eccentrism.

Meyerhold answered Sokolov in a lecture (November 6, 1922) entitled "Tartuffes of Communism and Cuckolds of Morality" (reported in Teatr i Muzyka, *no. 7 [1922] pp. 23–24), in which he stated that his system "had no scientific basis . . . other than a booklet by Coquelin on the subject." Meyerhold was referring to Constant-Benoît Coquelin's* L'Art et le comédien, *in which the concept of the duality of the actor as both "the performer, the instrumentalist, [and] the instrument to be played on" bears a striking resemblance to Meyerhold's own formulation $N = A_1 + A_2$. Meyerhold went on to assert that the basic objective of Biomechanics was to improve the health of the actors, who were often forced to play in extremely bad conditions, and to overcome the system of "inspiration" and* *"experiencing" (a reference to Stanislavsky's System) so that they would be able to perform under any conditions.*

In Meyerhold's Biomechanics, there is neither "bio" nor "mechanics." "Bio" and "mechanics" are the basis of all of our existence in general, but for some reason, Meyerhold's theatrical system stakes a claim on the term "Biomechanics." However, Meyerhold's system doesn't establish and doesn't advance even a single elementary law of genuine Biomechanics. And even more, it ignores the laws of biology and mechanics. It is clear that Meyerhold is attempting to use at any cost the great ideological and mnemonic power of that promising term "Biomechanics." Meyerhold's understanding of the term itself, however, is extremely general, amorphous, and hazy.

For Meyerhold, "Biomechanics" is nothing more than a metaphor. Of course, no serious scientific discipline can bear a clearly metaphorical name. This purely metaphorical term "Biomechanics" might, in practice, be developed over time into a full-blown allegory, but of course, no scientific discipline can function as an endless allegory, a total analog.

As a scientific term and a scientific discipline, biomechanics has already existed for a long time. Conte wrote of anthropotechnics and Ostwald about biomechanics. Work in the area of anthropotechnics was carried out by a whole series of major physiologists such as Marey, Meyer, Weber, Ranvier, Raoult, Chauveau, Traube, Atwater, Zuntz, Demeny, Sechenov, and Amar. During the war years the prominent French physiologist, Jules Amar, published a major work, *Le Moteur humain et les bases scientifiques du travail professionnel* (more than 600 pages). Amar objectively and experimentally studied man as a living machine. Now it would be only with great difficulty that we could go beyond Amar in order to discover or research something new.

At the first demonstration of biomechanical exercises on June 12, the promulgation of the theory of biomechanics took place. From notes, Meyerhold very simply read as theoretical propositions some chaotic, unrelated aphorisms by one of his pupils at GVTM. At the second program on October 18, Meyerhold announced that there was no literature on biomechanics either in Russia or in the West.

This is not so. There exists an astonishing literature on biomechanics, more than one hundred major works by Western European and, in part, by Russian scholars.

Of course, Meyerhold's biomechanics has nothing in common with the work of anatomists and physiologists in the realm of anthropomechanics. Meyerhold's system is, of course, neither genuine, universal biomechanics, nor is it metaphorical biomechanics of the theatre.

The general sociological position of Meyerhold's Biomechanics is a simple repetition of the well-known views of the chief director of VVO [General Military Training], N. I. Podvoisky, on the theatricalization of physical culture and on physical culture in the theatre based on the program of the work of the All-Russia Red Stadium. But these views don't coincide or correspond in the least degree with the body of Meyerhold's practical activities (his *Cuckold* production and Biomechanics).

According to Meyerhold, biomechanics must resolve the problems of physical education and theatrical art. These few biomechanical exercises can be divided into two types: physical exercises—Leap on Partner's Back and Transfer of Weight, Falling, Catching and Lowering of a Heavy Object—and theatrical exercises—Shooting with Bow and Arrow, Throwing a Stone, Blow on the Nose, Slap on the Face, Pushing Down a Kneeling Figure with the Foot, Leap on the Chest of Opponent, Play with a Dagger, Horse (for three), and Fool (for five).

From the point of view of physical education, Meyerhold's whole system is to put it mildly, a curiosity, a joke. It is understandable that Meyerhold's several biomechanical exercises won't be able to compete in any respect, not only with the old German, Swedish, and Sokol systems of gymnastics, the gymnastics of Lesgaft, Demeny, Dalcroze, and Proshek, but also with the vulgar systems of Mueller or Anokhin.

Practically speaking, biomechanics is outside any kind of physical culture. It is overloaded with huge, completely inadmissible shortcomings from the point of view of the elementary demands of human anatomy and physiology. All of the biomechanical exercises are extremely haphazard and absolutely baseless from the point of view of the anatomical structure and the physiological functioning of the human organism. Ordinarily, in all gymnastic systems, all of the exercises are precise and sequentially arranged in different groups and categories: exercises for the muscles of the lower extremities, the upper shoulder area, the neck, spine, diaphragm, side muscles, and so forth. But all of the exercises in Biomechanics are completely non-sequential, pointless, and unsystematic. Meyerhold's system is an unsystematic "system." Biomechanics is very superficial, purely external. The constructing of the biomechanical exercises was done in a purely amateurish way, by look and by feel, without any aim or consistency. Biomechanical exercises based on the carrying of human figures put an excessive strain on the heart and lungs through inadmissibly hard work. All of these falls, catching, and lowering of human figures without doubt harmfully affect breathing. If Biomechanics is going to be taught to the chorus at the Bolshoi Theatre, as is proposed, then in the course of a couple months it will irreparably ruin correct breathing. Incidently, in our time, gymnastics of the lungs according to the system of Leo Keffler was long ago introduced into the German army. Furthermore, the carrying of a figure abdomen-down on the shoulder of a partner causes completely inadmissible and definitely harmful pressure on the abdomen, or rather, it simply delivers an extended blow to the stomach. But on the other hand, as we know, in the section of free exercises in Sokol gymnastics, there is a class of gymnastics with a partner (opposite) where there are very interesting and completely natural exercises with the help of coexercisers such as "climbing the coexerciser," "carrying and lifting of the coexerciser," and so forth (see "Course in Sokol Gymnastics"). In Meyerhold's Biomechanics one can see a complete lack of knowledge and understanding of the elementary laws of anatomy and physiology. Biomechanics has all of the specific shortcomings of crude circus acrobatics. It is a definitely unnatural system.

Empirically speaking, Meyerhold's Biomechanics is a deliberate maiming of man under the cover of pseudoscientific terminology.

Even theoretically speaking, Biomechanics according to Meyerhold is a scientific joke. The theoretical bases of Biomechanics are "location of the center of gravity," "balance," "stability," "the law of leverage," and so forth. All of these principles are without principle. The center of gravity and the law of leverage never were and never can be principles for any kind of system of movement. And does Meyerhold know that scores of mathematicians, physicists, and physiologists in the course of several centuries have been trying unsuccessfully to find the center of gravity of the human body, and that the law of leverage is explained exhaustively in every textbook on anatomy or on physical education?

From the viewpoint of theatrical art, Biomechanics is in essence completely non-theatrical. Meyerhold does not even attempt to establish a modus of theatricality in the exercises. In the purely theatrical biomechanical exercises, illustrative, imitative exercises are introduced instead of exercises based on physical strength. Everything disparaging Meyerhold ever said about Duncan's plastics can be applied to Biomechanics. Why are Duncan's illustrative gestures imitating a breeze or a sea wave bad, and the illustrative movements of shooting the arrow (!) or play with daggers (!) in Biomechanics good? Why? The principle of imitative movements is one and the same in plastics and in Biomechanics. The only expedient circus stunts—a blow on the nose, a slap on the face—are, of course, in no way biomechanical.

The wretched Meyerholdian "parade" during the exercises doesn't achieve even one one-hundredth of that theatricality which exists in the artistic and varied figurative marching (in a circle) of the Sokols. The childish exercises "The Horse" for three and "The Fool" for five (what poverty!) are far below the effectiveness of children's active play and the perfection of Sokol group exercises with many-leveled pyramids. By the way, the biomechanical exercise "The Horse" can't be compared to expedient, genuine equestrian acrobatics, or even to the effectiveness of exercises on a simple gymnasium horse or trestle.

In spite of the fact that Biomechanics is based on elements of circus acrobatics, plastics, active play, plus Sokol pyramids (a little from everywhere), Meyerhold, for some reason, attaches to his Biomechanics the so-called rationalization of muscular movements. All Biomechanics is blatent anti-Taylorism. None of the biomechanical exercises has anything in common with the principles of economy, simplicity, expediency, and precision of movements. Biomechanics as a whole is not an economy of strength but an exorbitant waste of it. Of course, Biomechanics cannot have anything in common with the precise principles of automation, economization, and rationalization of movements in labor gymnastics.

Right now, Biomechanics according to Meyerhold's system doesn't exist at all. Meyerhold's Biomechanics is an example not so much of good dilettantism as it is of simple philistinism in matters of science and the art of movement. The insignificant number of biomechanical exercises shows Meyerhold's complete lack of innovation and originality in the realm of movement. Meyerhold has too many pretensions when he calls the dozen or so circumstantial, aimless, meaningless, and worthless exercises a system of training for man and actor. The old system of Swedish or Sokol gymnastics has as many as 40,000 strictly thought-out and well-constructed exercises. I'm afraid that thanks to Meyerhold's system, the scientific term "biomechanics" will soon become an odious expression.

This same lecture, which Meyerhold has repeated several times lately, is loaded with false and distorted facts in the realm of physiology (for example, on the question of the physiological functioning of the actor's nervous system according to the theory of "intuition," "experiencing," and "reflex arousal") as well as in the realm of the scientific organization of labor, (for example, on the question of fatigue in connection with Edison's work and relaxation). Meyerhold must definitely publish as soon as possible those results of the scientific work at GITIS about which he has talked so much and which thus far he hasn't reported anywhere.

["Biomechanics According to Meyerhold," *Teatr*, no. 5 (1922), pp. 149–151.]

Taylorism on the Stage
by Arkady Pozdnev

Arkady Pozdnev, another one of Meyerhold's students, was commissioned to reply to Ippolit Sokolov's attack on Biomechanics. As Pozdnev notes in his reply, the work gesture in the theatre and in the factory share the common objectives of eliminating superfluous movements and of conserving energy. But whereas work gestures in the factory are directed toward reducing movements to the "least and shortest trajectory," in the theatre, movements must be "broad, open, and natural," so that they will be visible and expressive. Only then can they fulfill their function, which, in contrast to the "product" produced by the factory worker, is not a tangible object but an emotional reaction aroused in the spectator.

When the Meyerhold Theatre was on tour in Kiev in June 1923, Pozdnev, who by then had left the theatre, wrote in a letter to Meyerhold, "I often observed mistakes in your work which seemed to me — why hide it — unforgivable. Now I see that even if your work were nothing but mistakes it would still be valuable. . . . I'm happy, Vsevolod Emilevich, that I'm your pupil. Perhaps it's a little late now, but allow me to thank you for those lessons you taught us as future servants of the new theatrical auditorium."[4]

When I encounter Ippolit Sokolov's verbose judgments in the theatre journals about mechanics, Taylorism, and the work gesture, I am no less amazed than I would be if I were to see Kachalov [a leading actor at the Moscow Art Theatre] in Foregger's *buffonades*. What is there in common between what Sokolov preaches and the theatre? He stubbornly attempts to combine the uncombinable — the "theory of the work gesture" and the theory of the *theatrical* gesture. There is obviously a misunderstanding here, and I shall attempt to clarify what it is.

"The theatre can and must teach all of us to Taylorize our walking and gesturing" (*Zrelishcha*, no. 2 [1922]).

In the first place, not everyone, but *only actors* — persons who are physically and psychologically suited for the stage according to the strict laws of professional selection. As for the general pedagogical, nontheatrical dissemination of the concept of geometrical work processes, that is the objective of the TsIT [Central Institute of Labor] instructors in work gymnastics, the school of Taylorized gestures and the like. In any case, not the theatre's.

Sokolov introduces the principle and definition: "The geometric and most efficient Taylorized gesture is the straight line plus the right angle."

That is true in regard to work gestures of *workers*, but is by no means true in regard to *theatrical* work gestures, because while the *work gesture* is directed at the formation of material outside of itself, the theatrical gesture is at the same time both the *tool* and the *product* of theatrical work.

The basis of all stage gesture is its effect on the spectator. That is its main objective, for the achievement of which the actor must orient his movements toward the scenic design of the production, and coordinate them not to degrees, right angles and straight lines, but to the elements of the scenic design. These elements are not determined by straight lines and acute angles. All deliberate squeezing of theatrical gesture into straight lines and acute angles inevitably leads to stylization, which, by the way, Ippolit Sokolov demands in *Zrelishcha* no. 1. That will be "Kamernizing" [a reference to Tairov's style at the Kamerny Theatre] inside out. Instead of Kamerny ellipses, circles, "children's scribblings," this is the angle and the straight line. However, whatever its source, the theatre must and will fight against all forms of stylization.

Meyerhold's *Biomechanics* flows from the *natural* possibilities of the human body. (*Natural* not in the naturalistic sense, but in the sense of the physiological potential of the structure of the human body.)

Taylor built his theory on the economy of the workers' energy, mainly by the rational reduction of the work gesture toward the *least and shortest trajectory*. In the theatre that is not only *not needed*, it is *harmful*.

I will explain with an example.

In pounding a nail, for economy of energy the worker must move only the forearm and perhaps only the wrist. In pounding a nail on the stage, however, the actor must deliver the blow with a *broad, open, and natural* gesture, not taking into account the theory of the shortened trajectory, because: in the first instance, one must pound in the nail, whereas in the second, one must show (and at a great distance) that the nail is being pounded in.

These are two different things, a fact which is not understood by comrade Sokolov, who dreams of Taylorizing the stage gesture and hasn't explained to himself the different concepts: the worker in the factory and the worker (actor) on the stage.

Another example:

The actors' blue costumes in *Cuckold* are excellent costumes, capturing theatrically the contemporary spirit, but in terms of "work clothes [*prozodezhda*]" they are based more on the principles of work clothes for factory workers than for workers in the theatre for whom the best work clothes are "shorts" or tights....

Of course, Taylorism and the theory of work gestures are good things, and it would be good for Ippolit Sokolov to study them. But the *theatre* must have a different, "*theatrical Taylorism*," its own theory of *theatrical gestures* and movements. This Taylorism will be directed exclusively at naturalness, emphasis, and the broadness of gestures. Its goal is the struggle against *superfluous* and *unnecessary* "gestures for the sake of gestures" on the stage.

That theory is *Biomechanics*.
The Taylor of the theatre is Vsevolod Meyerhold.
["Taylorism on the Stage," *Zrelishcha*, no. 5 (1922), pp. 8-9.]

PROJECT: PROFILE OF THE ACTOR GRADUATING FROM THE MEYERHOLD STATE THEATRE SCHOOL

Although incomplete, Nikolai Basilov's "Profile of the Actor" offers the fullest description we have of Meyerhold's program of actor training. Prepared in 1935, it is striking testimony to Meyerhold's faithfulness to the principles of the actor's art he had begun working out as early as 1907: the mastery of movement in relation to the stage space and to one's partner, and the ability to control each part of the body. In the "Profile," Meyerhold rejects any artificial means for the arousal of feelings, either through systemic narcosis (as employed by actors in the nineteenth century) or through the hypnotic training of the will (the Stanislavsky system). He maintained that both are equally dangerous for the psychological health of the actor.

In their place, Meyerhold proposed his "biomechanical system" based on the principles of reflexive arousal of emotions through proper placement of the body in space.

The "Profile" also outlines Meyerhold's program for the construction of a role. Rich in practical advice to the actor, it is of as much relevance today as it was when it was written sixty years ago.

Objective: to create a highly-qualified professional actor, who is a politically conscious, artistically active participant in the construction of socialism, an actor who is a well-rounded craftsman, who has mastered the cultural-artistic heritage, and *who knows how to create stage images* on the basis of Marxist-Leninist methodology.

The graduating actor must:

1. (a) *Master his human material* (the discovery and control of his inherent psycho-physical characteristics).
    Make his body healthy, well-trained, with good coordination of all parts of his body.
    Develop good attention (organs of feeling),
    memory,
    observation,
    quick wittedness,
    orientation in space,

imagination,
fantasy, and so forth.
Develop a proper, fast reaction to external stimuli.
Know how directly and freely to express and manifest his wishes, in actions, in deeds.
Know how freely and directly to express any emotional state.
and

(b) *Master the technique of the actor's craft*
The mastery of rhythm and the fundamentals of music.
The mastery of movement (Biomechanics, boxing, dancing, rhythmics, fencing, and so forth).
In stage behavior.
In speech (genre, verse forms, and so forth).
In the handling of objects, makeup, costume, etc.

2. *To know*
   (a) The basic stages in the development of the artistic culture of the past;
   (b) The major theatrical cultures of the past and present-day theatrical systems;
   (c) The evolution of the basic acting systems (Russian theatre, Western European theatre, and the Japanese-Chinese theatre).

3. *To know how*, on the basis of Marxist-Leninist methodology, to recognize reality. To know how to use historical, scientific, literary, iconographic, documentary, and other materials for a correct understanding of the epoch, society, and so forth, reflected in the work/play/production and for the extraction, the selection of essential material which can help to form the image/play/production.

4. *To know how* to understand, to analyze a work (a play, a production) and the artistic idea of its manifestation; to know how to analyze a play, the idea of the director, artist, composer, and choreographer from the point of view of the ideational-thematic tendency, stylistic, technological aspects, and so forth.

5. *To know how* to reflect correctly the cognitive reality in the images.
To know how to create an image: to present the personality traits of the role being played, to reveal the social typicality of the individual, unique personality; to master the method and technique of building a stage image; to define the stage behavior and the choice of devices for scenic expressiveness and so on and so forth.

6. *To have* a repertory worked out (no less than four roles)
In various genres
Classic and contemporary repertoire
To define one's *emploi*

NOTE: the profile presented here serves as a basis on which the *general teaching program as a whole and by subject* can be worked out for each discipline separately. It indicates only the objective of the education and *only* the essential results of that education.

Nikolai A. Basilov, August 1935

The Actor

The status of the actor graduating from GEKTEMAS [State Experimental Theatre Workshops] under the Meyerhold Theatre, compiled by Nikolai A. Basilov [and Meyerhold and others].

1. The work of the actor is the awareness of oneself in space. One must study one's body in such a way that in taking one or another position one knows precisely how it will look at any given moment.

2. The art of the actor is manifested in movements, which by means of "will," convey a brilliance, a vividness, and a facility for infecting the spectator.

3. The peculiarity of the actor's art, in contrast to the art of the playwright, the director, and other artists, lies in the fact that the artistic process unfolds in front of an audience, as a consequence of which the actor and the spectator find themselves in some kind of relationship, and this puts the spectator in the position of a living resonator responding to all the manifestations of the actor's craft. Conversely, catching with a subtle ear his resonator (the auditorium), the actor instantly reacts by mean of improvisation to all the demands coming from it. By an entire series of signs (noise, movement, coughing, laughter, and the like), the actor must accurately define the attitude of the spectator to the production.

4. The actor must be rhythmical to the highest degree; he must hear not only with his ears, but with each point of his body; it's not enough to listen, he must *know how to control* each part of his body: he must combine rhythmics and gymnastics.

5. In the art of the actor we distinguish acrobatic, musical, and dancing parts, the art of wearing a costume, and the art of relating to objects on the stage.

6. For the actor, a study of the body also means a study of the costume, which for him is, as it were, a part of the body; the inability to master the costume is reflected in his acting, as for example, if the actor puts on his hat incorrectly, it means that he's insensitive (unresponsive) to his body.

7. In the complex of factors making up a production, where each of the component parts has a strictly defined magnitude, the actor's playing is one of the elements of the production which is in an unavoidable coordinative relationship to the whole.

8. The material of the actor's art is the human body, that is, the torso, the extremities, the head, the voice. In studying his material, the actor must proceed not from anatomy, but from the preparedness of the body as material for stage play.

9. One of the most important elements in the mastery of one's

material is the ability to place and shift one's body in the stage space, that is, to play *raccourcis*.*

If we take a toy, a "Bibabo" [a hand puppet], we will see that the toy is perceived by us as laughing, crying, and so forth, in spite of the fact that the Bibabo mask is immobile, the changes depending solely on the change of *raccourcis*: the secret isn't in the mimicry, but in the bodily movement; with skillful use, the mask can express everything that is expressed by mimicry.

10. One must study the mechanics of one's body in such a way that one knows precisely the dependence and the system of each separate part of the body. Each movement, if only of the little finger or toe, must immediately be reflected in all parts of the body; each movement of one of its parts must immediately reshape the relationships in which the parts of the body are arranged. One must grasp the laws of balance and know how to command the body so that at the needed moment one immediately finds the point of stability.

11. The extremities (the arms and legs) are one of the means for determining balance and for enabling one to find the center of gravity of one's body.

12. The hands of the actor must be trained so that besides serving the function of overall balance they can play an independent role in the acting, as an element of expressiveness. Examples: the hands of Eleonora Duse, of Konstantin Stanislavsky.

13. In addition to the aforementioned function of the legs (No. 11), they also carry out the role of springs supporting the torso of the actor; consequently that part of the body must be ready like a spring, prepared at any moment to receive a stimulus.

13a. For an actor, an unattractive body doesn't exist — there is only the inability to carry oneself and an inability to use it.

14. The correctly located center of balance of the entire bodily system gives a sense of well-being to the expressive means (legs and arms).

15. One can distinguish a good actor from a bad one by the eyes: you never see the eyes of a bad actor. It is necessary to train the eyes, focusing one's gaze on specific objects; if the eyes want to wander from the object, one must by a strong will train the eyes to keep them on it.

16. The actor when entering from the wings must keep the eyes on the line of the horizon; when he holds them on that line, then all the other positions of the eyes can be perceived as *raccourci*.

17. The eyes and mouth must be trained to an extreme degree of

---

*Raccourci — *the foreshortening, the visual change of the form of an object placed in an unaccustomed position for the observer (primarily on the horizontal place of vision)* [N.A.B.].

expressiveness. Any weariness of these organs deprives the actor of the possibility to use them to the fullest, thus denying him the possibility to take part in the production.

18. The head is one of the expressive means of the actor's material; it can only be used when it is placed in the appropriate *raccourci*, after which elements of the face can be used in the acting: the facial muscles, eyes and mouth.

19. A gesture which results from the movement of the entire body of the actor is a response in relation to the movement of the body. It must also be built according to the laws of balance of the given movement.

20. The technique of the actor not passed through the *spectrum of life* can lead him to abstract circus acrobatics.

21. In his artistry, the actor, in addition to the technical reserve, also uses that material of the "observations" he accumulates in the course of his entire life. We need "observations of life" not in order to bring them to our work (to our "acting") with photographic preciseness, but in order to use them as material on which we can train our technique. For the actor it is extremely important to know how to work with fabrics, how to finger a fabric; any Chinese merchant knows how to do that so well that you can see how he feels the material of the fabric with his entire body, its weight; and all of his feelings receive a vivid external expression; that is precisely what the actor needs when a fabric enters into his playing. The actor must use the manner of the Chinese in working with the fabric, not in order to imitate him, but so that it enters into the list of those training materials which he uses. Each object obliges a special relationship and these fabrics produce in the actor a skill — how to take hold of them — and thus he masters a thousand different skills, and these skills intuitively awaken in him; if he doesn't already have them, they are mastered by him; in this way he will acquire much experience, and with this experience (taken from life) he will go out on the stage.

22. In his work, the actor uses not only a reserve of technical habits and observations from life, but also those reserves which he acquires in developing himself with the aid of reading books, travels, the studying of all kinds of memoirs, diaries, and so forth.

The Actor's Acting

23. The ability to discharge through reflexive arousal a reserve of energy is essential for the actor. A person lacking this ability cannot be an actor.

24. In the *internal* and the *experiencing* systems of acting, this is

replaced: in the first—by forcing the will by means of artificial arousal of feelings enervated beforehand; in the second—by the formation of feelings by means of hypnotic extraction of a will enervated beforehand.

25. In the *internal* method, arousal beforehand of enervated feelings is achieved by systemic narcosis (alcohol, smoking, drugs). In the *experiencing* method, one's will and feelings are accumulated through the hypnotic training of one's imagination. The devices of both methods, equally dangerous for the psychological health of actors, must be rejected.

26. At the base of the acting system must be placed the principles of a biomechanical view of the nature of man. By virtue of training of arousal in the actor (the ability to reproduce in feelings and movements and in words an externally-received task), psychic processes become the result of physical well-being.

27. The biomechanical system of acting is based on the fact that correct arousal is brought about by the proper placement of the actor's body in space. Furthermore, at each moment there will be a correct relationship in the actor's movements to all the performers and objects around him.

28. The coordination of the manifestations of arousal also makes up the actor's acting. Individual manifestations of arousal are the essence of the actor's acting.

29. The actor himself is the material of the actor's acting (his work). As a result of that, we have a phenomenon where in one person is concentrated both the material and the constructor of it. Thus, we can represent the actor by a formula where A_2 is the material, and A_1 is the constructor, the controller, and N is the aggregate of these two elements in work.

30. Each element of the actor's acting is invariably (vitally) made up of three obligatory factors: *intention, realization, and reaction* (author-playwright, director, initiative of the actor).

The *realization* is the cycle of volitional, mimical reflexes (movements arising on the periphery of the actor's body, also movements by the actor in space and related to speech).

The *reaction* is the submission of the volitional reflex according to the realization of the mimical and vocal reflexes and in the preparation for the receiving of a new task (the shift to a new element of play).

Reflexive arousal is the reduction—to the minimum—of the process of realization of the task (time of simple reaction).

Schema

31. It is this arousal (emotion) that distinguishes the actor from the marionette, giving the former the possibility to infect the spectator and

arouse a reciprocal emotion which is already nourishment (fuel) for the succeeding play (an ecstatic state).

32. For verification of the degree to which the actor's A_1 is working one can make the following test:

You admit the person being tested through the antechamber of a room where one of the doors is mirrored (the subject doesn't know this) and curtained. At a certain moment, as the subject approaches the door, the curtain falls away, revealing the mirror. The subject in whom A_1 is working correctly will at that unexpected moment somehow react, become wary, organize himself externally. He will take a correct position with regard to the space around him. Passing by that door with the mirror he will continue further in his imagination (to see, to know) himself in relation to his surroundings. It is clear that the further he moves away from the mirror the weaker that state will become. Thus we can even establish a law, namely: the length of the path taken during which is felt that aforementioned state of control of A_1 is in reverse proportion to the strength of that control. The actor must train his A_1 so that the force of control doesn't diminish, but on the contrary, increases.

The path of the subject.
The moment of revelation of the mirror.
The moment of reaction.

33. A_2 — the material, must be brought in the actor to such a state of training that it is possible for him to juggle the combination of his skills. These skills make up the technical stock of movement (of the body, voice, face), of volitional impulses, and the work of the nervous system, all of which he orients, giving the basis for his A_1 to carry out a task, to create the construction of his role.

A_1, in giving a task to A_2, not only constantly sees A_2 on the acting platform, but also draws deductions from those or other positions of A_2 which give an impulse toward new, still unknown to A_1, *combinations of technical skills (improvisations)*.

34. The realization by the actor of his role is conditioned by (1) that *emploi* within whose framework it is squeezed, and (2) the dramaturgical and directorial score.

35. The *emploi* helps in the realization of a role by the fact that it combines a series of signs issuing from the external appearance and the scenic functions.

The dramaturgical and directorial score, constructed on musical principles, allows the possibility to find the correct assignment of stage time of the overall movement and of each individual movement, and to find the correct deployment and use of stage time-space. Thus the correct understanding of "the score as a whole" gives correct rhythmical alternation of the remaining states, of individual manifestations of "reflexive exitation." In other words, the internal side of constructing the role, as the result of the entire form, is the rhythmical alternation of various intensities of individual states.

36. Observations drawn from life which the actor accumulates are, along with the technical reserve, the material that the actor dispenses according to the plan of his role. These observations result in enabling the actor to catch from each living phenomenon that alternation of points of balance, legitimate for each given position. In completing his observations of life, the actor must above all have in mind an approach as a rhythmic manifestation of the particularity of one or another *individuum*.

On the Construction of the Role

37. The plan of construction by the actor of his role arises during the period of rehearsals with the director. The independent realization of that plan and the construction of the superstructure of the actor in the role begins from the moment when the director announces that it is his last rehearsal.

38. In constructing his role, the actor starts from:

(1) *The emploi* (external appearance, stage function).
(2) *The Directorial schematic of the dramaturgical material.*
(3) That sketch of the role proposed to him by the director.
(4) The entire complex of elements making up the production.

39. In constructing his role, the actor is guided by the following principles:

(1) A strict economy of movements and gestures (miserliness of expressive means), that is, one allows oneself only those movements and gestures sufficient to convey to the spectator what the actor needs to convey. This is called for by the tendency to tire quickly, which is characteristic for an actor's work; in order to avoid it, since an actor in a weary state cannot manifest maximum excitability, it is essential to calculate strictly (to rationalize) his movements, allowing only the extremely essential, avoiding movements which have no objective.

(2) The actor uses his reserve of observations from life with the objective of finding the rhythmically characteristic peculiarities of the construction of the role, for which the gait, as an element of dancingness, is mainly used.

40. An actor approaching work on a role makes his own notes on his copy of the text of the role.

A model page of the text of a role:

        Text of the role   Actor's notes

In his notes the actor records:
(1) Movement, both spatial and temporal;
(2) Speech from a musical point of view, and with respect to its coordination with the movements.

41. Just as a pianist, before beginning to study some song, trains himself with exercises, the actor, too, before beginning to study a role must work on the technical training of his material. For that, he must put himself in the appropriate psycho-physical conditions. No craftsman, no artisan can advance his craftsmanship if he does not have a workshop; similarly the actor, too, must have a room which he uses only for his work. This room must be empty, free of all furniture, papered with plain white wallpaper. In this room is located gymnastic equipment. The floor must be covered with carpet (cleaned daily with the help of a vacuum cleaner) or, in any case, the floor must be such that it isn't slippery under the feet. Instead of furniture, there should be in the workshop geometrical objects (a sphere, cube, cylinder, cone, and the like). The actor must have in the workshop a basket full of rings for the game of *cerceau*, a cap, hats, remnants of fabric, balls, rags, and other objects that can serve for his training. The actor works in an outfit which does not in any way hamper his movements, and which fits his body well (but not a knitted fabric), (nor should the body be bare); with or without shoes.

Part One — General

42. The auditorium always has such a significant influence on the stage and on the actor working on it that the latter is always either the prosecutor or the defender in relation to the role he is playing. In this respect the artist's craft is always tendentious. By means of this tendentiousness the actor's playing is determined for each part of the auditorium. The same could be said for the work of the director.

43. If the production is built musically, then the actor must unfailingly know the precise time for his entrances and exits in order to get into the rhythm of the production.

44. A pause is conditioned by the rhythm, by a feeling for time. It is necessary to train a feeling for time, so that all the pauses answer your purpose; they must be automated.

45. The art of the theatre can be studied and known not only through theory, but also through practice.

46. One must reject the old concept of the term *"intermission."* Previously, the intermission was a break between two acts during which the audience did whatever it wished, distracted from the direct and full

perception of the production. Up until now, the intermission has distracted the spectator, bringing in influences alien to the subject by means of conversations with one's neighbors and the like, thus interfering with the spectator's involvement with the rhythmical content of the production.

The fact that they in no way serve the technical demands of the production speaks against intermissions. Since this is the case, then it is clear that the intermission must not be merely a break, but must play the role of a connecting link between two scenes. Taking into account the musical nature of a production's structure, we see that the intermission must be one of the musically constructed elements of the entire production. The theatre of antiquity, the Japanese, Chinese, and Spanish theatre all had a correct understanding of the meaning of the intermission. For example, the *entremés* in the Spanish theatre had as its objective to carry the spectator into a contrasting state of mind.

In the contemporary theatre one of the first attempts at a correct resolution of intermissions was made by.... [Private archive, Moscow]

PROMPTBOOK FOR THE MAGNANIMOUS CUCKOLD: LETTER SCENE FROM ACT II

Fernand Crommelynck's The Magnanimous Cuckold *is the bizarre story of an Othello who is his own Iago. Bruno, the village scribe, is passionately in love with his devoted and obedient young wife, Stella. He is so infatuated by possession of such an attractive woman that he boasts of her charms everywhere. But once his jealousy has been aroused by his friend Petrus' attention to his wife, Bruno cannot rest until he has put all doubts to an end with absolute certainty. He therefore compels the suffering Stella to sleep first with Petrus and then with all the men in the village as he pursues the phantom of a nonexistent lover. True to her husband to the very end, Stella finally runs off with the Cowherd.*

In the following scene from act 2, the Cooper appears and asks Bruno to write a love letter. When Bruno learns the letter is for Stella, he reacts by slapping the Cooper on the face. The text is from Meyerhold's Promptbook for The Magnanimous Cuckold, *originally published in* Meyerhold's Magnanimous Cuckold, *a program booklet for "An Evening of Russian Constructivist Theatre," held in conjunction with the exhibition* Art of the Avant-Garde in Russia: Selections from the George Costakis Collection *at the Solomon R. Guggenheim Museum, New York, December 10–13, 1981, and at the Museum of Fine Arts, Houston, March 25–28, 1982.*

BRUNO *stares straight at the* COOPER. *He walks around him and stops between him and* ESTRUGO, *two steps downstage from a line between* ESTRUGO *and the* COOPER. *The* COOPER, *following* BRUNO *with his eyes, turns his back to the audience. He takes his pipe out of his mouth during the turn, in view of the audience.*

THE FIRST SLAP ON THE FACE.

  Wheels: White — (*plus*)   *Turn on*

BRUNO

And you aren't afraid?

BRUNO *gives the FIRST SLAP ON THE FACE. The* COOPER *lets out a low one-toned sound.* BRUNO, *a little frightened by the sound, retreats from the* COOPER *a little downstage left and says, looking at him, "And you aren't afraid?" He walks to* ESTRUGO: *"He's not afraid." A momentary play of perplexity — toward the audience.*

He's not afraid.

THE SECOND SLAP.

He walks to his previous place and gives the second slap. The COOPER *lets out the same sound.*

You're not trembling. He isn't trembling.

BRUNO *repeats the play*: *"You're not trembling?" "He's not trembling."*

Well, I'll let him have it.

He says to the audience: "Well, I'll let him have it." He walks around the COOPER *from the outer side and gives him the* THIRD SLAP. *The* COOPER *gives forth a sound.* BRUNO *plays as before, he doesn't retreat downstage right from the* COOPER.

BRUNO

Well, I'll let him have some more.

  He says to the audience, "Well, I'll let him have it again." The FOURTH SLAP ON THE FACE. *The same sound from the* COOPER. *The* FIFTH SLAP ON THE FACE. *A pause.* BRUNO *looks at the* COOPER *in perplexity, then at* ESTRUGO, *and speaks to the audience.*

Who is this? Is this the Cooper? No, it's not the Cooper. It's the Aeolian harp. The most beautiful, the most beautiful.

A pause. He goes over to the top of the millrace and leans back on his elbows. The COOPER *walks slowly to the door and exits through the left half.* BRUNO *turns and looks at the door. The* COOPER *returns through the right half of the door and leans his elbows against the door jamb. He pauses and looks at* BRUNO, *then walks slowly toward* BRUNO *and suddenly leaps on his chest. (An exercise in Biomechanics from Di Grasso.)*

The COOPER *raises his fist over* BRUNO'S *head.* ESTRUGO *runs to the slide, skirting the bench. He gives a panic-stricken yell and with gestures pleads with the* COOPER.

Excuse me, It was an attack of lyricism.

After BRUNO'S *words, "It was an attack of lyricism," the* COOPER *slides down to the floor. Both stare at each other eye to eye, turning three times like cocks (clockwise). The* COOPER *stops and suddenly extends his hand to* BRUNO, *kisses him on the right nostril, then sits down on the bench at the millrace with his back to the audience.* ESTRUGO *returns along the bench. He stops to the right of the* COOPER *and looks at him in astonishment.* BRUNO *comes close to the* COOPER *and also looks. Everyone is embarrassed.* ESTRUGO *guffaws.*

Chapter 9

Eisenstein: On Biomechanics and Expressive Movement

Introduction

As the first documents in our section on Eisenstein, we have included the notes he made for his lectures at the Proletkult Theatre: "Notes on Biomechanics," "The Principles of Movement in Our Theatre" and "What Is a *Raccourci* and What Is a Pose?"—all published here for the first time. Eisenstein's definition and analysis of the *raccourci*, and the difference between it and the pose are invaluable for an understanding of Biomechanics. These lecture notes are followed by Aleksandr Levshin's lively description of Eisenstein's work with the actors at the Proletkult Theatre following the latter's appointment as a director there in the fall of 1922.

Although much of the Eisenstein/Tretyakov monograph on Expressive Movement is of a rather theoretical nature, we have nevertheless included it with the other documents by Eisenstein because of the light it sheds on the basic principles of Biomechanics. Of especial interest for the student of Biomechanics are the section on methodology and the many notes that accompany the essay.

In his lectures at the Institute of Cinematography, Eisenstein always accorded an important place to many of the theories fundamental to Biomechanics and the principles of Expressive Movement. Eisenstein's development of the concept of the recoil, one of the cornerstones of Biomechanics, is fully explored in the selection "On Recoil Movement." This lecture was to have been a part of the first chapter of his book on directing. In it, Eisenstein carries the idea of recoil movement far beyond the physical level to encompass the dynamics of the psychological process as well.

The final Eisenstein document is his lecture on Biomechanics at GIK (The State Institute of Cinematography) on March 29, 1935. This informal talk is of especial interest because Eisenstein is explaining Biomechanics to a group of students who have just finished their first biomechanical training session. In this more relaxed setting we find Eisenstein expressing his ideas and opinions with considerably greater clarity than is often the case in his more formal writings. His comments about Meyerhold are especially revealing. Particularly valuable is his discussion of Biomechanics as the basic principle underlying Expressive Movement.

NOTES ON BIOMECHANICS
by Sergei Eisenstein

Stanislavsky and Komissarzhevsky followed the psychological teachings of the vitalists. Meyerhold followed the teachings of the mechanists-materialists.

Biomechanics was earlier considered in connection with man's spiritual life. Only later did it remain exclusively as the training of man's physical life.

Biomechanics can be considered from two points of view:

1. As mechanical-physical training for man.
2. As a method for acting.

Essential for acting are:

1. Arousal.
2. Orientation and correct placement of oneself in time and space and in relationship to other persons around one.
3. The means for achieving arousal in the old theatre were:
   a. Stimulants.
   b. Nervous self-hypnosis.
   c. Non-organized physical arousal.

Biomechanics is a method for giving the actor healthful excitation (which is a condition achieved by means of organized muscular activity). (A man's physical movement gives birth to excitation peculiar for that movement. Thus, laughter evokes a happy mood, tears—sadness. William James.)

When acting, the actor must have an extended state of excitation. It cannot be achieved from one single muscular activity. Therefore the entire production must be built on uninterrupted muscular activity. The fixation of uninterrupted muscular movements is achieved by means of a *raccourci* of the body and not a pose, that is, by an active, nonstable body in space. A position of *raccourci* is impossible without the biomechanical method. The *raccourci* position is the only position of the actor's body which dynamically acts on the spectator. In this lies the meaning of Biomechanics for the spectator.

Of all the means of physical training, Biomechanics is the only one that teaches the actor the orientation of the body in equilibrium and in conditions of nonrisky circus tricks, as distinct from acrobatics. (It is for each actor individually.) Furthermore, Biomechanics helps the actor to share the orientation in time and space of those acting with him. Mises en scène can be built starting from *raccourcis*.

All forms of acting can be broken down into categories: repulse, run off, kiss, bow, etc. There are about thirty such devices, just as in dramatic works there are variants of only forty-two plots.

Biomechanics teaches a conscious approach to these movements and offers a method for doing them. For example, a drunk says, "Hello," and stops. Usually actors do this unconsciously or by an empirical approach. But Biomechanics shows the method for how to do it. The sound of the voice, as a physiological phenomenon, is the result of physical movement. Because the entire production is built on the sound of the voice made during the course of the production, the entire production must be built on muscular activity which is broken into individual parts—the *raccourci*. As a result of the *raccourci* comes the organically correct sound of the voice.

Biomechanics and the Theatre

Not every theatre needs Biomechanics. For certain theatres built on the pose (see "What Is a *Raccourci* and What Is a Pose?"), it is harmful. Biomechanics is essential for each new theatre with a special objective, since the actor in such a theatre must be healthy. And the only healthful excitation in the actor is biomechanical excitation. For the old, realistic theatre, Biomechanics would not be at all harmful.

At the demonstration of Biomechanics at Meyerhold's studio, all of the old actors admitted that this system was useful and could even make easier the work of the old theatre. According to Inkizhinov, there is no position or movement either on the stage or in life which Biomechanics as a method could not help. In the theatre, there are in all fifty movements. Stanislavsky cannot determine what acting consists of and what are the components making it up. Vakhtangov also could not say it. Meyerhold, breaking up acting into three basic positions, and finding that each of these positions is the result of movement or the awareness of movement, approached the question of Biomechanics scientifically, but experimentally. This was his merit.

Biomechanics as a Control of Movement

Biomechanics teaches how to consciously break up movements into elements from which at any moment the actor can reconstruct or put together the movement he needs—a *raccourci*. The ability to analyze, synthesize, and construct a movement, consciously to develop and use the *raccourci*, is achieved by training. From here comes the physical training aspect of Biomechanics. Biomechanics is the superstructure of physical training. Physical training is the fundamental subject of physical education, and Biomechanics is already a speciality. It includes all of the basic principles of physical training such as: correct relationship of the internal and external organs, audacity, lightness, flexibility. The analyses of *raccourcis* and the breaking up into component parts in Biomechanics distinguishes it from physical training and sports, which deal with movement as such.

Biomechanics and Music

Music aids in Biomechanics, as in all movement, the development of the rhythm which is needed for the positioning of the body in time and for establishing of the tempo needed for that positioning.

Biomechanics and the Nervous System

Biomechanics trains the nervous system since it teaches how to consciously control movements and produce them. Man must not be at a loss. He knows how movements are made and at a moment of danger—for example, when falling from a streetcar, on a tossing ship—he calmly places himself in the least dangerous position, knowing how it must be done.

Biomechanics and Rhythm; Biomechanics and Life

Besides the importance of Biomechanics as a method of acting and as the objective of physical training, it has also a utilitarian significance in life, in everyday situations, for example, in the training of the physical life of man:

1. Orientation in time and space, essential training for *raccourcis* not only on the stage but in all life conditions;

2. Accidents and the training of the nervous system;
3. Correct sound.

These are the elements of the training of an organized and well-equipped person.

Objections to Biomechanics

Biomechanics raises objections because of its harmfulness as physical training. Jumping on the shoulder blades harmfully affects the lungs and heart. A year after biomechanical studies, a medical examination took place and it turned out that the doctor permitted even those suffering from tuberculosis to practice Biomechanics to a limited extent. An American doctor prescribed the practice of Biomechanics as medication. From the point of view of physical training, there are no harmful movements. It is considered that Biomechanics produces acting clichés. But actors of the psychological experience school of acting also develop clichés of their own, even Mikhail Chekhov in *Eric XIV*.

Meyerhold is a follower of the French school (Coquelin). The great actors of the French school always approached acting consciously, and when on the stage were very well aware of and could control their surroundings. For example: Chaliapin in his relationship to his colleagues; Sarah Bernhardt during the tragic death scene in *The Lady of the Camellias* clearly saw someone sleeping in the stalls.

[Notes of a lecture by S. M. Eisenstein at the Proletkult Director's Workshop, 1923–1924, private archive, Moscow, published for the first time.]

PRINCIPLES OF MOVEMENT IN OUR THEATRE
by Sergei Eisenstein

Each movement is the result of the work of the entire body. The extremities play the role of a pendulum (Kleist, 1810, his letter and discussion about movement). A marionette cannot err in the mechanics of movements because of the physical disposition of force.

Here, correct and exact work is done.

Man is distinguished from the marionette by the fact that he can consciously make movements, but still he makes them incorrectly.

The expressing of an expressive movement are notes of a rhythmical, temporal, and spatial structure.

Man can consciously build a movement, change its direction, speed it up, slow it down, and so forth. Thus the expressive schema changes.

The persuasiveness of motor work is convincing if the motor elements are being performed in all seriousness. If the inertia is interrupted, then the possibility of an enormous dynamic effect is achieved.

The Recoil

The register of force is made from the point of support. A small movement at the point—this is a recoil.
Vsevolodsky-Gerngross: *The History of Theatrical Movement [sic] in Russia.** The recoil has a dynamic force.
An example:
The recoil is connected with the new movement.
All movements must be connected with each other.
Between the recoils, the movements, and the following movements, there must be an organic connection.
The force work defines the rhythmic scheme.
According to James, an imitative movement is evoked in the spectator.
This is because the recoil contains an element of the new movement.
Work rhythm establishes the beginning quite consciously.
Later it becomes mechanical....
Meyerhold's Biomechanics is based on a metrical structure. An example of recoil—a machine gun.
A special quality of muscles lies in the springiness of the reaction.

WHAT IS A RACCOURCI AND WHAT IS A POSE?
by Sergei Eisenstein

1. What is a *raccourci* and what is a pose?

In fine arts, a *raccourci* is defined as the position of the body as depending on the point of view of the spectator. If we look in a horizontal position then we see it in a foreshortened form (of the position of the body and the observer of the body—in recoil).

A pose is the arrangement of the body in a harmonious whole, pleasant for observation, without a utilitarian objective.

**Translator's note: The correct title is* The History of Theatrical Education in Russia.

A *raccourci* is the arrangement of the body for maximum expressiveness, the essentiality of the movement being mechanically made acute.

A pose has no relationship to the general movement, it is static, contained in itself and for itself, an end in itself, complete, nonutilitarian.

A raccourci is a fixed movement pulled out from the general movement, a point of break between two movements, a potential movement, the dynamics frozen for a moment. It is always utilitarian. There are also secondary *raccourcis*.

In a pose, the movements are blurred and defined by a curve. In a raccourci the mechanics of movement are not blurred. They (the movements) are defined by a broken line.

2. The *raccourci* and the actor.
Why the actor needs the *Raccourci*.

a. For arousal (see lecture on arousal of the actor).
b. For the actor's movements on the stage.
c. For the organically correct sounding of the voice.

3. How the actor builds a *raccourci*.

a. From observation in life.
b. From Biomechanics, as a collection of recipes (mechanics is regarded here from the point of view of story line).
c. From knowing how to catch the idea given by the director, or felt by the actor himself.

The collection of observations plays a very important role here. In order to affect the spectator, the actor must give form to a *raccourci*. The actor need not repeat what the director does, but he must feel in himself the ideal and afterwards put it into form.

A *raccourci* without words, solely for arousal, is used in pantomime.

4. The *raccourci* and the director.
Where does the director get the *raccourci*?

a. From experience as a director.
b. From director-actor intuition and organic perception.
c. From scientific principles and the course (on word-movement.)

The director must know how:

a. To catch an idea for a given movement.
b. To give it a form.

S. M. Eisenstein, Proletkult Theatre
[Private archive, Moscow, published for the first time.]

At Rehearsals of "The Wiseman"
by Aleksandr Levshin

I want to tell about a period of Eisenstein's work that is hardly known to us — about the preparation and creation of his first independent production, *Enough Stupidity in Every Wiseman* which Eisenstein himself, and after him, we too, the participants in the production, and later the press, called *The Wiseman* for short. It laid the groundwork, in my opinion, for many of the elements in *The Battleship Potemkin*.

Sergei Mikhailovich Eisenstein was approved as director of the Proletkult Theatre. We, the workers in the theatre, did not yet know what play we would be working on. He devoted several days to conversations with the actors in which he laid out his understanding of contemporary performance and his credo as a director.

In those conversations, he started from the proposition that the Revolution had defined a new stage in the development of theatre art, and that it was to lead the theatre of that time out of the dead end of an acute ideational and artistic crisis. He saw the basic abnormality in the professionalization of different types of outlived theatrical forms.

If earlier (in the Middle Ages) dialog, dancing, singing, acrobatics, demonstrations of strength, exotic animals, and in general, anything unusual all made up a single theatrical whole ("the theatre of charlatans," "Commedia dell'arte"), then later the theatre split up. Drama, ballet, opera (the "higher" arts), circus, farce, *balagan*, and animal shows (the "lower" arts) all became separated. In his first production, Eisenstein intended to synthesize the elements of both "high" and "low" art. Eisenstein planned to mobilize all the features of various forms of spectacle in order to affect the contemporary spectator.

In these conversations with the actors, Eisenstein also formulated a new concept of the director's role in a production. He proceeded from the importance of leading the spectator through a series of psychological states ("the meat grinder"); he wanted first of all to "shake up" the psyche of the spectator in order to get the necessary result. Usually directors look at the stage during rehearsals and observe the work of the actors. Eisenstein wanted to sit with his back to the stage, facing the audience, and proceeding from the dramaturgy of the production to observe the spectators in order at the proper moment to give them a portion of tears or an armful of laughter, and occasionally force them to leap out of their seats in horror. This is how the famous theory of the Montage of Attractions came into being, a theory which for the first time was revealed with particular clarity in *The Wiseman* in the realm of "the production, directing, design of the arena, costumes, and props" (from the poster and program).

In these conversations, the role and meaning of the actor was also clearly outlined.

Up to that time the Proletkult Theatre was under the influence of the Moscow Art Theatre: the director was an actor from the First Studio, Valentin S. Smyshlyaev; under the supervision of an experienced teacher, Vladimir N. Tatarinov, Stanislavsky's "System" was solidly studied. And suddenly there was a sharp swerve to the left.... To "high" art, it seemed it was vital to add on the "low": to learn in a hurry acrobatics, balancing, trapeze art, juggling, clown entrances.

Classes in the "System" were dropped. Also thrown out was plastics, which Eisenstein called "plastitution" because as Eisenstein considered then, it didn't strengthen the actor's musculature but weakened it, and consequently nothing but harm could come from it. Instead of plastics a subject completely new to us was introduced — Biomechanics. Eisenstein devoted a great deal of time to the theoretical basis of that subject with references to Meyerhold's work, to Diderot's *Paradoxe sur le comédien*, to Coquelin's *L'art du comédien* and to the Kabuki theatre....

Practical lessons in Biomechanics were conducted by a specialist in that subject, Valery I. Inkizhinov (later an actor — the hero of Pudovkin's film *Descendent of Ghengis Khan* [Storm over Asia]). In Biomechanics we were won over by the logical formation of an actor's movement, the possibility to analyze its sense and efficiency for obtaining the desired effect, and we were intrigued by the rational approach to working with a partner.

We threw ourselves into all those "supports," "settlings," and "recoils." We were literally bewitched by the relatively easy, but for the performer, tangible mechanics of switching the movement from the support — the feet — to the tips of the fingers. I recall the various exercises in which those propositions were made sharp and clear: "Slap on the Face," "Stab with a Dagger," "Carrying a Partner in One's Arms," "Race on All Fours (with a Person Standing on Your Back)," "Fall to the Floor." If earlier when we had to fall, it was with fear, with risk of hurting ourselves, and we fell "any which way"; now we did it brilliantly, with pleasure, without bodily harm, "according to the rules."

Under the supervision of Pyotr K. Rudenko [professionally known as Zhorzh, or Georgy Rudenko], one of the best circus performers of that time and head of a troupe of trapeze artists, "The Mountain Eagles," we actors ourselves outfitted a circus arena in the Morozov stables; we put up trapezes, stretched wires for tightrope walking, wove safety nets, and with enthusiasm, and as the saying goes, we willingly and freely began learning. New terminology rang out. Instead of "faith," "naïveté," "imagination" it was "lunge," "perch," "swagger," "*salto*." ...

How was our working time divided? From nine until one we had classes in gymnastics, rhythmics, boxing, fencing, and circus work. In addition to these "classical" subjects in physical culture, Sergei Mikhailovich insistently urged us to learn horseback riding and acrobatics on horseback. (He himself went with us to the riding school, and he wasn't a bad rider.)

For us it was completely incomprehensible that rowing and fancy diving had anything to do with the theatre. However, Eisenstein was very pleased when his actors became proficient in this type of sport. (It came in handy for Aleksandrov and me when we stood in for all the officers who were thrown overboard in *Potemkin*.)

In general, though, Sergei Mikhailovich wanted for us not to portray, not to play physically adept people, but "to be them in actuality." To play an awkward person demands even greater craft, and he introduced into *Wiseman* an example of a "bad" clown-cyclist, a role which was played by the best actor in the troupe. One time, an actor was late for a rehearsal of *The Wiseman*. He made the excuse that he was on the streetcar without a ticket. He was caught and taken to the police station.

"Didn't you try to jump off the streetcar?" Sergei Mikhailovich asked.

"It was going too fast...."

"You shouldn't be working for us then, but for the Art Theatre: Kachalov there also doesn't know how to jump from a moving streetcar!"

Bearing in mind our disdain at that time for the "Aks" (Academic theatres)—that rejoinder was a total knockout.

From one until four we had dinner (those who had something to eat). After dinner, forty-five minutes were devoted to volleyball. The captains of the teams were Sergei Mikhailovich and Tretyakov. Tretyakov was head of the "writing" volleyball players, Eisenstein the "directing" ones. Frankly speaking, our captains weren't the best players, but each winning point was accompanied by a verbal bomb from one of them and with a resourceful answering "firecracker" by the other. And so we tried to score points in order to enjoy those witty improvisations. The passersby were our audience. The whole sidewalk was full of them. They watched through the wire fence near the Proletkult building (the present "House of Friendship").

Our frequent guests on the volleyball court were Mayakovsky, Brik, Demian Bedny, all of whom reacted wildly to the playing. At the inexorable bell both Sergei Mikhailoviches went to the rehearsal of *Wiseman*, which would run until midnight (if there wasn't a performance or a concert).

Curiously enough, we never knew any weariness! For us, it wasn't work, it was pleasure.

[Excerpted from "Na repetitsiiakh *Mudretsa*," in *Eizenshtein v vospominaniyakh sovremennikov*, ed. Rostislav N. Yurenev (Moscow: Iskusstvo, 1974), pp. 136–150.]

EXPRESSIVE MOVEMENT
by Sergei Eisenstein and Sergei Tretyakov

In connection with the Left Front's work in the realm of movement in the theatre—Meyerhold, Eisenstein—new works by two German scholars about expressive movement are of exceptional interest.

One is *Ausdrucksgymnastik* [Expressive Gymnastics] (1922), whose author, Rudolf Bode, has been teaching his system of movement since 1921 in the Deutsche Filmschule (School of Cinematography) in Munich.

Bode bases his work on research by Ludwig Klages as presented in the book titled *Ausdrucksbewegung und Gestaltungskraft* [Expressive Movement and Creative Power], 4th edition (1923).

It must be pointed out that neither scholar regarded his work as intended specifically for the theatre, but as a system of general training.

The metaphysical terminology used by the two authors may cause confusion. They use the words soul [*dusha*] and spirit [*dukh*]. Furthermore, their basic idea can be reduced to the notion that movements dictated by the soul are in constant conflict with movements dictated by the spirit. In examining what these two terms actually mean in the two authors' presentation, we see that the soul is a term referring to the realm of the subconscious, instinctive, the purely biological, whereas spirit is the realm of the conscious, controlled, coordinated, and restrained. We may call the realm of movements having to do with the first category reflexes, and the second realm, the consciously directed, consciously coordinated.

According to both authors, a small number of reflexive movements provides the raw material for all possible movements. All other movements are built from them by calling into use the controlling and coordinating work of the consciousness [*soznanie*]. The consciousness (or in their terminology, will [*volya*] or spirit) cannot produce independent motor [*dvigatel'nyi*] combinations which are not caused by primary biological reflexive movements. Moreover, relying on the authority of medical research, the authors point out that movements dictated by the will of a relatively pure type (movements exercising one or another group of muscles in gymnastics devoid of any goal orientation) are harmful to the health: the biological basis of the organism resists and protests.

Theory

Until now, the science of movement has been built on the anatomy of the human body and on physiology. The choice of exercises was based on the possible combinations of muscular movements and on a knowledge of the physiological processes. Man was treated as a kind of machine, independent of the surroundings in which he acts and outside the concrete forms of this action, forms which had been biologically shaped. Science cannot even describe natural movements, much less create exercises which would qualify these movements, since these movements relate to a muscle or to a group of muscles, and not to the entire muscular system or to the actually acting organism. In corroboration, excerpts from du Bois-Reymond (*Spezielle Muskelphysiologie*, Berlin, 1903) are cited which say: "Individual muscles are anatomical units, and not mechanical-physiological ones" (p. 245). "One may suppose that if the muscular mechanics are not defined by the anatomical arrangement, then they should be defined by the physiological interaction of the muscles. But this is completely impossible since the physiological interactions are not constant.... And, finally, the limits of the physiological coordination of muscles cannot be established in general, since with each change in the position of the body they are different" (p. 246). "The muscular system of the back and the neck, no matter how many individual muscles anatomists divide them into, must be regarded from the physiological point of view as a unified mass. But it by no means follows that this unified muscular mass always acts as an entity. On the contrary, the back musculature along the spine, the spinal column, may in each separate section be independently active" (p. 254) [note 1].* "Instead of constructing the mechanics of body movements according to anatomical groupings, which at best could serve for the creation of a special physiology of movements, one should systematically reduce all of the endless variety of movements to individual forms of movement, and each of these should be studied as an independent entity" (p. 321). "Furthermore, one must take into account that the entire body, according to the position it is in, takes part in each separate movement. This interaction, however, due to constant practice, has become so habitual that it takes place unconsciously and almost unnoticed" (p. 277) [note 2].

Tigerstedt (*Lehrbuch der Physiologie des Menschen*, Chapter 15, Leipzig, 1915) expresses analogous ideas. "A contracting muscle pulls not only from the point of its attachment, its end, toward the origin of the muscle, but the opposite as well, it pulls from the origin toward the end,

---

Original notes to this document are reproduced on pages 190–192.

thus acting with two equal, but mutually contrasting forces on both points of attachment. It would be possible to ignore the dual movement of force only in that instance where one of the two points is artificially, with the help of an external force, brought to a state of immobility, for only in this way could the muscular force acting on the origin of the muscle be brought into equilibrium.

"It follows, then, from the above that a contracting muscle exerts influence as well on the joints not directly connected with it."

Further, Bode polemicizes with the representatives of a purely mechanical view of the human body which ignores the entire enormous area of instincts, reflexes, and everything which is unified under the general term "organic" and which arises not in the process of conscious combination but in the lengthy historic process of selection and adaptation. Mechanists, rejecting all phenomena of an organic order, base their teachings about movements of the human body exclusively on anatomy and physiology (Bess Mensendieck, *Körperkultur der Frau*, München, 1900, writing about the mechanical expedience of the structure of the human body). Bode bases his method of development of the human body on the position expressed by G. B. A. Duchenne in 1885 in his work, *Exposition d'une nouvelle méthode de galvanisation....*: "Isolated muscular movement is not found in nature."

Duchenne proceeds from the proposition that by the action of an electrical current on individual muscles he will be able to evoke artificially movements unconnected with the emotion of the subject of the experiment, to reproduce them, and in this manner to establish further the physiology of movements. The result of the experiments with local excitation of muscles was unexpected for Duchenne, since he suddenly became aware of a number of unforeseen circumstances which confused all of his mechanical calculations and led him to the following final conclusion: "Electro-physiological experiments and clinical observations reported by me," he writes, "threw light on each impulsive muscle group (impulsive in contrast to muscles which act automatically). These experiments and observations showed that partial muscle contractions (isolated contractions of individual muscles) are not inherent in nature and can be produced artificially by means of a local electrical charge or can arise under certain pathological conditions and bring about harmful consequences and organic deformation" (p. 597) [note 3].

Citing these arguments and also a number of others not quoted here, Bode makes his final conclusion in the following words: "Just as the development of the voice cannot be based on the physiology of the voice, so also the development of the body cannot be established on the physiology of movement. Both are based on the flow of correct, that is, natural movements. A natural movement is one which is at the same time a movement of the body as a whole. Only artificial movements can be constructed with the help of anatomical-physiological research. All of these artificial movements cannot achieve what is needed first of all in any system of physical culture: further development in the organic sense. For organic movement is the obligation borne by man as a whole" [note 4].

Bode rejects anatomy and physiology as the determinants for working out a method of exercises for physical development. He places at the base of his teaching about the development of movement, which includes all special realms of physical culture (work movement, expressive-theatrical movement, etc.), the principle of totality (*Totalität*). In physiological terms, this means the unity of stimulus (*Geschlossenheit des Triebgefühls*). In physiological terms this is the mechanical unity of the process of movement, and anatomically, it is the unity of the purposeful arrangement of the muscular apparatus determined by bodily movement.

Bode speaks of the unity of stimuli inasmuch as he is interested in the expediency of the structure of elementary movements, rejecting emotional-expressive movements as well as gestures of a communicative type. These latter could be constructed in two ways: in some instances they are a simple consecutive combination of elementary movements, and their expressive significance is defined solely by the conditions of the movements of which they consist; in other instances (especially in the case of complex emotions, passions), we have movement built from an elementary emotion, the stimulus of which is intersected or deformed by another restraining stimulus. The latter can be expressed by the non-correspondence of directions of both movements—the basic organic (reflexive) one—and the other, arising as the result of restraint, inert resistance and differences in speed.

To further cite Bode: "The principle of integrality [*tselekupnost'*] is connected as an absolute necessity with the principle of the center of gravity (*Schwerpunkt*), since a unity of movement can exist only when the will-stimulus is directed at the center of gravity of the body as a whole. In this instance, the entire motor system is moving in space, without destroying its unity, or equally, the internal distribution of the basic impulse by extraneous stimuli which exist in individual impulses. In the latter instance, we would have artificial movement, deprived of organic unity. From this alone, it follows that natural gymnastics must turn its attention to the muscles grouped around the center of gravity, that is, the major muscles of the body. From the fact that the will acts by interfering and changing the direction of movement, follows the principle of release [*razryazhenie*]. The movement flowing between two moments has a tendency to return from the deflected form to a natural one. The release follows the contraction produced by a voluntary act. The releasing movement always has a rhythmical character. The releasing movement must be distinguished from a "state of rest." The latter is always only apparent, for there is no such thing as absolute rest.

Herein lies the source of the greatest misconceptions proposed by research about movement. From the fact that we seemingly, by a voluntary act can, for example, raise an arm which is hanging quietly, it still does not follow that the ability to engender movements lies in the nature of the voluntary act. This assertion would be psychologically true only if it were possible to prove that the hanging arm is in absolute rest. Since the hanging arm is at rest only in a relative sense, each change in this position must be considered a digressive movement [note 5].

From this comes a conclusion fraught with consequences for physical education: the agent of rhythm is not voluntary acts, but that which lies between consciously fixed metrical intervals, that is, natural body movements. The degree of rhythm depends not on the exactness in time of the will's impulses, but on the quality of the motor preconditions on which the impulse acts, that is, on what more or less unconsciously transpires between the accents [note 6]. There is given a movement, which proceeds in certain definite forms, whose rhythmical structure no one is capable of changing. The sole possibility is a conscious influence on the amplitude of large or small rhythmical fluctuations in order to place the movement in a narrow framework, as a consequence of which, by virtue of the concentration of movement, it also gains in intensity.

On the basis of all the aforementioned, we may call the principle of releasing the rhythmical principle. Symbolically, this process is best expressed by the image of a flowing river. Influence in this case is analogous to transforming the river into a canal. Making the shores and the bottom smooth destroys the rhythmical individuality for the sake of expediting of the process of movement; by that same image we can also clarify what take place in any sports or gymnastic activity that is goal-oriented. Whenever we train the will, we run up against the necessity of breaking, that is, of transforming the original movement into organized movement.

Further, turning to the question of training the will, Bode cites Möller (F. A. Schmidt, R. Möller, H. Radezwill, "Schönheit und Gymnastik," *Zur Aesthetik der Liebeserziehung*, Leipzig, 1907), who writes: "When one is speaking of the training of the will (for example, if we want to train boldness—courage in the trainee), we must set a goal which has a direct relationship to the will, not touching on so-called mastery of form [note 7]. (Form, here, is the aesthetically pleasing visual arrangement of the elements of the body.)

But the demand for the expenditure of all reserve, the discharge [*otdacha*] of energy, is at the same time related to the training of the will. And the perfection of the whole is contained by no means in producing some preset form (taken as a pattern, etc.), but in expressiveness which is free, not consciously set, is constantly flowing, but nevertheless is strictly controlled by the will. (That is, the source of expressiveness is not the aesthetically perceived form, but the entire flexible system of expedient and goal-oriented movements.) This expressiveness, which also was present in the palestra of the ancient Greeks, is most valuable in that type of work, and therefore must be maximally cultivated in our work as well.

The next step now will be the "mastery of form" (*Formbeherrschung*, that is, the organization of the movement process from the standpoint of spectacle).

These two different disciplines—the training of the will and the mastery of form—are built on one and the same basic psychological process, because the same voluntary act is the basis for the mastery of form, just as it is for the mastery of anything else. The only difference is in the material. While under pure training of the will, form (in the aesthetic sense) is sacrificed completely, in expressive gymnastics it is sacrificed only to the degree necessary for greater expressiveness. The latter is possible only in the case where the initial rhythmical movement acquires greater resistance, greater in any case than under pure gymnastics of the will. The means for increasing this resistance is music, which strengthens the rhythmical principle, the fullness of movements. In this way we achieve goal-oriented movement that does not break with basic organic movement. Thus we establish the study of expressive gymnastics as lying between dance (aesthetic-emotional) on the one hand and sport (mystery and goal-oriented movement) on the other. It is at the same time the threshold for either, containing both components: rhythmical-movement excitation and the voluntary act.

In the conflict between reflex and consciousness, expressive gymnastics not only does not facilitate the destruction of one for the sake of the other [note 8], but on the contrary, it develops both of them, making these forces oppose one another. Bode makes so bold as to interpret the words of Schiller, "Man is only wholly man when he plays," to mean that play is nothing more than an artificial calling forth of the aforementioned struggle. The protest against music as a demagnetizing agent is incorrect, for expressive gymnastics strives toward the goal, not of passive submission of movement to the power of music, but on the contrary, the overcoming and the organizing of the movement aroused by the music. Furthermore, the meaning of music is very great in another respect: encompassing the entire motor system, it has the closest ties to the principle of totality established by us. The entire system as a whole reacts to music and not just the arms and legs! This is the basis for the effect of music on marching soldiers (Bode, p. 24). One can add that for the circus acrobat working to music, it is not only a sound-support, but also an arouser of motor energy.

Criticizing the gymnastic method of physical education, Bode analyzes the types of basic adjustments by the body and finds two such types:

1. Adaptation, adjusting to the resistance.
2. Overcoming the resistance.

The first divides into adaptation to the resistance which must be overcome, and adaptation to a solid support [resistance] (the floor, arms of a chair, etc). The overcoming may relate to the weight of one's own body or to some object. In shot put, all four phases occur; in jumping and running: the resistance [to be overcome] is to one's own weight, and the adaptation is to the ground underneath the body. In gymnastic exercises with an apparatus, the resistance is the weight of the body, the adaptation is to the apparatus. But in existing gymnastics, everything is wrong, because the weight of the body is not borne by the springiness of the legs and the waist, but the shoulder girdle. From this suspension (from the shoulders), the movement takes on a mechanized, unnatural character, and as a whole results only in building up the muscles. The same function, with no less success, is achieved by sports which place man in natural conditions that respond to the basic demands for the correct placing of the body and for a normal gait.

Methodology

Expressive gymnastics as taught by Bode does not touch on the expression of specific, verbally-defined emotions, or on the working out of set patterns of movement for expressing feelings. This is a matter for acting schools. He sets himself the task of bringing the human organism into a psycho-physical condition which will simultaneously liberate its motor potentialities and develop the ability to control these movements consciously. Bode's methodology sets itself the objective of selecting exercises which will serve the above goals. We present here the simplest movements (*[Ent]spannungsübungen* [releasing exercises]; *Abprallübungen* [repulsing exercises]).

The exercises in "releasing" are not directed toward complete abolishment of muscular tonus, which would be physiologically impossible, but toward elimination of false tensions. Under the latter, one should understand tension arising as the result of muscular innervation (the innervation is manifested as a result of the physiological connection of neighboring muscular zones with the basic innervated zone), which does not fully follow the normal system of muscular contractions. Similar false tensions, created by prolonged voluntary pressure, lead to muscular spasms and a catalyptic state of the muscles. This occurs because the false tension interrupts the normal rhythmical muscular "relaxation" — the moments of rest by the muscle — as a result of which there occur muscle fatigue, cramps, and temporary paralysis. It should be pointed out that these phenomena adversely affect the psyche as well, inasmuch as psychological activity is expressed in movement. When the latter are frustrated, the voluntary impulse and nervous expenditure turn inward, so to speak, disorganizing the reflexive apparatus. (Compare with "conversion" of the psychoanalytic school).

It is evident that expressive ability is sharply weakened under such protracted tension, inasmuch as the muscles, as a result of immobilization, drop out of the general motor activity, or they lose their elasticity. The muscular extremities are most prone to this, since in civilized society voluntary impulses are directed at them and not at the body as a whole. (The overloading of gesticulation, which is so characteristic, for example, of second-rate actors.) In the normal force-position on the center of gravity, such an accumulation of voluntary impulses would be impossible because of the weight of the whole mass of the body which it would be necessary to overcome each time. On the other hand, physiologically, the movement would proceed correctly, reaching to the extremities, and vibrating more or less strongly, depending on the character of the innervation, would be nullified. Under false innervation, however, each fluctuation is the result of a *special* voluntary impulse.

The contemporary civilized German works and moves totally ignoring his body. One must turn to artisans and peasants in order to find correct work movements. In their ideal form they can be discovered by observing animals.

We must develop the ability of quick reaction by the muscle to the voluntary command, while not losing the muscle's ability to return easily to a state of repose. An example — in playing the piano or the violin, if it is done incorrectly, that is, playing in which not the entire body, but only the fingers take part, such playing evokes muscle spasms in the fingers which have to be treated, not however, by medical but precisely by gymnastic means [note 9]. These spasms occur because the opposition of a moment of gravitational force is not sufficiently taken into account; and exercises in "releasing" are created precisely in order to reestablish a normal interaction between voluntary impulses and the natural force of gravity. Bode, incidentally, cites the following text from the book by C. Colditz,

Bewegungskunst oder Kunstbewegung (Musikpädagogische Blätter, 1921): "The fact that obese people in most instances possess greater agility of movement, while thin, lightweight people are characterized by awkward movements." This, in itself, is sufficient proof of the importance of the technique of control over the weight of the body as a whole (*Gewichtstechnik*) as applied to any motor task, including musical fingering. The basis for educating a musician, singer, actor, conductor must in the future be the normal training of the body as a whole — the freeing of the motor apparatus from unconscious psycho-physical restraints.

The exercises in "releasing" could also be called "pendulums" (*Pendelübungen*), since after the deflection of a bodily extremity and its return to the original position it does not fall at once into the original position, but makes several wavering movements.

These same exercises train the ability to automate quickly any temporal and spatial task, thus developing in the gymnast corresponding spatial-temporal "postures." In sum, the system of exercises amounts to the incorporation of material forms in a spatial framework and of organic processes in a temporal framework *(Die Eingliederung einer Naturform in ein Raumnetz und die Eingliederung eines Naturablaufs in ein Zeitgitter)*.

Opposed to this system is Dalcroze's metrical gymnastics and the so-called gesticulative gymnastics where we are dealing with an arbitrary placement of the extremities in space which is not connected with the principle of unity [note 10], and which is mechanically broken up according to the smallest units of a predetermined metrical network (Bode, "Alte und Neue Pädagogik," in the collection *Künstlerische Körperschulung*, published by L. Pallat and F. Hilker, Breslau, 1923).

The special characteristic quality of Bode's exercises is the absence in them of transitional gradations from easier to more difficult ones. All of his exercises are of an equal difficulty and they are equally easy depending on the degree of mastery of his basic principle. It should be recalled again here that Bode builds his system not at all in the interests of stage expressiveness, but in pursuit of general pedagogical objectives. For us, however, Bode's research is of the utmost interest precisely in the realm of theatrical work, and hence we draw from his work only those propositions which may form the basis of a scientific theory of stage movement.

Bode's system, therefore, is summed up by three basic propositions: the ability for muscular "release" (détente) [note 11], the ability to direct a voluntary impulse at the center of gravity, and the ability to convey and distribute along the periphery (the extremities) the inertia of the gravitational center. Here we consider it important to point out that these propositions were already recognized and confirmed by observations of the marionette theatre made by Kleist, who made notes on it as early as 1801. Here is what is contained in Kleist's notes. (See Kleist's *Grillparzer, Immermanns und Grabbes Dramaturgie*, published by W. Von Scholz, München und Leipzig, 1912, Vol. 3 of *Deutsche Dramaturgie*.)

Kleist was sitting on the boulevard with a dancer from the opera and watching the marionette theatre. In talking about dances, Kleist's companion observed that a dancer could learn a good deal from marionettes. Precisely what, Kleist understood from the following examination of the mechanism of movement of marionettes. He was interested in the means by which it was possible to control the movements of the limbs and the joints without the aid of countless strings attached to them, and at the same time to achieve the necessary rhythms of movement or dance. The dancer replied that Kleist mistakenly imagined that during the movement or dance each limb was put into motion separately by the marionette operator. Each movement depends on the center of gravity. It is sufficient to find this center in the doll and to find the means to control it. The limbs, dangling like pendulums, mechanically follow the center of gravity without any additional intervention.

The dancer added that basically the movement was very simple — each time when the center of gravity shifts on a direct line, the limbs make a curve, and with the least chance shaking, the whole marionette assumes a certain rhythmical movement resembling a dance. In those cases when the movement is not on a direct line, the character of its curvatures does not rise above the second degree, and most often it is elliptical, a form which is characteristic of the human body, and which, because it is determined by the construction of the joints [note 12], is especially easy for the *nervopast* [note 13].

The same phenomenon is observed in constructing artificial limbs, where the ability to perform the most varied movements is achieved by proportionality, mobility, and the light weight of the prosthesis, but mainly by the distribution of the centers of gravity, which must be analogous to the natural distribution.

The advantage of a marionette over a live dancer, according to Kleist's companion, is first of all a negative one, specifically this: its inability to be "pretty" as is the case when the motor force (*vis motrix*) is applied not to the gravitational center of movement, but to another point. Since the marionette operator, with the help of wires or strings, controls only that one point (i.e., the gravitational center), the other parts of the body become what they should be — dead mechanisms, pure pendulums, obeying only the law of gravity, a quality which we look for in vain in contemporary dancers.

"Look," Kleist's companion said, "at Madame P., when she dances Daphne and, pursued by Apollo, she looks back at him. Her soul (*vis motrix*) is located in the vertebrae of the small of her back and she bends as if she were going to break in half, like a naiad from the school of Bernini. Look at the young dancer F. when he dances Paris, and standing among the three goddesses, he hands the apple to Venus: his soul (oh, horror!) is located in his elbow. Such blunders are inevitable since the time when we 'ate of the tree of knowledge.'" (That is, since we have introduced intention into the conscious structure of movements—note by the translator of Kleist.)

Further, Kleist goes on to the question of how the intrusion of consciousness disorganizes man's natural gracefulness. He cited an incident that had occurred to a young man in his presence. The young man was drying his foot, and glancing at himself in the mirror, he said to Kleist, "Isn't it true that I resemble the famous sculpture of a youth pulling a splinter from his foot?"

Although Kleist had noticed the same thing, he wanted to tease the youth and he began to disagree. The young man attempted to repeat the pose, checking himself in the mirror, but he did not succeed in spite of numerous determined efforts. Not only that, but Kleist noticed that from that time on, the young man began looking at himself in the mirror all day long. Self-consciousness, constraint, and artificiality appeared in all of the movements the young man made, and little by little all of the former charm in his movements was lost.

The companion then answered Kleist with the following episode: an outstanding fencer, he was once forced to fence with a bear on the country estate of a Livonian nobleman. The animal faultlessly parried all of the attacking blows of the foil, but did not react at all to the so-called feints (the essence of which is that they are completely harmless and have as their purpose only to distract attention, since they are produced artificially and deliberately.)

In this way identical views were established by Kleist and his companion about the nonorganized naturalness of reflexive movements. And from this, Kleist's final conclusion becomes clear: that perfect movement is characteristic only of completely unselfconscious beings (animals, puppets), or of a being who has absolute consciousness—according to Kleist— "a divinity" (pp. 19–25) [note 14].

Since the aforementioned "releasing" has decisive importance for expressive gymnastics, Bode introduces a kind of preparatory class in which exercises are grouped according to the following four categories: exercises in "releasing," swinging, tension, and repulsing. (*Entspannungsübungen, Schwungubüngen, Spannungsubüngen, Abprallubüngen*).

Conclusions

Although, as Bode insistently emphasized, his system was not in any sense designed for solving the problems of stage movement, it nevertheless contains all the mechanical prerequisites for the correct organization of stage movement. This theory merely underscores our following basic assertion: maximally expressive (affective) stage movement can occur only in those instances where the actor, instead of copying exactly the result of motor processes (leg movement, grimace, gesture), performs the motor process itself with organic correctness. As a result of this, the affective design will be achieved by itself.

Any ideally purposeful movement (standard-movement) can be considered an expressive movement. But if we are going to speak of stage movements, about specific movements having as their objective to affect, to create emotional charges and discharges, then in contrast to all other movements, we agree to call their expressiveness the specific quality of these movements to evoke in the spectator a predetermined reaction, to create an impression (the attraction potential of movements).

Besides a complete exactness of the mechanical scheme, any stage movement, in order to be an attraction, must carry a certain accent. It is not enough to do a somersault correctly, to sit on a chair, to walk a wire, to make a threatening gesture. The movement must also be "sold," as circus performers express it; the movement must be *underscored*. This underscoring is achieved by the most varied devices—in particular, every instance of a so-called *recoil*, which accentuates the approach to a movement, is a device for this underscoring. It should be said that this emphasizing attractionizes all stage movements in general, but it has decisive meaning for movement presenting complex shifting (acrobatics), not having any kind of plot-meaning function, as for example: walking, lifting, a push, a blow of the hand, bending of the body. If the movement is produced properly, then involuntarily, on the basis of the organic unity, a certain condition arises which is characteristic only of this motor process, and which Bode calls the feeling of plasticity. This condition can be strengthened by music, and under the influence of restraint, it defines the plastic expressiveness of the simplest movements.

Then there are a number of ideas indicating that together with music, collective work is also an organizing means. In the first place, in collective work there is present an infective emotional interaction. On the other hand there is also the strengthening of the reflexive processes under the awareness of movements going on next to you. The difference between expressive-gymnastic exercises and military as well as gymnastic exercises of the usual type (demanding complete uniformity of the mechanical coincidence of each movement) consists in the fact that the former are regulated only according to the time-measure, and the fulfillment of the tasks within the limits of the time-measure is individualized for each performer (the individual rhythm). The more participants in the exercise, the stronger is the manifestation of individuality, as analogous with the effect of music, the effect of a mass of people on each performer increases the organic resistance to conscious impulse [note 15]. It is precisely in mass exercises that the ability for temporal and spatial orientation is worked out.

Another category of expressive stage movements is that in which are present a conflict between reflexive movement and the voluntary impulse restraining it. Here, one must have in mind that reflexive movement has as the point of application of force the center of gravity of the body as a whole, whereas the voluntary act is realized through movements by the extremities. The extremities either restrain the general thrust impetus, or strengthen and change its direction. The first instance — restraint — is most characteristic for expressive movement. And it is that collision of two motor movements which gives that muscular distortion which characterizes "expressiveness" (mime, gesture).

Bode establishes (Bode, p. 19) a curious subdivision of the parts of the body into performers of utilitarian, mechanical work for maintenance of the body and its automatic movements; and, so to speak, *"déclassé"* parts, which in civilized society, freed from these obligations, serve the function of "intelligence" [note 16]. Such parts of the body are the hands, after man stopped using them for stepping on the ground, his face, in as much as it stopped being a maw intended for grabbing food or for fighting. It is these *"déclassé"* parts where man's voluntary, conscious stimulus which creates expression is mainly realized.

Citing Tigerstedt (*Trägheitsmomente*), the same Bode (p. 19) points out the manifestation of voluntary impulses (of expression) through the preservation of inertia in the extremities, which are brought into movement by the general thrust. Such are: bared teeth (expression of fury) — under restraint of the general motor thrust, the jaws preserve their movement forward; eyes bulging from horror or astonishment, following that reflexive thrust which has the objective of enabling man to look over an object more closely, to become oriented to the situation; angrily spreading the fingers of hands which are closely pressed to the sides (the thrust is realized only in the fingers).

All of the aforementioned principles and observations make possible the construction of motor expressions of the most complex psychological phases (emotions), characterized by duality (the struggle of motifs) simply as a kind of "dual" gymnastics of two antagonistic forces corresponding to reflex and conscious impulse (Schiller, in Bode p. 19). It is the factual

"Slap on the Face"

fulfillment of this struggle which is the sole material content of acting, completely independent of the psychological conditioning of each phase of such "acting." Thanks to such a construction of stage movement, there is no more need for an actor's emotional experiencing [*perezhivanie*] of type, image, character, feeling, situation, since as the result of expressive movement by the actor, the emotional experiencing is transferred where it belongs, specifically to the auditorium. For the actor, there remains the work, completely analogous to the work of the circus performer or the athlete—the same overcoming of the obstacles which have been set up—and the objective is expressive movement as a factor of visually perceived [*zritel'naya*] emotion [note 17].

There are two very essential supplementary observations: 1. Expression is always a motor element and never a static one (it is a process); and 2. In every expression, from the very mechanics of this process, one can single out the moment of "fixation"—the moment when the forces are balanced, after which the expression passes over either into a real act, symbolized by the expression (victory of the reflexive thrust), or into a state of repose (victory of the voluntary stimulus). The teeth bared in fury either will bite, or the lips will close over them; the hand, with fingers crooked symbolizing grasping will either grasp, or the fingers will relax and return to normal.

The attractionness of an expressive movement (that is, the psychological, previously-calculated effect on the spectator) is assured in the first place to the extent that each phase of struggle or real, goal-oriented work attracts the attention of the spectator; and in the second place, to the extent that the expressive movement assures the arousal of the intended emotions in the spectator [note 18]. It is precisely expressive movement, built on an organically correct foundation, that is solely capable of evoking this emotion in the the spectator, who in turn reflexively repeats in weakened form the entire system of the actor's movements: as a result of the produced movements, the spectator's incipient muscular tensions are released in the desired emotion. James' view of emotion (with additions from Klages) as a subjectively psychological state derived from a physiological one here finds complete application. One must only avoid the incorrect interpretation of James according to which the bearer of each given emotion will as a result be the actor. One must suppose that the purely productive tension in which the actor finds himself in the conscientious carrying out of the designated attraction scheme, leads to the minimum situational emotion [note 19], which in turn grows and develops at the expense of the unused muscular energy in the spectator. Thus arises the aim not for the "sincerity" of an actor's movement, but for its imitative, mimical infectiousness (see Lipps).

Unorganized movement does not evoke a direct emotional reaction — the gesticulation in a ballet may create an aesthetic effect based on admiration, or an erotic effect, but it does not call forth a dramatic emotion conditioned by the struggle of motifs and based on expressive movement.

Turning to the realm of speech as used on the stage, we do not find anything which might prevent expressive speech from also being constructed on the same principles as expressive movement. Stage speech is, in essence, only a variety of movement, and its expressiveness, consisting of intonations, is above all a motor expressiveness [note 20].

If we take the simplest work and emotional sound signals (interjections), then we see that in them a certain remnant of energetic tension is realized, and that the greater this remnant, the more tense its use is, the more expressive is the signal itself. Here, the voice is a kind of "sound extremity" in which motor opposition is realized especially easily and freely.

By its mechanism, speech (especially in its simplest form of direct sound, and intonation of direct effect) is formed from the very same two elements as is movememt. In the first place, we have the reflexive pressure of the piston-diaphragm in the cylinder-rib cage, pressure in which the entire group of stomach muscles takes part. Furthermore, this pressure is only a partial realization of the general reflexive thrust, with the body as a whole taking part. On the other hand, the voluntary, interrupting act is located in the vocal chords (voice intonation) or in the muscles of the tongue, lips, palate, jaws (articulational intonation). The basic pressure flow of air is thus introduced into the narrowed channel of the larynx and is cut off, or its character is changed, by obstacles in the voice box.

Expressive dramatic intonation can be achieved only in those cases where the basic pressure forcing the air is given by the thrust of the entire body and not by only one group of muscles — in the latter instance, we will have declamatory (that is, purely aesthetic) rather than dramatic intonation. This basing of speech on the moving plunger of the diaphragm is characteristic for singing. Isn't that the reason why our singers are so inexpressive in their intonation? And isn't the secret of Chaliapin's style in the fact that he introduced voice (pressure) intonation into his singing? Let us note as an example the fact that expressive words (onomatopoeic) are those in which the antagonism between the airstream bursting from the chest and the obstacle of the articulative muscles is expressed most sharply.

Several words about gestures accompanying speech. The entire mass of these gestures, judging by their function, easily falls into three groups: representational gestures (I trace a question mark in the air, I point to the thing about which I am speaking); symbolic gestures (an obscene gesture of contempt, counting a wad of bills with the finger, making the sign of the cross over someone, a threatening fist, and so forth); and verbal-mechanical gestures not having either representational or symbolic meaning (for example: oratorical "chopping" with the hand, declamational jerking of the head, rising on tiptoe like a tenor, clenching the fists, facial mimicry of a person speaking). The latter category is especially vital for us. It realizes in the bodily extremities that *general* thrust by which the musculature of the body achieves speech pressure. These are reflexive waves which have reached the shores of the body, that is, which are distributed throughout the extremities and thus assure the participation of the entire body in the movement.

An example of an expressive intonation accompanied by a representational gesture: you say, "But there are two," on the last word showing two extended fingers. And how much the persuasiveness of the phrase itself will be strengthened, the expressiveness of the intonation, if on the first words, you make a recoil movement with the body while raising the elbow, and then with an energetic movement you throw the torso and the hand with the extended fingers forward. Furthermore, the braking of the wrist will be so strongly directed that the wrist will vibrate (like a metronome). In the first instance, you are dealing with partial thrust, in the second with organically [word omitted] movement of maximal exertion. Thus the expressiveness of movement, and with it, intonation as well, is not created by representational exactness, but by the energetic intensity of the gesture which helps to develop the general thrust.

The same principles of movement are operable in everyday life as well—in work movements. The same Central Institute of Labor, that same scientific organization of labor, teaches us to use primarily the mechanical inertia of the body's mass in work movement and to move with general thrust and not partial thrust. But everyday movement pursues entirely different objectives than does stage movement. Its object is not at all to infect the spectator with emotion. The product which the work movement produces (a material object) is entirely different from the products of an emotional and reflective character (psychological states) the evoking of which is the objective of stage movement. Without going into detail on the organization of everyday utilitarian movements, we merely consider it our duty to forewarn against confusing these two types of movement on the stage, keeping in mind that fundamental objective of "expressiveness" which stage movement is after. Utilitarian, everyday movement is incapable by its very purpose, by its very form (not by its mechanics which as we have said are the same for all types of movements) of being an attraction, that is, of being emotionally affecting. And it is pointless to think that the sawing of wood expressively on the stage will earn for that actor a high rate on the sawer's labor exchange, just as the best qualified sawer will make a minimal impression on the stage.

Sergei Tretyakov
Eisenstein

Notes

1. The origin of the muscle in flexing muscles is thought of as a relatively unmoving point, the end as movable. The origin of the biceps muscle is in the shoulder bone, and its end is in the elbow bone.

2. In support, we point out the ineffectiveness of individual movements insofar as we break their instinctively automatic connection with the body and bring them into the realm of consciousness. To lift an object in real life (automatically) is easy, but to lift it on the stage, consciously comprehending for oneself the entire chain of interrelated movements and the mechanics of the body's mass, is extraordinarily difficult, as anyone knows who has had to have anything to do with the theatre. Formerly, the theatre strove for correct movements, building them on remembered experiencing [*perezhivanie*], that is, on the emotional tonality which gives to a movement the automatic character (and therefore the authenticity) of real life (but by no means the expressiveness of affecting the spectator). The new theatre, on the other hand, sets as one of its objectives the development of the actor's ability, independent of emotional tonality (remembered experiencing), to break down a movement and reproduce it.

3. Industrial movements are the best examples of such artificial movements. The historical adaptation of man's muscular system to environmental conditions and by the process of selection do not keep up with the adaptation of movements to the system of industrial tools and machines. Movement has to be constructed, to be adapted artificially to the tools alone without taking into account the organic nature of movements. The results are the professional distortion of the bodily system and the professional illnesses with which NOT [Scientific Organization of Labor] must struggle by studying that normal material from which must be built all industrial movements not contradicting human nature. For illustrations of these positions see Hueppe in his work *Die hygienische Bedeutung der erziehenden Knabenhandarbeit* (Leipzig, 1899), where he was the first to put forward the concept of gymnastics at the machine. The aforementioned work is also in his *Hygiene der Körperübung* (Leipzig, 1922), pp. 22–24.

4. Hueppe, for instance, gives parallel examples of the wrong way of using a plane (only the arms are moving, which produces the position of the body and the asymmetry of the shoulders), and the right way to work (arms moving under the pressure by the torso striving upwards on the bending and unbending leg). Incidentally, the latter action is typical for exercises in Bode's method. Hueppe is a military doctor and sportsman, sixty-two years old, who received a gold medal for physical control of his body.

5. See the supplementary ideas in Ludwig Klages' *Ausdrucksbewegung und Gestaltungskraft*, p. 47.

6. Only an absolute lack of understanding of the nature of rhythmicality makes possible the verification of "rhythmical feeling" with the aid of a metronome (!) in the sport-psychological laboratory of the Higher School of Physical Culture in Berlin. The same fundamental misconception prevails in the methodology of Dalcroze, which is mistakenly called rhythmical gymnastics (Eurhythmics) but which in reality is a method based on musical time measurement, exhaustive criticism of which is given (Bode, page 22).

7. This can be elucidated by examples from the circus, theatre, and sports. For example, in boxing there are a number of rules (the so-called "magic of boxing"), based on the purely visual effectiveness of poses and gestures. In acrobatics and for professional circus performers, it is not enough to know how, for example, to walk the wire well. One must also "sell" (in theatrical jargon, "present") the act, that is, make it visually interesting and exciting. Here is the basic difference between Russian and French circus performers. Under the same exertion of will, the same clarity of the act, there is a total abyss in its effect on the spectator because of the character of the "selling." For the theatre of attractions, this moment of "presenting," that is, of the direct reflex effect created in the spectator, is a question of first importance.

8. In support, a citation from Robert W. Schulte, *Leib und Seele im Sport* (Charlottenburg, 1921), p. 10, on the fact that in sport, activity of the will achieves the highest degree, frequently violating sharply the normal organic processes for the sake of achieving a record. An example is the moment of crossing the finish line in a marathon race. The psychology of a record breaker sacrifices the normal rhythmical-organic processes for the egocentric impulse of will. The aforementioned marathon runner is proof of the fact that the process of the will acting on the organic not only violates it but can also lead to its total destruction.

9. Observation of pianists shows clearly the degree to which mechanical finger play is characteristic of pupils, and play by the whole body, of virtuosos.

10. Instead of a single dynamic movement unfolding in a series of interacting phases, we have here a static series of "poses" inwardly disconnected from each other. Examples are the work of the Kamerny Theatre and Foregger's machine dances.

11. "Release" (*Entspannung*) we use in a sense opposite to "tension."

12. See the research according to the cyclograms by the TSIT [Central Institute of Labor].

13. Nervopast — the person operating the marionettes.

14. Attention MXAT and A. V. Lunacharsky: even from the point of view of 1801, wouldn't modern acting "from within" and the insistent demand for "soul" in acting prove a clear preference for the bear to the maximally organized person?

15. Compare elemental movements of the body, panics, lynchings, orgies.

16. In the same way that the four-footed animal's duty of signaling belongs to the tail — the only "intelligent" part of the animal's body.

17. Mechanism of the expressive — conflict of sailors [*sic*]; the reflexive impulse not brought to a conclusion because of braking is realized in a series of distinctive, objective signs — expression.

Standardized movement is ideal from the point of view of economy of means, for complete fulfillment of the utilitarian task.

Expression is the complex of objective signs on the basis of which one can judge (intuit) objective states.

18. All forms of tics, convulsive twitchings, aimless movements invoke a feeling of revulsion.

19. The work of an actor is poor and inexpressive when he lapses into emoting and in an emotional outburst tears not only the hat from his antagonist, but also the wig.

20. I purposely disregard speech as sound complexes having stylized-symbolical meaning. Their emotional effect is minimal.

On Recoil Movement
by Sergei Eisenstein

That movement which, when you wish to make a movement in one direction, you initially make in the opposite direction (in part or completely), is called in the practice of stage movement a "recoil."

This is one of the fundamental laws inevitably met at all levels and in all varieties of expressive movement.

In practice, in its simplest form on the stage, the "recoil" consists of the following: when you need to go from point A to point B, you initially retreat to a certain point C which lies in a direction opposite to B, and then breaking off the movement in the direction of C, you move in the opposite direction, and passing again through A, you come to B. That is, you follow the path A—C—B.

        A ······▶ B
        ○————○

   ······················▶
   ○———○————————○
   C ◀···· A   B

    This phenomenon in spatial displacement, which at first glance seems unlikely, turns out, however, on close examination to be unusual only because of its unexpected area of application, and not "in itself."
    Indeed, when you must strike something with a truly large expenditure of energy, you make a threatening gesture with the fist, hatchet, or hammer in the opposite direction, and from that extreme point you then deliver the blow. If you need to jump across something, you take a few quick steps back in a direction opposite to the obstacle, in order to get a running start.
    This is one of the basic laws of movement, and as soon as you must make a movement with a genuine expenditure of energy, you immediately feel, instinctively and correctly, that organic law; without observing it, you simply are unable to carry out the desired movement—to jump over an obstacle or to drive a nail into a board.
    The unexpectedness begins the moment it is pointed out to you that this organic law applies always, everywhere, and to all kinds of phenomena.
    And if a recoil movement is needed for hitting a nail on the head, then for a "blow" on the psyche of the spectator, when you have to "thrust" one or another expressive scenic element into it, your action must resort to the very same recoil principle, and according to the very same principle of direction (although, of course, not comparable in terms of quality).
    A stage approach has a dual function: the actor must approach, and simultaneously the action must "enter the consciousness of the spectator." In order to realize the second objective, the action can never, and must not, begin from a dead point, from a blind phase. It must begin so that the starting point of the movement in question (C–B), a movement which enters the consciousness, proves to be not amorphously static, but a dynamic point of break between two directions (AC and CB).
    (The recoil AC as an independent transition doesn't enter the consciousness.)

N.B. *There is also a recoil directed forward—the first of two blows; but about it at the appropriate time. —S.E.).*

That by no means signifies that the recoil must inevitably be equal to the whole length of the stage transition. [A movement from one point on the stage to another.] For four steps forward, one may make any number of recoil steps—three, two, one, and finally, not a single one: it is sufficient, prior to a step forward, simply to lean back distinctly.

In the transition itself, temporal continuity is not obligatory. On the contrary, the visible mechanical continuity of the recoil and of the action itself makes the recoil deliberate. However, that doesn't mean that the recoil must break the inertia from one transition to another. The unevenness of tempo of either of them, a slight pause ("pensiveness," "distraction of attention") at the point of the break (C)—all this contributes to a meaningful concealment of that transition's helpfulness.

But God save us from working out the action in such a way that the inertia of the flow from movement to movement is at some point ruptured. Then its functional interconnection will rupture, and there will be a wavering in the straight line of march.

The recoil must be what is called "veiled." In its objective there is something rather similar to what we attempted to explain in speaking of elements of calculated effect on the consciousness and of no less calculated effect on what we call the subconscious.

The plastic objective of the recoil, its technical, applied function, is to endow the detail necessary to the action with the maximal, efficacious distinctness.

The law of constructing the recoil is a necessary condition for expressive resolution. It is made up, as it were, of elements of contrast, one of the sharpest means for attracting attention, elements included within the action itself—a certain "auto-contrast" in the action being carried out.

For that reason, the recoil is a technical support, but it is also a condition of expressiveness with an independent decorative value. Like a backbone or a skeleton, it is called upon to maintain the structure. It is like the mannequin under a garment.

Its role in facilitating perception is the following: not to overload the consciousness, but unconsciously to instill the spectacle into the feelings.

But if the recoil is structured so that it enters into the consciousness of the spectator as an end in itself, the structure will be just as unsightly as a building under scaffolding where a finished building is envisioned.

In practice, that means that the recoil must be "acted out" and developed in the performance to such a degree that with its content it provides a basis for the technical stability of the construction.

The ideal would be that situation where the sequential phases of the development of the elements of acting serve as each other's recoil pre-acting.

9. Eisenstein: On Biomechanics and Expressive Movement 195

The chain of uninterrupted thematic development of the content is set forth in such a case without superfluous offshoots, and as for the process of instilling the form in the perception of the spectator, it takes its course within the most favorable structure.

Precisely in this way was the first element of action by our woman constructed: consistently "recoiling," without "formalisms" and without tension, either psychologically or socially. [Here and in the discussion that follows, Eisenstein is referring to a scene from *The Return of the Soldier* which he is working out with his students.]

When she [the mother] heard the baby cry, she looked over her right shoulder. Then she wearily and reluctantly turned in the opposite direction in order to get up. We have already established above in detail that precisely such a construction within the framework of our resolution best answers the demands made on it. And from the technical point of view, the first turn of the woman's head works as a recoil movement in relation to her getting up and going to the baby.

Meyerhold's great merit was to resurrect in stage practice the conscious usage of that element of technique which has long been known to theatre art, but which like many other elements, had become stuck in the *amorphous, muddled conditions of naturalistic acting*.

It is true, Meyerhold went no further than adding the recoil to movement and to gesture itself. He confined himself solely to the purely spatial awareness of the recoil, without giving it a deeper meaning in terms of its energetical and dialectical generalizations. (On that concept of the recoil see below.)

In this form it has been known for a long time. Lessing already called attention to it in the supplementary pages (*Nachträgliches*) about the actor ("Der Schauspieler," III) for the *Hamburg Dramaturgy*.

And it was discussed in great detail by the Jesuit Father Franciscus Lang, the well-known writer on drama, an authority and pedagog of the so-called "school theatre," who between 1664 and 1725 (the year of his death) wrote a tract on the art of the stage with the curious title:

An Essay on Stage Performance with Illustrations of the Same, and Containing some Observations on the Art of Playwriting by Father Franciscus Lang, S.J. To which have been added Symbolic Figures for use in Theatrical Performance and Costume. Munich 1727 [Dissertatio de actione scenica, cum figuris eandem explicantibus, et observationibus quibusdam de arte comica. Auctore P. Franciscus Lang Societatis Jesu. Accesserunt imagines symbolicae pro exhibitione et vestitu theatrali].

In expounding the rules of the so-called "stage pace [*passus scenicus*]" Franciscus Lang gives the following description of the recoil as its essential element:

If the actor on the stage wishes to cross from one place to another, or to step forward, he will do it clumsily if he does not first draw back a little that foot which is placed in front. Thus the foot formerly placed in front, must be drawn back and then again moved forward, but further than it had been placed previously. Then the other foot follows and is placed in front of the first one.... Thus are made the first, second, third, and fourth steps. Then one must stop briefly, as if taking a pause. In the case of a larger change of position, the actor, if he is not exiting from the stage, must after the fourth step take a fifth step back, and then move as before, and then stop again. Then he can continue as described, but with the other foot...." (V. N. Vsevolodsky-Gerngross, *Istoriya teatral'nogo obrazovaniya v Rossii*, Vol. 1, St. Petersburg, 1913, p. 37.)

The principle of "taking a step on the stage," as formulated by Lang, has a longer history. In an analogous description it figures in the technique of the Russian "School Performances," just as it was also cited in *Amphione*, a work on poetics, 1692.

And finally, it exists in the same form in the laws of movement on the stage in the Japanese Kabuki theatre. Moscovites may recall how the principle of the second part of the description of Lang's description of the stage step was executed with brilliant technique and with dazzling temperament by the great Ichikawa Sadanji during the Moscow tour of the Kabuki theatre in the autumn of 1928 — his matchless, increasingly effective run along the hanamichi ("the flower path"), along the bridge into the auditorium: three steps forward, a large step back; and again three forward, and a step — twice as large — back. All at a growing tempo. All at a growing intensity. And the comparatively short *hanamichi,* in the conditions of the former Nezlobin Theatre, grew in length, and the short stage transition became a powerful event of enormous importance.

The description of Sadanji's stage transition and the characteristic itself of recoil movement (I would say even more: recoil phenomenon!) — doesn't it remind you in its formation of something which you have been used to hearing in a different context?

What discipline unfailingly uses a similar formulation?

Answer from the floor: Dialectical materialism.

Eisenstein: Where, precisely?

Answer from the floor: In the law of the negation of negation.

That's absolutely correct. We could say about our stage transitions that they are carried out in accordance with the full development of the process of the negation of negation: You are planning to go to point B, but you negate it by going in the opposite direction — C, and again, negating the direction toward C by a new movement toward B, you remove the first negation and you realize the initial intention but with a qualitatively new meaning and significance.

We can say about the recoil that through it one of the basic laws of dialectics is revealed in the organics of movement—both as the process of moving from one place to another, and as an object of precise perception. In almost the same words, Lenin writes of the highest form of movement—of cognition: "The movement of cognition toward an object must always proceed dialectically: to go back in order to better hit the target, to step back in order to jump better (to know?) . . ." (Lenin, *Collected Works*, Vol. XII, p. 229).* This citation points out the universalism and dialecticism of such a process and the very inevitability of such a course of dialecticality.

And indeed, in life, we inevitably encounter that phenomenon as soon as we deal with the necessary expenditure of a greater effort for gaining our objective.

What happens in those instances when there is not too great a need for physical strength? From the complete development of the overall picture of the course of movement in all three phases, you shift to a more economical type of manifestation of energy. If in the course of everyday life, you must approach some place and *not* jump across it, or you must lift a light object, then why develop the entire three-stage process to the full degree? In terms of physical demands it isn't required, and the action can be accomplished without it.

Such seems to be the case. But in actual fact *any kind of* manifestation must *always* and *inevitably* go according to the same law of the negation of negation. It is only a matter of the "mass" involved in the various stages of the process, and in the amount of energy expended on them.

On the stage, too, in recoiling you can take a very tiny step back, or you can run back to such a degree that it is many times greater than the act itself, for which the run back serves as a recoil. (Sometimes the run back can encompass the entire play, functioning as a recoil, so to speak, for the final denouement! But of that, later on.)

This is the situation in real life. Even in the simple act of taking hold of the back of a chair, let's say, you *cover* it with your palm. To do that, the palm must be at least slightly *raised* over the object: in order for the descending hand to take the object, it must inevitably be raised slightly, that is, must move away from it. Of course, that is less apparent than running back five steps. But the principle is the same. The difference is only a matter of the "degree" of the manifestion allowed for that action.

And finally, there can be an instance when absolutely nothing takes place spatially, and that entire process of the negation of negation is carried out mentally without any external manifestation.

*In the original in French: ". . .reculer pour mieux sauter (savoir?). . ."—S.E.

A person thinks: "I'll go. No, I won't go." Then he goes. The first two elements are that same recoil with the very same function, but in a different dimension, in a different quality.

A person steps back and approaches—this is a spatial recoil movement.

A person thinks. He gnaws on his finger. The recoil takes place in the gesture (the gnawing on the finger is, in essence, a movement of the hand in the reverse direction—the hand meeting the body and the face).

A recoil resolved in a gesture is a new quality in relation to a spatial transition.

And finally, a man stands "with his hands in his pockets" and thinks: shall I go or not? This is the third quality. But in each instance equally, that same process takes place with a different degree of movement back. (Pondering is also a means of "stepping back," in order to *jump* better.)

In everyday situations, it all amounts to being able to achieve a maximum effect with the least expenditure of energy. It is trying to get results by moving less and by expending less energy.

Therefore a movement such as changing position we try to make a conscious one. Rather, we don't allow auxiliary elements of the actions to spread beyond the limits of consciousness, that is, we *think* them over. We don't adapt by running here and there, but as much as possible without changing position in space, we do it by the quickest means, with the more active "extremities," with most active apparatus of the body—in the brain.

And so the full picture of the process in life appears where possible in an extremely contracted form.

How beneficial it is for mankind—the possibility of turning a greatly expressive running transition into a gesture, and a gesture into a movement of the voice (for mutual communication), and into a thought (for personal use)! You can appreciate this when you have occasion to meet people who lack this ability.

I was once at a performance given by deaf-mutes. Both the audience and the actors were deaf-mutes. That was an astonishing spectacle (not so much the actors as the audience...). Hundreds of flashing hands, synchronically shooting out and going back. It made the audience look like that narrow band of the Pacific Ocean shoreline somewhere on the Mexican coast where millions of birds are flying about, reminding us with their thousands of flapping wings of an unending whirlpool. The only difference is that in the theatre all that proceeded soundlessly, and everything, even the most passionate expression of emotion by the audience through its agitated silence, in no way interfered with the actors. But in observing the enormous expenditure of motor force in their mimicry and arm movements,

I could not help but feel a certain sense of shame: only in such situations of the physical heaviness of expression, do we sense clearly how much unnecessary talking we are used to doing....

The extreme activity of our tongue, the ease of its "peristaltics," has spoiled us so much that the real weight of each word has long since gone from our usage.

How useful it would be if for only a week or so we were to force our good "prattlers" to speak on artistic subjects with their entire bodies, using the techniques of the deaf-mute.... However, that already becomes a moralizing digression, and it would be better to stick closer to the subject.

The very process of thinking, the realization of purpose through conscious thinking, also follows that very same schema of the negation of negation. This is theoretically clear and certain, since here too we are dealing with an organic process, and therefore inevitably a dialectical one.

But aside from that, there is still other curious material for direct observation of the workings of the consciousness and the manifestation of will, which indicates that the complete picture of the process of a consciously willed act even in conditions of instinctive manifestations, inevitably follows that same formula. One can cite examples from various realms.

In one, the first negation—excitation—plays a part, that is, the presence of a counter-motif; in the other example, this counter-motif reaches the point of discrediting the initial intention.

But one way or another, in both instances the intention is immediately followed by the negation of it. Subsequently it is already interrupted by a new negation, now leading to the realization of the intention.

The first example comes from the interesting observations of the reaction process carried out with the late Doctor Otto Kohnstamm, head of the Königstein Sanatorium in Taunus. A specialist in the destruction of basal-motor phenomena, he extended the field of his research, for which he used the method of hypnotic analysis, to include the observation of psychological processes. In patients who were more susceptible to hypnosis, he succeeded in arousing the ability not only to carry out one or another action, but also to describe the process of that action in the most rudimentary phases of its coming into being.

Although a method such as this isn't entirely canonical, on the other hand, these experiments are nevertheless free from any prior suggestion by the hypnotist as regards that part of it which interests us.

The character of the process thus obtained not only wasn't foreseen by the hypnotist—it was for him simply unexpected (Typical is his N.B.

after the account of the evidence of a female patient: "At first that was for the author completely unexpected"), and he made note of it as an auxiliary result to those special questions which he was basically studying.

What, then, is characteristic of the work of the internal mechanism, for example, even in such instinctive reactions as laughter at a witticism, that is, in the seemingly maximally involuntary and direct reaction.

In his research, "Das Unterbewusstsein und die Methode der hypnotischen Selbstbessnung" (in the *Journal für Psychologie und Neurologie*, vol. 23), or in the posthumous edition of Dr. O. Kohnstamm: *Erscheinungsformen der Seele*, München, 1927, p. 479, where we read in paragraph 27, "Der Witz und das Lachen" [Wit and Laughter], a transcription of a patient's words. N.B. The account, as with any description of internal processes, lacks both the terminology adequate for it and a precise formulation, and it is unavoidably "personified": "The brain finds that," "The brain had just given the order," the account is unavoidably figurative, a type of mythological tale where the brain is presented as a character, as it were. In attempts to describe similar states, there is always a reliance on older forms of thinking: see, for example, the account of experience under narcotics or the notes of persons coming out of a state of ecstasy or an epileptic seizure. In relation to the material itself, we would like to protect it from extreme skepticism and underestimation. In this regard, it would be easy to fall into the same estimation of it with which Engels had already sharply criticized Utopians:

"We leave it for the literary merchants to juggle these ridiculous fantasies and to delight in the sobriety of their own way of thinking compared to such craziness. . . . It is also more profitable to find among them indication of the actual characteristics of the processes in order to master them, the characteristics which the 'blind philistines' don't see" (Engels, *The Development of Socialism from Utopia to Science*).

And so I cite the material of Dr. Kohnstamm:

> And so, the anecdote is told and understood and the smile is achieved by the usual route: the brain conveys its order to its own organs which carries it out. During this execution, the brain continues to work and to find that a smile is not a sufficient reaction to the anecdote, and it wants to strengthen the affective reaction to it. And so in place of a smile one gets laughter. I find in this process that between light merriment or a smile and laughter as such, a specific act of will also intrudes. The brain senses the difference between merriment and laughter as such. And a specific action is needed in order that laughter as such is produced from the prior stage of merriment. The very same distinction, that is, "the necessity of the inclusion of a secondary excitation," exists in equal measure between walking and running, whispering and loud speech. . . . This occurs so quickly that it is completely impossible to establish how much time is expended on carrying out that action. . . .

9. Eisenstein: On Biomechanics and Expressive Movement 201

That is, in examining laughter, loud speech, running, as fully valid and maximally expressed manifestations, we see that they are preceded respectively by a smile, a whisper, a step, as the primary objective, which is then cancelled by the moment of critical doubt, in order that later by a new negation it will be affirmed with full validity.

NOTE: One should keep in mind that the incident described by the patient in no way refers to a case where a similar process is carried out consciously or intentionally: that is, where a person feels awkward for insufficiently reacting and he artificially, intentionally begins to strengthen his reaction. (This point is especially emphasized by the researcher.)

Here it is interesting to note that in such a case, "the artificial process, the intentional one, is merely translated from a deliberately conscious plan, a graph according to which the process flows in normal, organic conditions." In this case it clearly acquires a qualitatively different reading. But here it is valuable to note the particular connection between both types of manifestations commensurate with the qualitative differentiation.

If what has been shown here proves to be insufficiently canonical as research material, then the correctness of precisely this schema of the course of the act of the manifestation of its psychic activity can also be followed in detail in the process already observed from the outside, that is, already in the conditions of objective research.

We are speaking here of the process of the creative act, and moreover, under conditions of its public course: artistically inventive directorial work in the conditions of rehearsal and of staging a work on the spot.

To start with, I will draw on my personal experience. For my work, it is very characteristic that when I get an idea right on the spot, I never immediately "accept" it. I always ask for advice, for verification, for encouragement from someone standing near me at the filming.

Also, characteristically, it makes almost no difference to me who it is, and what is even more remarkable, it's not at all important what that person says, or even whether it is a positive or a negative answer. Those who have worked with me can undoubtedly confirm this. (That by no means signifies that I allow advice or observations from my collective or from outside to go in one ear and out the other. I have in mind here a very special set of circumstances, and no more. S.E.)

What does this mean? It means, evidently, that in this turning for advice, for encouragement or verification, it is not the answer that is important to me: for the full realization of the process of invention, one needs this transitional stage of the negating of the invention, which is here expressed by "doubt." Sometimes this doubt grows into a direct contradiction of my own intention, when my initial idea too quickly finds a positive confirmation.

I vividly remember that gray, foggy Leningrad morning after a night shooting in the Winter Palace, when in looking at the opened Palace Bridge, I got the idea for the scene with the cab horse which was shot. The dangling horse. The cab falling off the one half of the drawbridge. The slowly opening jaws of the bridge. And the long hair of the dead animal, stretching from one half of the bridge to the other.

I remember a similar moment of uncertainty when I was deciding (also right on the spot) whether or not to do the "The Odessa Steps" in *Potemkin*, which was not provided for by any kind of "firm" or even written scenario, and the indolence (an unconscious braking counter-action) with which I devoured a kilo of grapes in Alupka, fighting myself: whether or not I should go and film three palace lions in order to merge them into the three-part montage of one marble lion leaping. Evidently this moment of recoil doubt plays a role not in itself, but only as a necessary phase in the creative process.

I am even more convinced of that by the fact that a very similar phenomenon, although in a different key, also exists in the rehearsal work of the director Vsevolod Meyerhold.

Anyone who has had the opportunity, or more accurately the genuine fortune to be present at his rehearsals, these most remarkable events among theatrical experiences, undoubtedly remembers the habit of the maestro [Meyerhold], after the preliminary outline of an especially successful moment, always to turn to the "chorus" of those present at the rehearsal with the words: "What nonsense! What foolishness!" Or something of that sort. However . . . neither that "nonsense" nor that "foolishness" would be dropped. On the contrary, after several minutes, the polishing would begin to develop them further—and in the production they would unfailingly be among the best examples of unforgettable details in Meyerhold's craft.

Here we have features of that very same negation (through discrediting an invention), a complete lack of attention to the enthusiastic replies: "Oh, no, Vsevolod Emilevich. That's amazing!" And a completely organic return to his original intention.

If from that point of view one looks at a certain amusing profession in the American cinema, then it may not seem quite so ridiculous. This profession turns out to be well-grounded; it was brought into being by the well grounded organic principle of the artistic-inventive process, and its foolishness turns out to be no more than the result of hypertrophy, a phenomenon which is legitimate and reasonable in itself. I have in mind the role of the so-called director's "yes-man" in America. The role is one whose function is automatically to say "yes" to whatever the director says.

In light of what has been said above, a certain justification for the presence of this strange figure and the absolute justification for its automatic character already seems less unexpected. I repeat, the nonsense is in the hyperbolization of the touchstone for manifestation of recoil by the director carried to the degree of an entire institution, profession, and role!

In normal, everyday conditions, the intention immediately turns into realization without any evidence of negation within the very act of carrying it out. The process takes place in a contracted form.

When you come up against art, that phenomenon must be presented in the maximally developed form.

Here is found one of the criteria for the similarity and the difference between real phenomena in everyday life and real phenomena as worked out in art. It is erroneous therefore to juxtapose in principle these two spheres.

If it is true to a certain extent, as Coquelin said, that "on the stage they don't speak, but pronounce, they step out and don't walk," and so forth, then life and art as a result seem to be opposites. In actual fact, they are only polar points of one and the same process — from maximal reduction of it in life to extreme development in works of stage art.

If on the path of cognition, as Engels said, the limits of mere everyday common sense are insufficient, so also in the realm of art a phenomenon in a composition must appear, not in its weakened form, but in the fullness of connections and phases of the process inherent to the given phenomenon.

The same happens in the destiny of some Ivan Ivanovich living quietly somewhere on a Moscow street, or to Monsieur Chalumet from the Rue Ste. Honoré, until the moment when one of them gets the idea to become the hero of a story as a social type. Then he must appear in the fullness of that hero's typicality, in typical circumstances and interrelationships, without which he could not become established in the pantheon of literature. Of course, even here, there can't be and there isn't a full development, but the economy which is prescribed in art is completely different. It in no way corresponds to the economy of movement in life, and more often than not it is directly opposite to it.

In life it would be economical, that is, it could be done with a minimum expenditure of energy, simply to approach the table. But for economy on the stage one must take several preliminary steps back toward the opposite corner. Try *not* doing that and see how much the energy loss of audience attention exceeds the amount the "economical" actor saves in not observing that condition of preciseness in his work.

You see that in the presence of different types of polar points, the line remains basically the same, that is, it is the usual dialectical picture.

Here it manifests itself in its two-stage form in the course of movement.

The second secret of the necessity for such a development in a work of art is that the developed process better answers the requirement for less economy, less rationalizing-sensory thinking, that is, thinking which is maximally saturated emotionally.

It is this type of thinking to which a work of art appeals in the first place, in contrast to a scientific tract.

I think it is clear to you that the emotional effect is always stronger when the process is more developed. To make a threatening movement with the finger is one thing; to make a threatening approach is stronger; but to approach and give you a "punch"—that will really be something. This is in the category of influences on the emotional level. But if I "contract" and mutter, "You bastard," in terms of *absolute* meaning, that will not in any way be less strong. And sometimes there is an even more terrible supposition, that I or someone else would be capable of *thinking* that about you (that is a contraction to an extreme degree).

These are simply different qualities of affective force, in various dimensions: one leans in the direction of the intellect, another in the direction of emotional penetration of action into the the human psyche, where the emotional and intellectual realms are indivisible.

[Sergei Eisenstein, *Izbrannie proizvedenia* (Selected works), vol. 4 (Moscow: Iskusstvo, 1964), pp. 81–90, with cuts restored from original manuscript.]

Lecture on Biomechanics, March 28, 1935
by Sergei Eisenstein

I must disappoint you because I came alone. The thing is, the Chinese are hurrying to get ready for their performance and so they couldn't be here. But even if they had come, they weren't planning to show or tell you anything.

Today we're going to talk about Biomechanics, since you are breaking your bones over that thing, and you should know what you are sacrificing them for.

Before starting on that, I want to ask you: the way we conducted our discussion last time, was it too tiring for you?

Voices: No, it was very good, we were very pleased.

This method of mine to wander into various related and unrelated areas may at first frighten you and seem distracting. The basic objective is to bring everything to one and the same point, irregardless of how remote an area is located. Because in our practice, this fanaticism of focusing on one idea is a terribly important thing. And when you are full of one aspiration or one objective, then from that position you must basically look at the whole surrounding world, always from the point of view of applying it to what is needed. When I asked here about what you know from literature, I was interested for the same reason: in what way does the sense of a relationship of a certain moment in literature, painting, or other art touch you from a theatrical point of view? For example, Zola can be read as literature; it can be read as it would be by a professor of the history of literature, with all the precise historical data, and so forth; from the point of literary research; and Zola can be read from a cinematic angle, stripping away all its literary pluses and minuses, and taking it in a barbarically practical way from the point of view of our interests.

Have any of you tried looking at Zola like that? If you look at it that way, you'll find that there are few writers who have such a brilliant array of close-ups and the knowledge of how to use them. It would be difficult to match such written descriptions in terms of visual sensation and of illuminating a scene. If you remember, in *His Honor Eugène Rougon* [Son excellence Eugène Rougon], there is a description of how he speaks in the chamber. These pages could be cut out of the book and given to the artist and cameraman, and you could shoot straight from the page. You've read *The Earth* [La terre] — who has read it? (Three persons.) Without *The Earth*, Zola isn't Zola, because there in one ultimate clot are all of Zola's pluses and minuses. For example, in *The Earth* there is a perfectly remarkable description of a scene of alienation of land in a notary's office, when the old man turns over the land to his children in imitation of King Lear. It is written with such subtlety that when a man sits down on the windowsill (in the room there is a little window with a low sill) and from this the lighting in the room changes, it serves not only as a detail of material for the description, but as a specific psychological nuance. You could literally do a notation for lighting the scene from that page. You must pay attention in this respect, because sometimes the usage of seemingly quite unexpected and insignificant things in the interests of the thematics we are discussing is not simply a manner of exposition or purposeful glibness, or lack of organization, or lack of consistency in outlook, as Sutyrin said, but of bringing closer all the things and looking at all of them from the point of view of the theme we're interested in and working on at a given time. That applies to the form of exposition.

Now, directly on Biomechanics. Has Zlobin told you anything about it?

Kustov: He has said almost nothing, no theoretical facts.

Maybe we can work out a summary of what is known about that subject. Who can say something? What basic principles of movement are found in Biomechanics, what basic tenets?

Tryaskin: Movement with a minimal expenditure of energy.
Ivanov: Everything is from the big toe.
Gakel: Springs.
Tokmasib: The working out of precision in movement.
Tryaskin: Coordination of all movements.
According to what principle?
Volodarsky: In Biomechanics there is maximum efficiency. It is like a worker's lathe: without taking emotion and experiencing into account.
Kustov: According to the most simple route.
And what is that most simple route?
Kustov: The most economical, the most expressive.
What else?
Goltsov: Probably with the least expenditure of energy.

How is it achieved? What is the motor base from which these things naturally flow? Right now, I understand you don't want to move in Biomechanics. It's a confusing thing: evidently, with the least expenditure of energy in the future, but for the moment with bone-breaking. I must say that your information, to put it mildly, is superficial.

The point is that Biomechanics is the very first step toward Expressive Movement. Also, beyond that first step, which was basically not a very large one, Meyerhold himself never went. He remained within the limits of that special biomechanical gymnastics and he didn't take any further steps in the direction of a system of Expressive Movement. In essence, Biomechanics is valuable only because of one basic principle that lies at the base of Expressive Movement—Expressive Movement is that movement which proceeds according to organic rules of movement. The most expressive, the most attractive movement is one which flows according to natural and organic norms. Because if the influence of the actor-performer works primarily and in most cases along the line of provoking direct or reverse imitation in the auditorium, then it is quite logical that the more inherent in people the movement presented as an object of imitation is, the more attractive it will be. When we say a character is "convincing," we mean it is a character one may not necessarily meet, but according to human psychology, a character one could meet. When a person is presented who bears no relation to the possible appearance in nature of such a person, then he doesn't affect [us] grippingly or infectiously.

You know, the colossal effectiveness of [the Vasilyev brothers'] *Chapaev*, in part because of Babochkin's acting, is built on the fact that you have here without any question a 100 percent hero, but presented in such a way that almost everyone feels he could be such a person. This taking of a heroic figure off of such high stilts onto which the ordinary person can't climb—that is one of the strongest things in *Chapaev*. You feel that this is a man who is actually beside you, he isn't separated from you by some heroic shell. That is, everyone feels that if he were a better person, if he demanded more of himself and regarded with greater passion those problems he should be passionately concerned about, he could approach that. That is an especially valuable contribution that Chapaev gives to the images of his heroes. His hero isn't an abstraction, he isn't forced on you, and therefore he has such a colossal effect. Because it's easy to experience along with Chapaev, to feel at one with him during the action.

If that element of empathy is important when it comes to the image or the character as a whole, in terms of the character being believable and gripping, then that is also quite true at a lower level of the working out of an image: not only the character as a whole, but also the least detail, precisely in the technique of working it out. There remains that same law: that a gesture, an expressive movement, mimicry, is easily imitated, is easily perceived organically when it is executed according to the organic laws by which they occur in nature. If they proceed from other laws, then one can imitate them, but then they are divorced from the psychology of the perceptual apparatus.

You know that well-known question of which comes first: gesture or emotion. *Voice*: We had a discussion about that today.

Oh, you are up-to-date on those special questions. And so, then, according to James' theory, movement comes first: a person is sad because tears are falling from his eyes; but another theory says that the tears flow because the person is sad. Actually, both of these are seemingly correct. The thing is, the very posing of the question bears in it the traditions, the remnants of a dualistic worldview, that is, the ripping apart of the unity of these manifestations, the psychic and the motor, as a single process. And depending on whether the focus is more mechanical or more idealistic, one person prefers to emphasize the leading role of movement, and another likes to assign the leading role to the primacy of emotion. If you look at where one theory or the other occurs, then the class antecedents and historical period of them are quite clear.

But the point here is that we are not at all concerned with the primacy of one or the other of them. In the complex as a whole, you have an indivisible unity. And as I define it, the question here is one of approach. Just as there is a back door and a front door, one can reach the unity of psychological and motor phenomena by one staircase, or one can come at it from the other side. In one case, one of them is first and in the other, the other one. If you begin to shiver as you do when you are cold, you will develop that unpleasant feeling you have when you are cold. On the other hand, if you place yourself in a certain emotional state, willy-nilly you will immediately translate it into movement. When a director has to demonstrate to an actor for whom something doesn't work out, he jumps up from his place in the auditorium, and by the time he runs up onto the stage, he is already in character and he shows how it must be done. That is, there arises in the director's mind an image of the character, of his personality, of his psychological state, and it is immediately translated into action. And so, the argument of there being opposing sides is incorrect, because that suppresses one component in favor of the other. It's not only that this unity is indivisible, it's not only that you can reach this effect in another way. Here, there is something else that's important: it's very important where you apply one or the other point of view. That is, when exploring problems of expressiveness, where should the expressive material given by James be applied, and where the material of other points of view?

Here it becomes clear that the Jamesian point of view has a correct expression in the theatre. Where? Not on the stage in the sense that now the actor has made a correct movement and he immediately experiences the proper emotion. But that it happens in the audience, because the audience reproduces the movement it sees, and besides, not in an expanded form, but concentrated, and through that the audience enters into that emotional state which the actor is demonstrating to it. That is where the secret of form lies.

If you watch children in the theatre, you will see that kids not only manage to reproduce one person with all his movements; they manage simultaneously to reproduce everybody on the stage. On their faces, all of the characters flash by. Children fully and completely reproduce that. The same happens, let's say, with an expansive audience. I must point out that the audiences in our major cities are extremely difficult. They are extremely reserved. If you compare them with the usual American audience, they bear no resemblance. Some nonsense at which we only smile, there in America the whole audience reacts with a roar. That's why in our audiences it is more difficult to see the elements of reproducing. But if you watch carefully, if for a moment you turn your attention away from the stage, then sometimes it is downright funny.

They once almost threw me out of the Art Theatre. You've seen [Hamsun's] *At the Gate of the Kingdom*. There's a moment where a couple is dancing and singing. And for some reason, I looked at the audience right at that moment when the couple was humming the waltz. When I saw how everyone was repeating it, each in his own way, I couldn't keep from laughing. I gave such a guffaw that they almost threw me out. And so, it is through reproducing those things that the psychological complex is triggered which is evoked by what the actors are doing on the stage.

We aren't concerned here with the question of whether the actor is experiencing an emotion or not. Right now I am only speaking of the result. The actor has convincingly and organically portrayed something on the stage. The spectator perceived that something through the way it was manifested, and from that arises, according to James' formulation, the very same state. Of course, that can't be considered apart from the plot, the preconditions, the rendering of the plot and so forth. Moreover, the textual content of a line and the presentation of a given line are the same content shown in different dimensions. The word gathers that into a formulation, and movement and acting, simultaneously with the delivery of the formulation, presents that in action, in feeling, and in appearance. They all work in one direction, although they are located at polar points. Movement here is the word delivered without emotion, from that side. And both extremes work equally well.

And so the element of imitation plays a very large role: from the convincingness of the character right down to the smallest expression. Because just as soon as a person makes an unorganic gesture, it immediately seems that he isn't experiencing, or it's incomprehensible, or not convincing, or as they say in the Art Theatre: "I don't believe it." Aside from whether the actor is supposed to feel or not to feel, certain organic expressive phenomena have a number of laws, a number of propositions. By observing and studying man's expressive manifestations, one can find the laws according to which they take place.

And here we arrive at the discovery of a whole series of laws. Keep in mind that, generally speaking, most people don't possess the precise organics of expressive movement. That is quite understandable, and understandable in conditions of everyday life, in conditions of social milieu in those conditions in which they exist. We know very well that in terms of physical development, people condemned, let's say, to office work, tend to lose their motor facilities. On the other hand, we know that people who perform physical labor exclusively have certain other components that are insufficiently developed. And the arrival at the proper balance so that each element with which man is physically endowed could be equally and properly developed, can happen only at that point where social conditions are such that the social system also concerns itself with the development of man and presents him with all the necessary conditions. We know very well that with regard to workers at a Ford plant what the concern of the management is: it's not merely to develop the physical work apparatus to the detriment of moral and spiritual development, but to train to perfection only one professional movement which destroys all the remaining facilities and turns man into one of the components of the conveyer belt.

If you simply take a man from the street, you will never find in him an organically expressive manifestation in its pure form. The organically

Students practicing various biomechanical movements at Meyerhold's studio on Novinsky Boulevard, 1922.

correct expressive movements that are endowed in everyone by nature are in some way distorted. At the very extremes will be the professional distortions. You know there are people who have an overdeveloped right arm or shoulder. Then you will have particular circumstances, for example, a broken arm or leg, and so forth. They destroy that basic system of manifestation with which man is biologically endowed. Here is the explanation of why, for example, they say that children and animals come across well on the screen. The point is that the organics of movement are not destroyed in animals. Of course, I don't mean some cart horse, but when you are going to film wild animals, some leopard, then they don't have any distortions. The same is true of children. They move much more harmonically than they will later on when they bear the mark of some quite specific pressure from the social conditions in which they further develop.

And the question arises: what basically needs to be known, what are the ideal conditions for the organic manifestation of movements in order to master them, and having mastered them to be able to build on them consciously that suprastructure of distortion which occurs in one or another situation. That is, to have a neutral system of movement which is basic for all manifestations, and to know how, from that view point, to see what deviations will occur in one or another direction. Moreover, these deviations in the general expressive schema can be considered as individual additions to the given image, to the given character, defined nationally, professionally, socially, whatever, since each of these elements leaves its mark. There is nothing terrible if we say: borrow your manner of moving from the Mongols. It's clear that they bear the mark of certain national or racial elements. That softness which Mongols have, beginning with Mei Lan-fang, they are endowed with that. On the other hand, take the Negroes. The feeling for rhythm they have, which is organic and not mechanical, that imperceptible rhythm with which Negroes in a jazz band perform, that's not easily achieved. I saw the way fellows in the American South work. For our dancers to achieve such a mastery of rhythm, they would have to study for twenty years.

And so, to the basic schema of movement you have adjustments in one direction in one situation, and adjustments in another direction in another situation. In portraying on the stage a Chinese or a Negro, you know that to the basic schema of expressive manifestations certain adjustments are needed so that the portrayal will approach, for example, the characteristic movements of the North American Indians. It is the same as regards any characteristic movement. Take, for example, professional movements. Supposing you are filming mowers at work, and two months later a matador at a bull fight. Each has particular movements. If you know the basic organics by which the body must move, you will find which general rules to apply to the particular manifestation.

Here it is a matter of certain average laws which in the ideal, pure form don't exist, but which show through in all individual manifestations. This is that same generalization of all possible individual manifestations which at a particular stage in the development of mankind manifests itself in all realms. You know that in primitive or early speech the word "to walk," the concept of "walking," doesn't exist. But there exist forty designations for various forms of walking. If you go swinging along, that has one designation, or if you walk quickly, if you walk stumbling and so on. There are thirty–forty designations for the slightest variations, but there is no overall concept for walking. With us, it's like this: an overall concept of walking and a series of divisions: fast walking, slow, limping, leaping, and so forth. You have a concept, a generalized idea, and its particular applications. The development proceeds in such a way that at first there is an array of separate instances, and then a general concept is formed.

The same kind of generalizing, organic law exists for all systems of expressive movement; and in each individual instance, through those laws which you know, you can uncover, reveal, and reproduce them. The director and actor must master these laws, not only theoretically, but physically. Because if a person, let's say, is as bound by his own characteristics as are the majority of people in real life, they don't need to know about their manifestations, or to master more than they have. But take a person who walks in a certain way and can't rid himself of that. How can he portray a man who walks differently? It is impossible for him to go from one characteristic walk to another unless he possesses a general language of movement. And so you must know: what are my habitual ways of moving, and what are his? What laws of movement are broken by him so that he moves the way he does? Only if you know certain general phenomena, common for various manifestations, can you work this out. That is, I can depart from my characteristic movement to the general movement, and then break to what is general for all of us, according to his particular case. And that's why we need that key to the laws of expressive manifestations: in order to analyze movements, to understand them, and in order to create movements.

And along the line of these laws, the first preliminary step was made by Meyerhold in his Biomechanics. Moreover, as with much in Meyerhold, it was arrived at by purely empirical means. Because Meyerhold was such a brilliant actor who could move brilliantly, he in essence turned his attention to certain laws which governed his own actions, and he fixed them as a law which is inherent to all expressive manifestations. Furthermore, in developing these principles, he wasn't original, as one might expect. All great actors in all important periods have known and possessed these features. Some formulated them, others didn't, and still others were able to bring them together into an orderly system. Parallel with Meyerhold, that was done—and to an even greater degree—by Rudolf Bode who developed with complete German thoroughness all those principles Meyerhold found in Biomechanics and turned them into a very detailed system of movement training.

What is the first law about which we are talking? For dialecticians, that law is, of course, very simple and graphic: in organic movement there is not a single expressive manifestation that does not involve the entire motor system as a whole. In other words, if you raise your finger, then in that movement the entire organism takes part to a greater or lesser degree. That position was formulated by the French in 1847 and was expressed by the famous formula that *"l'action isolée n'est pas dans la nature"* (an isolated movement is not organic), that is, it is contrary to nature. If you raise your arm using only the muscles that work there, this movement is contrary to the motor process. You find things like that in hysterics, in epileptic seizures, when there is an individual spasm, an individual muscle contraction. A spasm is an extreme muscular contraction isolated from all others. When in swimming you have a leg cramp, it is because the muscles are not working in harmony with the entire system. And when you make some individual movement in a muscularly isolated way, it is perceived as inorganic since it is contrary to the basic law encountered in nature. That is the basic law of aggregate manifestation which you as dialecticians should know.

In applying that law to expressive movement, that principle of unity is reflected in the fact that in a motor manifestation the body as a whole takes part in the very smallest individual gesture. That might at times confuse you: a person raises his eyebrows and there's no apparent change in his heel. Here it is a matter of the very minutest manifestation. You know that when you are excited, you move your arms about, and moreover, you do it this way (he demonstrates). In observing these things, you must always proceed from the more intensive example to the less intense one, because it is easier to see the law in the more intense situation. In the less intense one the same law exists, but it is less noticeable. I can give an example here of balancing a rod on the nose. If you take a rod about four meters in length and place it on your nose, it is easy for you to balance it because you immediately find that the center of gravity and your center of gravity and the fulcurm are on the same line, and you know very well that you work the pelvis, and sometimes the shoulder. But just as soon as you try to balance a tea cup on your nose, you're done for. The deviations here are so small that you have to have a highly-developed system in your neck, for example, down to the tiniest muscular element, in order to catch the slightest deviations. It is quite clear that the objective of the proper placement of all the centers of gravity and of the fulcrum is the same, but in the latter instance, it is much more difficult to execute. In the same way, don't worry when we say that in moving a finger, the feet take part, as well as the whole system of movement in general, because you can see that in examples on a larger scale. Try to lift a heavy object. You will immediately know how to do it: your whole system will immediately take part. First you place your feet, then you lift the object bodily, and so forth. But try to lift some light object. The order of movement will be according to the very same system, only so much more complex and refined in its course that you may not notice it.

And so Biomechanics is concerned precisely with training coordination of movement in that sense. That is, to train so that each movement which is made is the result of movement by the body as a whole. And from here comes our second question: if effort cannot be applied to particular points, where, then, must it be directed? What points of application of a given impulse are organic? And how is the center of gravity of the entire system organized? When you speak of balance, about work with balance, it is a matter of the mastery of the shifting center of gravity in relation to which the extremities work centrifugally. Basically, in translating that into a mechanical picture, you have here what is found in the old marionettes: when a doll is hung having in mind the center of gravity of the marionette, and it is made to jump by pulling a string, each movement repeats that rhythm with a certain delay, and with a jump and so forth, but preserving the very rhythmical picture of the general movement. The doll's extremities repeat the basic movement, and thus the marionette which is correctly hung always moves with perfect rhythm. If you take the sublety of movement in the Eastern theatre, in the Japanese or Chinese theatre, these movements are copied from marionette movements, and that special rhythmicality which they have, that special culture of movement, the coordinated movement of all parts of the body — all that is very deeply connected to those simplest rules of combinations of movements. The difference with marionettes is that there you have a very simplified kind of theatre.

These elements exist in nature, but not exclusively. Once you are concerned with the center of gravity, then it is quite clear where the motor impulse is located: resistance by the center of gravity to the center of the earth, that is, the entire movement is concentrated on those feet which are placed between your center of gravity and the surface of the earth. This never occurs without work. It seems to us we are standing calmly, but in actuality what are the legs doing? They are resisting the falling of the body. They aren't in a relaxed state, but in a state of tensity. And that weakened recoil prior to a movement by the body in one or another direction is also that same very simple mechanism through which the simplest movement up, down and to the side is executed.

It's a great mistake when they say that each movement must begin from the toe. The movement must come from that part of the body which serves to resist the center of gravity. If, for example, you walk on your hands, much as you like, it won't come from the big toe. It must come from the finger of your left hand. If you are in a crooked position, say you are bent over, then the feet won't help until you move your hand. That is, the starting impulse acts through those points through which the movement of the center of your gravity comes in contact with the external world around you. In other words, the impulse is sent there and then it spreads to wherever it is needed.

Here, more or less, are those principles of the organics of movement which Meyerhold worked out and the Germans too in even greater detail. What's more, Meyerhold worked out a system for its training. What you do in terms of story line isn't important. In all those movements, only one thing is important: to master that law. Biomechanics is one of those things you can't memorize, and basically you also can't learn those exercises by rote. In Biomechanics you must understand the principle according to which movement flows. There are in it a series of exercises which also develop the joints. For example, if you need to push with your hand, you aren't able to do it if the joints aren't trained to work properly; if the fingers can't be extended. At the Proletkult, for example, I had to deal with actors who worked at some speciality, I don't remember which, and whose hands were distorted professionally. Whatever the work process was, it wasn't important to them whether the fingers could be extended this far (he demonstrates) and it didn't occur to them to train the palm in the opposite direction. And so when it came to showing people how to spread out their fingers, some of them simply couldn't unglue their fingers. It was a matter of exercising the joints.

Say you have to make a movement with the shoulders. There are people whose shoulders and shoulder blades hardly move at all. And so in Biomechanics there are segments that are especially tormenting, such as that limbering up. You have to expend a lot of energy on that because your musculature isn't developed, the joints aren't developed. And so on the one hand, you have to become "hinged," so that the least push flows to every "hinge;" and on the other hand there is the mastery of that art of the "send-off," which then goes wherever it is needed. Both serve for mastering that first stage along the line of organic expressive movement which demands that the entire motor system of the human body as a whole participate in each part of an expressive manifestation. That is, it is the principle of the unity of the expressive system. This is what Biomechanics was built on and where it stopped.

When we speak about genuine expressive movement, you will see that the dialectics doesn't stop with the principle of unity alone. And about that second part, about the characteristics of that unity in opposites, and what it consists of in the particular case of human movement — I'm going to talk about that separately. That will be the second stage, and then I will speak a lot and in detail about that, because I myself worked on that part in the Proletkult Theatre. The detailed system of expression, the problem of balance and so forth — that is secondary to that question because you can freely work with the center of gravity of your body when you are trained for perfect balance; that is, when you can control the center of gravity of your body as you wish, then that center of gravity can't trip you up at some point.

All these auxiliary considerations are directed toward learning the main principle that everything takes part in a given movement. Then you will have the first prerequisite for speaking about movement. You can figure out what a person is doing when he makes a movement. For example, a certain way of walking. You will know precisely that first he bends his knee, that his center of gravity falls here (he indicates), and that this leg rises like this, and so forth. There is something to work with. And the same with each gesture. You know that you can bend however you like: in one case the area near the collar bone is bent, in another the shoulders are raised, and so forth. In each case you will know in which instances the bodily system is free and in which ones it is fixed. Biomechanics helps you to develop those things.

To what extent is this important? Along that line I have an old recollection from my visit to Berlin and of meeting Fritz Lang. Nizhny has probably already heard this at least a dozen times. I met Lang at a shooting of *Metropolis*. As I have characterized him in those years, it would be as if Kuleshov was given a lot to eat and wore a monocle—he would then be Fritz Lang. That man was a terrible show-off, but then all directors have that fatal flaw: they go on showing off until the time comes when they have to demonstrate the real thing. When an actor can't get something right, then you have to go and show him how it should be done. Well, Lang had that kind of difficulty. He had a scene where a millionaire's son comes to his father's factory and exclaims when he sees the enormous array of machinery. He is horrified and draws back. And it was filmed like this: they are shooting the person from here and he is acting out amazement. But behind the movie camera there isn't anything that could have aroused amazement. It was all filmed three months later in an entirely different location, and the actor hadn't even seen that factory. Later it would be incorporated into the montage. And so the problem was this. The actor was Freilich. He was to come and exclaim, but there was no factory. And so he entered and exclaimed; but it wasn't right. Lang got up there and he looked and exclaimed and it worked. He said to the actor: "Now you repeat it." The actor still couldn't get it. And it went like that for a long time. What was the secret? It was that Lang experienced the role correctly and played it. But what he did at that point, what movements he made, he didn't know, since he didn't control and didn't understand his motor responses.

There are many directors who do things intuitively, and then later they can't say how they did it. And Lang was like that. He saw that gigantic scene in front of him and he showed it correctly, but the actor couldn't picture it, or he was in a hurry and so it didn't come out for him. The actor did it like this (he demonstrates); and it gave the impression that he was looking at a clock somewhere above, or at best, at the clock's pendulum. Another time the actor did like this ([he demonstrates). It was quite clear that he was seeing something there in the distance beyond the camera. But here's the way it should be done: he should stagger back and make a movement with the whole body because then there is the feeling that he is looking at something from top to bottom, that is, he is seeing to the maximum everything he was supposed to be seeing according to the plot. You have to show that everything that can fall within the actor's range of vision is seen by him. And the director must say: you only threw back your head, and that gave the impression that you were looking at the clock. But when you step back, spread out your arms, and open your eyes wide, then there is the impression that you are seeing all that. There wasn't any especially complicated acting involved. Yet they lost hours rehearsing it instead of the director making the necessary corrections.

Moreover, if the actor is placed in the correct conditions, then it is much easier for him to act. The objective is to make it easy for the actor to carry out all the movements you demand from him. And in order to achieve this, you must in the first place give him the correct expressive schema. If you explain to him just what it is that will help him, he will calmly work out his experiencing of it. That's why it's important to observe and to know where the secret lies.

To find all the possible cases of movement is also impossible. But when you observe: Lang demonstrates and it works, but the actor demonstrates and it doesn't work, and then the fifth time he gets mad and it works out, and then again it doesn't work out — and you, comparing all these movements, must find the key to the whole thing. And once you have figured out that it worked when the actor stepped back, spread out his arms and so forth, then you begin to think — why is it so? When you step back and your character is in a recoil position, everyone will have the impression that you are seeing everything that that character could see. There can't be any contradiction between the logic of the movement and the expressive system. With movement you express the same logical idea.

And here we approach that very same problem we were working on last time: the problem of when an expressive movement works in such cases as a metaphorical image. Remember when I drew the schema of the mise en scène, it was the same thing. When you look only with your head, that outline of the head is translated by the spectator into what he sees. There can be an enormous vista before you, but you look at it only with your head, whereas it's important for you to convey to the spectator that you are seeing a great deal — all that I can convey by the words: "He was totally engrossed in contemplating the vista opened before him." That "totally engrossed" — how is that translated into movement so that in his look the entire body is emphasized? Here is where a metaphor is transferred into a series of actions, a transfer into a realistic execution of that objective. That is, the same principle applies here — to correctly define and correctly feel the situation, to correctly present it vividly — this is also appropriate here. Because if I want to see all that, I must present it very vividly.

That vivid expression or metaphor is always the point of departure for any expressive movement. It's a part of the language: "A person is depressed." For that depression you will look for a physical manifestation in the realm of depression. This "depression" expresses everything, and nothing. Only the basic schema is given. Inasmuch as this is a person who isn't going to try to expand, it will be something out of the realm of depressed things. In various situations that depression will be like this: in one case only hanging the head, then drooping shoulders, then knees bent, and finally a man completely prone—varying degrees of depression. But in all of them, one thing shows through: the task of concretely reproducing depression as a theatrical image.

Every expressive movement always has in it this motor prerequisite. Take, for example, aversion. The word itself indicates what must be done. That is, a movement in which there is an element of turning away. You are familiar with Darwin's little study, *The Expression of the Emotions in Man and in Animals*. Don't believe anything he says in terms of theory, but as a catalog of observations, this study is very interesting. Those laws according to which expression unfolds are extremely controversial, but the material is quite interesting. When you are going to express aversion, you will also have as a basis a movement of aversion up to the extreme degree when you turn away completely, because it's repellent to look. That word is the same in all languages: *aversion* in French, *Abscheu* in German. For such concepts there are usually corresponding words in all languages because they are constructed along the same line; and with a movement which had been formulated as a figurative designation, you must return to its primary point. From the movement which manifests it, it was reinforced into a term for designating it. And when you have to turn a stage direction into action it is always convenient to reveal its meaning. All words have frozen poetic images. At a certain point, it stops being an image, but when you are dealing with a schema, you have to return to the image from which the original meaning came. Take, for instance, aversion: you are interested in how that is done. When you need to create a new expressive situation, you need to find a basis for it through new imagery and then develop that into an adverb of action. Even the term "adverb of action" is preserved.

Now for the laws that are fundamental to this. The first is the one for which Biomechanics trains you. That is, so that you will be able, let's say, to work out how those elements are expressed in an overall individual schema. Later I will explain how all this is built on contradiction, and what that means—the unity of contradiction in movement—and how that is achieved. But you can only really understand that when you have achieved not a knowledge of Biomechanics alone, but when you begin sensing your movements as a single system. Then it will be easy for you to go on to the second level, that is, to understand how to read it as a unity in conflict.

Kustov: Biomechanics has always been accompanied by acrobatics. Here, that's left out. Evidently we need some kind of a supplement.

No, that's enough. Acrobatics makes it too heavy. Without a mastery of Biomechanics, you will never understand expressive movement properly, and you can understand expressive movement only when you can reproduce it. You need specific training. I hope that when you leave the Film Academy you will not be the kind of director who sits at a table and explains to the actor, and the latter pretends to think of something; and then when you have explained everything he tells you: I'm sorry, that can't be done; this chair can't be placed like that; how will I raise my leg, and so forth. You can best them only if you yourself are able to get up and demonstrate everything. Take Nemirovich[-Danchenko] — he can sit for two weeks talking about movement, but if necessary, he'll stroke his beard and then go out on the stage and execute everything correctly.

There are a whole series of things that are very easy to do and you must possess that knowledge. And the very first step for that is what you are doing in Biomechanics.

Tokmasib: They give us too much at one time.

Voice: Zlobin pays absolutely no attention to breathing.

There is one terrible thing about that training. In the Plastics Studio they try to develop your joints, and then you have to live with that macaroni.

Gakel: You convincingly told us about the sources of the system and its bases. But why is it that all of Meyerhold's actors move the same way? There's no individuality either from the characterization or from the actor as such.

Because in Meyerhold's theatre there's only one person who moves — and that's Meyerhold himself, and everyone reproduces him more or less successfully. If you have been at one of his rehearsals you know Meyerhold's way of moving, and then you can see how the others butcher it. They remember that he does something with his arms and they all attempt to do something of the same sort.

Meyerhold has one thing: he loves acting for everyone else. He's an absolutely brilliant actor, and when he's directing he's miserable because he's not acting. He acts for everyone. It doesn't matter to him what the actor understands, or what he feels. To him, what's important is that he do the thing himself: "Go ahead, do the best you can."

I must say that Meyerhold has a perfect knowledge of movement. And Ilinsky has taken a lot from him. But the fact that Meyerhold doesn't want to work out the individual characterizations and instead demonstrates them is a shortcoming that has nothing to do with his system. Besides, now Meyerhold is working on his vaudeville. That's *33 Swoons*—in which he is borrowing from himself. But it has nothing to do with movement.

I also have to say that Meyerhold has no luck with actors. I've had occasion to see many of his rehearsals. He demonstrates the characterizations quite remarkably, and those idiots stand around thinking: let him do what he wants, but I'm going to play it my way. But since the actor doesn't dare do it his own way, he compensates by not watching how Meyerhold does it. It's simply amazing the way they are unable to reproduce it. His actors are barely trained. Of his former trained actors, only Ilinsky remains. The rest either have very weak personalities, or they have gone elsewhere. The actors he has now really have very little in common with him, as for example, Bogolyubov; or now Gromov from the Art Theatre is working for him: it's as though an actor from another theatre had dropped in, and he has kept his old ways on the new stage. It's as if he had gotten into the wrong theatre, but so what, here I am and I'm acting. Meyerhold more or less worked on all that in 1921–1923. He's difficult to get along with, and so people leave.

Of the faithful keepers of that tradition remain Zlobin, Irina Meyerhold, and Inkizhinov, who has emigrated. There's also Urbanovich, who turned Biomechanics into physical culture; he had already turned it into a kind of regimentation at that time when we were all studying together with Meyerhold. He had that tendency even then. And when he left to go his own way, if he was a woodcutter then, in regard to Biomechanics he has now become a stonecutter. Later, there was a new tendency, to aestheticize those movements we had to do. I want to call attention to that—to that attempt to stylize the movements for the effect. What is important is to reproduce the mechanism by which the movement is done rather than capturing the external appearance and design. It is possible to reproduce not only the schema of movements but the individual form, and so in order to please the teacher they try to reproduce his manner. In Biomechanics that's very bad. That tendency toward mannerism, the aestheticization of external appearance, poses and so forth: that all occurred in his theatre. Meyerhold himself is to blame for that.

In *D.E.* a segment of Biomechanics was demonstrated in the course of the action. And since these exercises which basically should be done at home were put on the stage, there immediately arose that urge which every performer inevitably has: it's not enough for him to do it, it has to be "presented." And so that had a very negative effect on Biomechanics. Then too, Meyerhold got tired of all that business and he simply stopped training. And after that the situation got worse. Just today there was a discussion in the instructional section as to whether we really needed to hold onto Zlobin, and I insisted that it was very important. Zlobin is from the first crop, and the others less directly studied under Meyerhold. They didn't see how he did the exercises, and so there are all kinds of deviations in Biomechanics.

The most important thing is to ignore completely the subject matter of the exercises. Those exaggerated, slightly theatrical things on which these exercises are built, for example, that blow on the nose, that exercise with the top hat and so forth—forget all that. Those are random items you are practicing with. You could do that work equally well with a chisel or an ax. There is the danger that in doing the biomechanical exercises many are carried away by the remnants of old-time theatricalism, and they don't think about the technique of execution.

Goltsev: Zlobin wants us to add a kind of theatricality.

No. It's just that besides his knowledge of technique he has his theatrical ideals which for you are not obligatory. A distinction has to be made. What for him is an ideal of representation, you should regard as an exercise.

Voice: He demands exaggerated movements.

That, of course, is correct. In order to do the movement properly, you have to get into the swing of it. Exaggeration is always present in practicing.

Voice: We're going to be studying this for two years?

I think you'll be studying it the rest of your life. As I teach my students at GIK, you must use every opportunity to do motor exercises. For example, in jumping onto the streetcar, opening a door, climbing up on furniture and so forth. Each thing is an excuse for accumulating individual experience in movement. In each case there must be a particular motor objective which can be solved in one or another way. And that's why I say that it needn't be a complex of special exercises. What is important is to work out the laws and according to those laws to resolve what you come up against.

Voice: You say that the content of the exercises isn't important. And when, for example, Zlobin demonstrates a blow and a form of defense?

In jujitsu movements, he is giving you purely professional movements. But you needn't get carried away when he gives you, for example, a recoil in an exaggerated and parodic form. No one cares about that nowadays. You must select from that the technique of execution. Biomechanics mustn't be confused with acting. It isn't acting, it is only training. Sometimes the desire arises to act along with it, but that isn't necessary.

Voice: Would it be possible to arrange for him to state the meaning of each particular exercise?

I think now it is already more or less clear to you what you should watch for and what you should be concerned with. When he positions you, you should not worry about whether the feet are placed incorrectly. Instead, you must be concerned with what is the proper positioning of the feet. You won't get much out of him in terms of explanation because that's a matter which is very difficult to discuss. It's a little easier for me because I've been involved with that since 1923. I worked all that out and developed it at the Proletkult Theatre. And so I've shed a little blood over that matter. But take Meyerhold. He can explain almost nothing except for two or three basic formulations: look.

Voice: I tried to make notes based on Zlobin, but I couldn't put down anything.

It's impossible to write it down. It has to be filmed.

Ganel: There's a temptation to act it out.

Keep in mind that the system of movement basically arouses a desire to act and that's not at all bad, but the acting has to be kept under control. There is here the possibility for overacting. And then there's another thing too: it's all right to act, but there's a dangerous thing—that's the desire to experience the role. Here, you must differentiate somewhat. I had a chance to see that German school in Berlin. Mainly young women were studying there. They ran in a circle and they threw up their arms, and after three minutes they had already begun to pray: you know, those blue German eyes raised to the heavens. That's wrong. But the desire to compose movements, to complicate the outline of movements, to express oneself in a new variant on that basis—that's a slightly different matter. When you are seized by such a playful spirit, a desire to do something—that's correct. But when you are given the exercise of "Shooting the Bow and Arrow," and you see that people's eyes are clouding over and they are seeing in front of them a forest and a leopard, and their feet and stomach are trembling—at that point the important thing is a desire for self-control and a wish for training. Here it is important not only to have the organics of movement, but also to have it under some kind of control. Self-control is needed. Basically a psychological plot isn't given to you, and the schema which you act out is virtually abstract as a training system.

If I were now engaged in training an acting collective, I would discard all those figurative exercises from Biomechanics and would propose a completely different set of exercises from the expressive point of view. Because everything that is given now is the old, stylized Meyerhold material on which he has been sitting, *Love for Three Oranges* and so forth. For some reason it got bogged down in that period. I say it's all the same whether you whittle or do something else—you can also master movement that way. And so beware of that decorative aspect. When Meyerhold did that it was still all right, but beyond that it becomes a cliché. It's no use going after those clichés. They should be regarded as only a means to develop one or another movement. Perhaps when everything is fine in that respect, then perhaps we'll talk about the real system of expressive movement.

Voice: And so Biomechanics can be formulated as the mastery of mechanical movements?

It's deeper than that. As a term, Biomechanics isn't completely accurate. That's true, and since it was given a rather mechanical interpretation by its creators, it might actually be more correct than the actor supposed. In that ton of waste there is one gram of gold. But once you find that, then you can basically study whatever you want. That's not something to be afraid of. It's the same as if you took mathematics or music. When a problem is quite incomprehensible, and then you finally understand something, your mathematical perception has developed. It's the same with dancing. It happens sometimes you take a step, and then at some point you begin to dance.

Chapter 10

International Accounts of Biomechanics

> *To put it bluntly, this was the best body work for the actor I had ever seen.*
> Harold Clurman

Introduction

Although Biomechanics was designed with broad and revolutionary intentions, only a few thousand Soviet actors were ever schooled in it. To be sure, its novelty waned with the transformation of the Soviet theatre into a repertory of realistic satire and Socialist Realism. When the memoirs and autobiographical statements of some of Meyerhold's former actors and pupils began to appear in the 1960s, Biomechanics was regarded as merely another cipher of the golden age of the early twenties rather than as a serious system of movement training for actors.

For the foreign correspondents and Western theatre practitioners who flocked to Moscow between 1924 and 1936, however, Biomechanics held a constant fascination. Many of them believed that just as Meyerhold's use of Constructivist set designs had helped radicalize Western scenography, Biomechanics held the possibility of revolutionizing actor training. In fact, among the most interesting materials on Biomechanics are those accounts and documents left by international journalists and travelers.

Western interest in Meyerhold's theatrical innovations first began to surface in 1924 after the triumphant European and North American tour of the Moscow Art Theatre. The advent of NEP (New Economic Policy), with its limited free enterprise, and the maturation of "Bolshevik Culture," provided British, German, American, and Scandinavian reporters with fantastic raw materials, especially in the fields of art and theatre. Now, after Paris and Berlin—largely because of Meyerhold—Moscow became Europe's reigning theatre capital. Extreme distance and the inaccessibility of language did little to discourage the flocks of directors and producers, mainly from Germany and Central Europe.

The first accounts of Meyerhold's rehearsal techniques published in travel journals and political magazines like *Das Neue Russland* were little more than restated information in non-Russian languages. Biomechanics was always described as the "geometrization of movement," or as a mysterious avant-garde antidote to Stanislavsky's system of actor training. Occasionally, those who witnessed a session or two of the workshops would give a fleeting impression of the biomechanical exercises.

By the early thirties, as the political and economic situation reached a worldwide crisis, the majority of foreign theatregoers in Moscow were professionals from the United States and Britain. It is from this pool of visitors, who usually went to Moscow and Leningrad for only the brief period of the annual theatre festival, that we get the best eyewitness descriptions of Biomechanics. We have included six such accounts written between 1924 and 1935.

AN INTERVIEW WITH MEYERHOLD AT THE THEATRE OF THE REVOLUTION
by Lancelot Lawton

The British journalist Lancelot Lawton toured the Soviet Union several times between 1917 and 1926 and recorded his anthropological observations in The Russian Revolution (1917–1926). *Viewing the Revolution and its cultural institutions as exotic curiosities, he invited the ire of left-wing West European intellectuals, including the preeminent theatre historian Huntley Carter. In the spring of 1924, Lawton interviewed Meyerhold at the Theatre of the Revolution following a session on Biomechanics. Here one senses the immediate and humane scale of Meyerhold's work in actor training.*

I paid several visits to the Theatre of the Revolution and then arranged to see Meyerhold himself. After half-an-hour's tram ride from the center of Moscow, I alighted on a muddy road, and picking my way across a muddy courtyard, entered a dilapidated-looking building which served as the "laboratory" wherein the perfect actors and the perfect men of the future were in process of creation. I was shown into a large room. The floor was black and the walls and ceiling were stained. While waiting for Meyerhold I watched a tall, lithe, squint-eyed Tartar [Valery Inkizhinov] putting some half-dozen young men and women through physical drill. Here it should be explained that all Meyerhold's actors and actresses belong to the proletarian class, and that they work in the factories in the daytime, undergo training in their leisure hours, and perform in the theatre at night.

The young men and women whom I saw in training were lightly clad; the men wore shorts and shirts, while the women's attire consisted of bloomers and vests. Physically none of them approached perfection. The new man has not yet been made; he is only in the making. And even in Russia, where industry is still young and has not had time to break too many bodies, the raw material available is not plentiful.

Everyone was much in earnest. As a signal for the end of each movement the Tartar blew a shrill whistle. After the lapse of a few minutes, Meyerhold arrived, a man with a nervous, irritated face, a big nose, and eyes that looked into space.

"The Theatre of the Revolution," he said, "is the result of my study of the Commedia dell'arte, and of the Spanish, Japanese, and Chinese theatre — and finally of the cinema. My work so far is laboratory work and is empirical. Later I will form theories. I believe the theatre has possibilities to make not only a perfect actor, but also a perfect man. Two schools exist, (1) subjectivists, (2) objectivists. The first school is composed of vitalists, the second of Biomechanics. The former is based upon emotional movements. It imagines that these emotional movements are separate from physical movements, that the two are worlds apart.

"The other school to which I belong is based upon sure, firm ground: on the physical side of man. Emotions are the production of the nervous system; soul existence is not an element to be studied objectively. Here is the formula: N, the whole actor = a^1 brain (a quite clear element which gives order to the muscles and to the nerves of the actor) + a^2 element that fulfills action.... There is no place for the soul. Scientists who make a study of reflexology tell us that it is replacing psychology. My aim is to lay the foundations of a race of perfect actors, of perfect men. Biomechanics provides for every movement of the actor, but before he enters upon training in Biomechanics, it is essential that he should go through the discipline of physical culture, and acquire perfection in acrobatics, fencing and boxing."

"How about diet?" I asked.

"That is a question to which I am giving my attention. I am thinking out a suitable diet for the actor."

I then asked whether there was any truth in the criticism that the new system deprived the actor of all individuality?

Meyerhold replied that an actor was allowed to develop his individuality within the limits of his own part. Before we separated he praised very much the endurance of the new actor, who, he said, was able to play four hours at a stretch without feeling the least fatigue.

It remains to be added that frequently the actor in the Theatre of the Revolution is entirely without make-up, while sometimes only the slightest touches are employed to produce make-up. In some plays a special uniform resembling an engineer's overall is used; the color is blue and the skirts worn by the women are very short. The costumes are designed for the comfort of the actor, and they do not always harmonize with the play. In *The Earth in Turmoil* [Zemlya dybom], (which I witnessed) a special form of speech known as semaphore speech was used, the emphasis being placed on the vowels; the wailing sound produced was intended to be agitational.

The Theatre of the Revolution breathes the spirit of Revolution. For it, nothing is sacred. It has no plays of its own, but it does not hesitate to adapt old classical plays to the needs of the hour; dates and times are hopelessly mixed up. Art for art's sake is a bourgeois prejudice. Art for agitation, for the organization of social conscience, for the creation of a new man—these are the things that matter. The actor becomes a propagandist, the play a public meeting. There is no shrinkage from vulgarity, but it is honest, straightforward vulgarity. Do not forget that the proletariat is a virile class, one that has no use for sentimentality, and no patience with hypocrisy, or with the disguised sensuality of the old order. A new hero has arisen. A new romanticism has been created. The worker is the hero, his life the new romanticism. Not merely a few, but all workers are heroes, and the new Society, which is to be collectivist, is to be fashioned from this heroic mold.

The symbol of this new society is the Machine. The Machine is sober, reliable, heroic, powerful and productive, and it is composed of many separate small parts, all of which possess these essentially proletarian qualities. The machine-man is also sober, reliable, heroic, powerful, and productive. Free him from capitalist chains and, with the aid of the Machine that enslaved him in the past, he will build a new society. And so: Down with sickly, sentimental individualism, with all its puny efforts and all its petty strifes. Long live big industry, mass production, and riches for all! Long live proletarian Americanization! Long live Lenin, Marx, and materialism!

Meyerhold's methods, as he said himself, are experimental. That is not surprising, for he has been an experimentalist all his life. Where he may end, no one can tell.

[Reprinted from Lancelot Lawton, *The Russian Revolution (1917–1926)* (London: Macmillan, 1927), pp. 376–378.]

How Meyerhold Trains His Actors
by John Martin

Writing for The Theatre Guild Magazine *in anticipation of Meyerhold's cancelled North American tour, John Martin provides a sympathetic analysis of Meyerhold's training techniques. As a dance producer and a celebrated critic for* The New York Times, *Martin displayed a deep understanding of Biomechanics' philosophic underpinnings. Like many dance people, he was far more knowledgeable about avant-garde performance techniques than his colleagues at the Drama Desk.*

The forthcoming visit of Vsevolod Meyerhold and his company from Moscow will provide the American theatre with its first opportunity to observe at close range the third important system of acting which, with a bit of stretching, can be said to have arisen within the playgoing memory of our older inhabitants. It has been a short time, as such things go, since Delsarte reigned supreme over the stage of gesture and elocution; it was only yesterday that Stanislavsky superseded him with the theatre of naturalism and emotion; but already Meyerhold has swept aside the subjectiveness of his predecessor and laid hold of the throne in the name of Biomechanics.

It is indeed an accurate and descriptive title which Meyerhold has given to his method, and though one may not care to follow him all the way into the paths of behaviorism, it must nevertheless be admitted that the changes he has made in the course of the actor's art are in a forward direction. They are, as a matter of fact, so violently in a forward direction that it may be necessary for the next great leader who arises to lead them back a bit to set their feet on the true path.

A glimpse of the basis of training in this new method will serve to illustrate its radical departures from tradition. Biomechanical actors, men and women alike, are taught, first of all, to box; for Meyerhold sees the problems of a play as closely akin to those of a boxing match with its firmness of stance, its alertness, its exchange of blows, the continuous physical give and take, clean cut and accurately timed. Many traces of this type of training are to be found in the carriage of the actors, particularly in the classes devoted to exercises in Biomechanics as such. They stand with feet planted solidly, toes in and knees bent; their heads are generally forward and their shoulders up; the arms are bent either with open hands or clenched fists. This attitude, like an animal about to pounce on its foe, can almost be said to be typical.

There is also at times something of that fine relaxation which belongs to animals unannoyed by the inhibiting complications of higher intellectual processes and able to concentrate their muscular energy where they need it. This is especially evident in the supple knees and ankles of the actors and the loping ease of their stride. Some of the exercises are made up solely of variations in this stride and the ability to come to a complete halt easily and quickly on signal. Other exercises lean more heavily toward acrobatics, as when upon a given signal during the course of their march around the room, all the lighter members of the class leap lightly and without apparent effort upon the backs of their co-workers without pause and proceed to execute certain variations of balance while poised upon their shoulders. It is very similar to the routine work of the "understanders" and "top-mounters" of vaudeville tumblers and yet with the fundamental difference that here the tricks are not ends in themselves but are in a way — not always obvious to the observer but certainly so to the director and the participating actors — related to life.

Certain other exercises take a less abstract approach and are almost pantomimic. For example, there is one in which a man stealthily pursues a woman with an imaginary knife in hand; he stabs her, she falls, he lifts her rigid body to his back and carries her away. This is performed under the same muscular basis as the more frankly gymnastic exercises, and is based on no emotional premises whatever. It is interesting to observe, however, that emotional colors inevitably develop of themselves during the progress of the exercises.

All of these maneuvers are accompanied by music which serves to set the tempo and perhaps to a certain extent to suggest phrasing and accent, but most of all apparently to provide a continuous background of nervous stimulation. Each exercise is started by a signal from all the participants so that they may work in unison. This signal consists of a sudden bending of the knees followed immediately by two rapid and vigorous clappings of the hands with a violent downward movement as they separate.

The variety of the exercises in this class, their strenuousness and the agility with which they are performed, constitute something strangely off the beaten track in dramatic education. In addition, there are also classes in floor gymnastics and ballet dancing, the latter solely for the strengthening and development of the legs. Presumably, also, there are lessons in voice and speech, but these are not in any way extraordinary.

The theory of Biomechanics is apparently as much a manifestation of the religious, social, and political life of present day revolutionary Russia (at least insofar as it may be judged accurately from beyond its borders) as the theory of Stanislavsky was of the Russia of thirty years ago with its mysticism, its frustration, its suppressions. If God has been read out of the Soviet code as a nebulous ecclesiastic symbol, so the human soul, upon which Stanislavsky posited his method of acting, has been uprooted and cast out as an element in Meyerhold's. Surely, no matter how devout one

"Horses." In the upper photograph, the riders leap onto the horses. In the lower photograph, the riders are demonstrating one of the variants of the exercise. Exercises such as this were designed to train the actors in balance under varying conditions. They also provided training in coordinating movements in a group.

may be, the nominal godlessness of professed atheism is a step in advance of the abject superstitious enslavement to an erroneous conception of deity which belonged to the corrupt church of the old Russia; and in a like manner the emancipation of the actor from the bondage to his emotions (and this is roughly speaking what Stanislavsky meant by the soul) is a happy release, even if nothing has been supplied to take its place except a similar bondage to his nerves. This is a healthier, a more objective way of working than the introspective obsession with affective memory which has sent Stanislavsky's finest actor, Leonidov, three times to the insane asylum.

To enter into a detailed analysis of Biomechanics is straightaway to involve oneself in half a dozen other subjects, for it is based on an utterly different concept of life than we are accustomed to consider. Religion, political and economic doctrines and practices, social conduct, and philosophy all are implicated. It is likewise a grave temptation to draw from this single, perhaps detached, example of Russian thinking conclusions about the whole agitated Russian question. One must tread warily, therefore, unless one would call down the wrath of the experts in these particular fields.

To be as general as may be, then, Biomechanics is built on the premise that life is an entirely physiological condition and accordingly man is simply an animal a little more highly developed in certain directions than some other animals. His contact with the outside world is maintained through the elaborate mechanism of the nervous system which reacts automatically to external influences. All of what we are prone to consider his emotional life, all of what yesterday was thought to be the center and core of man, his immortal soul, is merely the aggregation of these impressions of the nervous system, just as the feeling of pain, to use an elementary illustration, is the result perhaps of pricking the finger. This is to state the situation very crudely, but clearly enough at any rate to make apparent the breadth of the chasm between the old method and the new.

The actor trained under this system does not learn to feel the life about him, but to see and touch it; he does not go about as his predecessors did seeking emotional experiences to store away against a future need, he bends all his labors to keeping his body alert and agile and his nervous responses keen. To this end he must undergo something of the rigid training of the athlete and above all he is forbidden to use alcohol or drugs that tend to deaden the nerves. If by some chance there should be an actor so out of step with his colleagues and countrymen as to resent being considered as an animal or a mechanism, he can console himself with the realization of how much better off he is than if he were subjected to the dangerous practice of autohypnosis which would otherwise have been his technical method.

Naturally enough, Meyerhold claims a nearer kinship to Delsarte than to Stanislavsky, from whose company he separated himself in disagreement many years ago. Delsarte was concerned with the outward sign rather than the inward urge and hence is more sympathetic to one who rejects the inward urge as a false and deleterious medium. But the magnitude of Stanislavsky's contribution to the actor's art was too great to be destroyed even by an antithetical force as strong as Meyerhold's, and in the Biomechanics we find some of the finest features of Stanislavsky's method firmly entrenched. For one thing, the importance of interplay between actors, which was one of Stanislavsky's strongest points, is as heavily stressed by Meyerhold. If he procures his results through the entirely external device of teaching them to box, it is a difference of detail but not of principle.

For another example, and a more important one: Stanislavsky tells us in his autobiography of his struggle to arrive at some definite means to retain the freshness of his acting after many repetitions. He wanted to give to each performance the character of genuine creativeness instead of merely repeating night after night what he had done before. This he accomplished magnificently, though at considerable cost to the actor, by substituting for the particular situation pictured by the author a similar experience which he had actually gone through. He did not attempt to recall and imitate the effect of this experience but to reproduce in memory the cause and let the effect follow of itself. Thus the performance was actually created anew nightly in the presence of the audience and to them it appeared to grow from the situation evolved by the author. In Biomechanics subjective feeling is taboo, the nucleus of expressing being the action and reaction of nerves and muscles. But the actor creates in the presence of the audience just as he does under Stanislavsky's method, for the reactions of nerves and muscles are equally the spontaneous outgrowth of objective stimuli, the only difference being that in this case the stimuli are physical instead of mental.

In this respect, Biomechanics is nearer to Stanislavsky than to Delsarte. It is true that Delsarte dealt with externals much as Meyerhold does, but with a difference. He had studied and tabulated an almost unbelievable number of gestures with their corresponding meanings observed from life, and these he applied simply as effects. He did not bother about recreating their causes at each performance. He did believe, however, that all gestures — and in this category may be included all external action — came from internal mental and emotional as well as external physical causes; and on this point Meyerhold and the behaviorists would probably be in disagreement with him. On the other hand, while Meyerhold in his Biomechanics deals primarily with physical actions and does not concede that they have any emotional reactions, he nevertheless supplies them with sources outside themselves so that they are not merely so many dead, stereotyped motions. These outside sources may be physical objects such as scenery and properties, they may be lines of the play, they may be other actors and their manner of carrying on.

Thus the stage belongs to the actor (as it does also with Stanislavsky) and if anything can be altered to the advantage of the actor, whether it is the set, the costumes, or even the play itself, it is sacrificed wholeheartedly. Indeed, the actor is more dependent upon his surroundings in this system than in any other, and is able in return to make the stage and decor play a more vital part than they are generally able to do. Hence the great variety in the mounting of the plays of the Meyerhold repertory is not only for the effect upon the audience, as with Expressionism, Constructivism and what not, but is also for the assistance to the actor.

[Reprinted from John Martin, "How Meyerhold Trains His Actors," *Theatre Guild Magazine* (November 1930), pp. 26–30.]

BIOMECHANICS IN MEYERHOLD'S THEATRE
by André Van Gyseghem

André Van Gyseghem's account is probably the most detailed and objective description of a Biomechanics session to be written by a foreign observer. Just twenty-seven years old when he first visited the Soviet Union in 1933, Van Gyseghem was the producer/director of London's left-wing Embassy Theatre. Searching for new sources of training for the British political stage, he frequented the rehearsals of all the major Moscow theatres, finally apprenticing at Nikolai Okhlopkov's Realistic Theatre.

Let us go along to the Biomechanics class one morning at ten o'clock.... At this time of the day, the long foyer around which the audience patrols in the evening before a play begins, is turned into a gymnasium. Chairs are cleared to the walls, and down the center are a series of mattresses such as are used in any school gymnasium. We are in the first course, so there are about thirty students—in the advanced course there are less. It is interesting to note that the predominance of girls from which every dramatic school in England suffers does not exist here: there are an almost equal number of boys and girls. Their ages vary from about seventeen to twenty-one or twenty-two, and they are a pretty average bunch of youngsters, healthy, animated, and varying in origin from the Mongol to the White Russian, with a French boy and an American girl thrown in to give it an international flavor....

The morning's session consists of a carefully graded series of physical culture exercises very similar to those taught in our ordinary schools, leading up to incredible acrobatics, jumping and somersaults which everyone enjoys enormously. Then follows an exercise in Biomechanics. These exercises consist of a number of prescribed movements in a certain sequence which tell a simple action-story: "Throwing the Stone," "The Dagger," "Bow and Arrow," etc., etc. Into these exercises are incorporated all the elements of stage movement and mind-state which Meyerhold demands of every actor in his theatre. The actor must be able to use his whole body as an instrument to play upon. His mind and body must be in complete harmony. What he understands with his mind he must be able to express with the movement or non-movement of his body. . . .

The whole technique of Biomechanics lies in the careful study of the time of *preparation* for a certain action: of the emotional and physical state of the moment of *action itself*: and the resulting anti-climax of *reaction*. On this Meyerhold has said that an actor should be trained, and on the conscious use of these three states or conditions he builds up his whole production. Naturally one of the basic laws for such a training is the law of balance.

Thus it is plain that the actor must be at the same time the organizer and the organized.

Biomechanics teaches the actor to use the space about him on the stage three-dimensionally, as a definite measurable commodity. Just as his feet measure distances on the floor of the stage as he walks, so the rest of his body is made to use the air about him for a specific effect. Through exercises he is taught to achieve the feeling of the place of the actor in space, time and rhythm. But more important still, he is taught how to coordinate his own body with other people on the stage, with the properties he handles and the scenery he is acting against so that he becomes a plastic part of a harmonious whole.

On the correct position of the body depends the correct quality of the sound which accompanies it (word, cry, shout, sentence, a laugh, etc.), and therefore all the movements in the exercises are based on the principle of the static position of the body in space. Let us take as an example the exercise "Throwing the Stone," and carefully enumerate each movement as it develops into the next.

1. *To concentrate the attention of the pupil*—the hands are clapped twice together in a downward movement, the arms hanging loosely.

2. *Preparing to run*—with a jump, turn and face the right, landing with the left foot in front.

3. *Preparing to run*—knees bent, right hand in front, left hand behind.

4. *Running*.

5. *To arrive where the stone lies*—stop running with a jump, landing on the left foot and with the left shoulder in front.

6. *Return to normal position.*

7. *Prepare to get the stone*—rise on the toes and drop onto the right knee. Lean the body backward and then forward.

8. *Lifting the stone*—pick up the imaginary stone with the right hand, rise, swing the right arm round in a wide circle—swing it round to the left—front and back again to behind the body, where it hangs. The left shoulder is high, the right low, the right hand at about knee level. The knees are slightly bent.

9. *Preparing to run with the stone*—move backward a few steps.

10. *Running with the stone*—the stone still in the right hand held behind the body, left shoulder being raised.

11. *Arriving at the place from which to throw*—stop running, always with a slight jump, landing with the left foot in front.

12. *Preparing to throw the stone*—swing the stone over to the left front and grip the right wrist with the left hand.

13. *Swinging the stone*—swing the body weight on to the right foot—sweep the right arm back and swing it in a circular motion, still clasped by the left hand. Release the left hand and the circle widens until the whole right arm is swinging in a huge circle from the shoulder.

14. *Looking for the object to be hit*—the circular movement stops, the right arm (and stone) held out in front while the student looks.

15. *Rejudging the distance*—run a few steps forward, jump and stop.

16. *Preparing to throw*—swing the stone back, and the right leg.

17. *Throwing*—swing the right arm forward and the left back.

18. *What is the result? Preparation*—kneel on the right knee, clasp the hands and listen with the right hand cupping the ear.

19. *The mark is hit*—point forward with the left arm, lean back with the right arm on the right hip.

20. *Finish*—rise, facing inward and clap twice as at the beginning.

It is difficult to give a clear picture of such physical exercises with the written word, and the explanatory sentences are only for the dancer or gymnast who has a technical knowledge which will make it easy for him to visualize each position and movement from the description, but the lay reader, simply from the numbered headings, can get a certain impression. This impression must be one of careful and gradual control—of preparation and action—preparation and action—of a rigid disciplining of emotion, until all chance of spontaneous and disruptive movement is entirely abolished. If he receives this feeling then he is nearer to understanding the essential quality of a theatre of convention.

[Reprinted from André Van Gyseghem, *Theatre in Soviet Russia* (London: Faber & Faber, 1943), pp. 27-30.]

Notes on Biomechanics
by Lee Strasberg

Long a disciple of Stanislavsky and Vakhtangov, Strasberg nevertheless felt a strong affiliation with Meyerhold as a director and actor. Stylization and theatricality, Strasberg believed, were not antagonistic to Stanislavsky's training. And in some ways, Meyerhold, as a student of Stanislavsky before 1905, could be thought of as an unconscious follower of Stanislavsky. Conversely, Strasberg was baffled by Meyerhold's notion of actor training. These clear and well-preserved notes of a lecture on May 11, 1934, by Nikolai Kustov, a teacher of Biomechanics at Meyerhold's theatre, testify to Strasberg's fairmindedness and objectivity in attempting to understand Biomechanics.

Chief characteristic of Meyerhold's school—subordinated to mathematics and mechanics.

* * *

In order that the actor be the most expressive means in the theatre—necessary to know everything connected with it—actor must be very vivid, lively and possess many means of expression.

* * *

Since we demand as much from the actor it was necessary to create some theory for his training—and Meyerhold took Pavlov's reflex system.

* * *

Meyerhold builds all his productions musically—these things made him create a school for training the actor.
Besides, the actor comes to the theatre with his own habits of life which have nothing to do with the theatre. And since he has those habits he sometimes loses his talent he has by nature.

* * *

Taylorism is taken as a basis for work. In this school we try to find the mechanical movements which should educate the actor.

* * *

There are elements of Kabuki, Commedia dell'arte, Shakesperean theatre in Biomechanics.
The main difference between classic movement and Biomechanics is that the latter uses knees as base (as in the Japanese theatre).

* * *

Chief means to make actor expressive is to get him away from everyday troubles.

* * *

We try to find out and reveal and build the laws of scenic time and space.

* * *

In so far as this is our aim, it is necessary that the body is able to find its place in rhythmic time and space.
1. The first rule is finding the center of balance.
2. The second task to keep (have) the body in a certain expressive position within a space.

* * *

Taking as a basis these correct movements we begin to teach the actor how to think correctly. After the actor has learned the movements we ask him to direct his mind toward the *theme* of the étude.

* * *

Besides the above-mentioned it is necessary that the artist also have temperament.

* * *

In connection with the reflexes [the actor] begins to feel the experience. So the correct and natural movement already opens the way for emotion.

* * *

Some artists, despite the fact that they know all the rules, remain cold — and then we find the correct way in music.

238 *Documents*

* * *

Music is built not on the basis of rhythmic movement but on the basis of [the actor's] emotional experience.

* * *

The basic rules for [the actor's] emotion and general activity are coordinations of his movements of hands, head, stage, etc.
The basis for mastership of coordination are polyphony and counterpoint, sound and movement, sound and movement and thought.
The main feature of actor's work is exactness — not more, not less than necessary.

[Lee Strasberg's notes were first published in a slightly different order in *The Drama Review* vol. 17, no. 1 (March 1973), pp. 110–112.]

NOTES ON EISENSTEIN'S LECTURES, 1934
by Marie Seton

Later to become Eisenstein's first biographer, Marie Seton first met the film director in Moscow at the beginning of August 1932. Depressed over the fiasco of his film Que Viva Mexico, *Eisenstein confided in Seton and invited her to the special lectures given at the Moscow Institute of Cinematography.*

For two years, Seton acted as a conduit for Eisenstein and his Western devotees, bringing him clothing and books. In October–November 1934, she attended Eisenstein's master course in cinema direction. The abridged version of her notes published for the first time here reveals once again Eisenstein's ongoing interest in Meyerhold and Expressive Movement in the theatre.

October 16:

Technique of Movement — Each individual instance of movement is regulated by its own logic — The students must develop the ideas which Eisenstein gives them.

Man and his superhuman actions — animal fear (Civil War) and class purpose — e.g., the elephant and the little dog — self-preservation and the hunting instinct.

Man composed of two elements, fear and purpose, the conscious and the unconscious—

STUDENT: Which is the dynamic?

100 percent of each and the crossing of elements—e.g., the bell which signifies the end of the lesson and the pleasure derived from the sound—

There are no static laws—A broken line in walking does not necessarily mean temperament—How emotion is expressed in movement—Characteristic walk—Instincts, the whole body—The conscious, the different parts of the body—The blurred picture analyzed—

Expression—of being repelled (previous notes)—The expression will differ with the social origin—and again the motives change—process repeats the development—instinctive without direction—If you operate on a woman at the seventh month there will be a total veinlike reaction of the whole body—

The simplest movement, the springing of the tiger reveals two motives, the animal psychology and the material weight of the animal. Evaluation of this movement through the ages has made it into a beautiful movement—To jump one line, to turn round the second—utilitarian and mechanical movements—The psychological cause comes from a single cause, the movements in contradiction—

When you pass to the human stage, thought enters—Man knows that something will happen—reaction-contradiction to impulse. The fulfilling of a double function—Which dominates? The emphasis may be on the instinctive, but that depends upon the subject and the objective and that which dominates at that particular moment. Snake causes a physiological fear—a bomb the psychological—the mind—the biting of the lip—either having said something or else holding something back. The back-forward movement in order not to express too much—the mind dominating the impulse.

Reaction and tempo.

Whether panical or rational will dominate—the same power may be pure instinct, or it may turn to the rational. Move in one or the other way—the same cause will feed both.

How to distribute power—whether it is instinctive or rational—The difference between the word and the movement—Words and intonations are the highest expression of an expressive movement—

Assembling of parts—the distribution of movement—one word or a whole phrase—sometimes the movement comes first, then the word or vice versa, or both simultaneously—A dull person makes the movement and then the word—the man with temperament the word and gesture together—it corresponds to character.

The character of facial expression—

October 19:

Basic English—it is like every movement, it can be expressed in a simple way, and as we try to explain all the simple actions from this movement so we try to do the same thing with language. We are trying to convert the logical formula into the formula of feeling—a combination of different parts (montage)—changing a complicated form into a simple form—basic English helps the development of thoughts. You learn the most complicated words first, not the first necessary words.

(The STUDENTS argue for and against the method and there are more cons than pros.)

GRAPHICS CLASSES—they must attend because without them the students can only make the most primitive drawings—They must understand perspective—Again the students argue the point—they are in a hurry to get to their practical work after January—therefore they want to miss this department.

EISENSTEIN then argues that they will have to rely upon painters and artists for their designs—And only a few understand the medium of film composition—Many can design a set on paper, but they cannot fit it together for practical use. One artist-designer, a follower of the naturalists, could not have his designs adapted for use. *Scenery* must be constructed in such a way that the *regisseur* can take it from every angle—*In the theatre the scenery is not so dynamic* as in the cinema. By that, he means that the scenery can be reassembled and taken at any moment from any angle—THE CONVENTIONAL [STYLIZED] THEATRE has certain characteristics in common with film—the close-up of a symbolic object—

Plan the mise en scène—The trial of the executioners of Pancho Villa's men—the dead as jury (*Viva Villa!*)—*the planning of the movement is more important than the perspective*—central Mexican plateau with hills, prairie, and maguey—the cubic houses—costume—work out color scheme—like different geometric forms—FREEDOM OF CHOICE IN DETAIL—Approach from the point of view of compositions not naturalism—There they have seven or eight elements—Don't invent any unnecessary elements, for the plan must be interesting because of its *composition*.

The general plan, the composition of the frame.

Sometimes in the newspapers there are published pictures which call forth entirely wrong impressions—(the worker finishing a wall and looks like a bomb-thrower)—the same occurs in the cinema—We don't only use the movement of the figure, but the figure in relation to the whole—*the position of the figure is as important as the movement*—

The praying woman who can look as if she is knocking nails into the wall — Don't use corners — the decisive position of the figure — the dynamic knitting the whole movement together — *Artistic composition is sometimes harmful* — e.g., the scientific film of horse disease — the impression on the peasant, you cure your horse and he will disappear into the fields — the shot introduced for variation.

Every expressive movement is a conflict between the immediate reaction and the rationalized reaction.

On the stage conflicting tendencies are performed by parts of the body selected by the actor — The question as to whether the actor must feel the fear expressed — where does the fear come from?

IF HE REALLY FEELS FEAR WHY DOES HE NOT RUN OFF THE STAGE — the external and internal theories (Meyerhold and Stanislavsky).

What must the producer [director] show? What must the actor show upon the stage? The actor feels himself as a single unit, the producer has to feel the whole. The producer cannot be the actor, nor the actor the producer — We can consider it from the point of view of the actor or from the point of view of the producer.

The Feeling and the Technique — The Combination STANISLAVSKY — primitively understood, it is that the actor must feel in the right way.

MEYERHOLD — knowledge and technique of the expressive movements — Biomechanics (Meyerhold told Eisenstein recently that there had been no progress since 1921). These theories of expressive movement have worked out so well that perhaps nothing more is necessary.

CHEKHOV and VAKHTANGOV endeavored to embody the mood with the technical form.

Though Meyerhold talks of the external basis of his work he has all the feeling — *internal as well as external technique is the secret of both masters — Both schools have the same elements and they stress them according to their philosophy which has been derived from the social factors of their upbringing* —

Their theories are often repeated parrot-like, the words, by people, one-sided people, who murder the theory — THE KAMERNY THEATRE only interested in the form.

Both theories date back before the Revolution and reflect the contradictions of the period — the same thing has happened in the cinema — Both theories reflect *part* of the total bourgeois tendency (Odessa notes).

Stanislavsky — the merchant with the shop full of actual wares —
Meyerhold — selling by check —
Dead Souls is the first struggle for trade —
The details of the MOSCOW ART THEATRE are connected with the

living surroundings of the bourgeoisie—property of the bourgeoisie, the merchant who in his leisure uses his thoughts—

CONVENTIONAL theatre showed only the symbol—a single arch for the whole cathedral—Sometimes the productions of the ART THEATRE have no definite form—so long as there is the right expression in the eyes the body can be held in any position!

JEWISH THEATRE—Emotions as such play no part, but the best of the artists there work upon the two principles of feeling and form.

VAKHTANGOV—took the middle way.... The question is whether Vakhtangov really achieved the synthetic form ... viewed the future of the theatre, but he had no basic.... The social factors of that time were too great for him.... Today we can speak of SOCIALIST REALISM ... which was impossible in 1922.

Vakhtangov's thoughts were logical and he was a success because he created an eclectic performance—the grotesque as a style is a combination of naturalism and the conventional—*Turandot*—

Before the Revolution there were some grotesque tendencies—Today everything is changed—Constructivism has got into the Maly Theatre and *The Lady of the Camellias* has got into the theatre of Meyerhold—

There are no typical features—for everyone wants to protect themselves against attacks—The Theatre of the Revolution uses real wood and the Art Theatre changes the set when it is not necessary.

After the Revolution the theatre was interested, or rather the audience, in seeing real things on the stage—the camel and the tractor—Now an educated audience can no longer abide that—therefore eclecticism has arrived as an escape from criticism.

The Theories of Three Periods

Mechanical combination—The mixing of elements—From which must emerge the natural combination—THE CINEMA—

In the cinema actors must have an ideal technique—Socialist Realism also has come into the film and it is good for the natural development of the art—If it is put together eclectically it will not be a success. In the theatre there is much scientific research—Synthesis is not the absolute truth but it is the main basis of our work.

Some people believe that Eisenstein is in the anti-e [...] group, but having collected all his experience together he is[...]. Stanislavsky and Meyerhold are developments of the same p[...].

Then compare with Marx—first two elements denying another—the third a synthesis of both.

October 22:

Necessary combination—the same principle is . . . naturalistic and conventional theatres. The synthetic [theatre] composes both elements equally.
OKHLOPKOV—
Marx said [large fragment missing]
Ten years afterwards Okhlopkov represents the first ideas.
EISENSTEIN and PROLETKULT—
There was a tendency to step out of the limits of the theatre, *a tendency towards the cinema*, as for instance, *producing a play in a factory*—the logical step in order to show the factory, in the cinema, *Strike*—On the stage there appeared real camels and tractors—
Influence of the cinema introduced by AKIMOV—
BIOMECHANICS—not only movement for the stage, but generally supposed to be the element of real life—
Slogan of the Constructivists: *"The set must be a machine on which the actor is working."*—The aim of this machine is to give the actor a chance to show off all his talents.
The first stage was a single wire—the elimination of everything that was not absolutely necessary. The second stage, the introduction of scenery, more wire than is absolutely necessary for the action on the stage. Sometimes *regisseurs* introduced (*The Dawns*) news from the front.
OKHLOPKOV is conservative in that he repeats the traditions—In the early days agitprop brigades asked factory workers to see performances—in his theatre they are invited to the theatre. Not all of the elements of the old theatre are charming.
MEYERHOLD was influenced by cinema montage—in the Theatre of the Revolution—*Lake Lyul*. Another example: EISENSTEIN's *The Wiseman* at the Proletkult. In the Proletkult a struggle between workers and Fascists was carried into the audience, they had a fight near the ceiling.
PUDOVKIN's montage is emotional montage.
Many people don't know the theatrical history of this period—At the Proletkult they had 250 seats under which were fixed shooting machines—They built bridges above the public (it is repeated in *The Rout* [*Flight* by Stavsky]) and bicycles. Do you realize that all the people with whom we worked are still alive?
Today the theatre has an entirely different character. *The necessity to express such things has become an external reality in the demonstrations*, so that the old mass performances of the Winter Palace are now expressed in demonstration or in the Park of Culture and Rest.
One line of the tendency to break the limits of the stage demonstrations, the other the cinema—

244 *Documents*

The Cinema was not beyond the limits of art—

Eisenstein tells of these things not as an historian but as a participant. This tendency of experiment in extremity only remains intact in the Krasnaya Presnya Theatre [Realistic Theatre], Okhlopkov—*The Iron Flood*. Inevitably the next period would be that the actor would steal from the spectator!

A STUDENT: Why do you go back into the theatre?

EISENSTEIN: The cinema has assumed two elements of the theatre, the line of montage and typage. These are not the sole elements of the theatre—actors, words and sounds were never so completely assimilated by the cinema, for a special cinema actor has not been created though roles are so often played by theatre actors. . . .

The theatrical performance in the cinema—nothing. Montage and mise en scène are entirely separate in conception—the tracing of the line is different, though *both typage and montage were first created in the theatre*. We can't yet see the difference in dialog.

COMMEDIA DELL'ARTE—the origin of both in the mask. But the eight or ten masks of the theatre have been replaced by hundreds of faces in the cinema. *Strike* expressed the straight transference.

The masks of Commedia dell'arte are conventional and traditional, but typage neither one nor the other. Typage is synthetic—for example, the Menshevik in *October* has all the characteristics, he is biologically and emotionally a synthesis. The complexity of physiognomy, of the physical type, from that point of view typage is not conventional, human beings—realistic tendency though not naturalistic. The choice of the most typical, those people with the synthetic features of all. The same elements are found in Commedia dell'arte, but there they are worked out through traditions—the Doctor is composed of the types of every Italian university, while the Captain is the figure evolved from the history of Italy's struggle for freedom from Spain. *Commedia dell'arte is an expression of collective work through many years*. . . .

Expressive movement is life. In real life we have an emotion which we express in some way—these are the laws of expression in actual life. On the stage we have no real emotional conditions—for example, the fleeing from fear—there is no real fire. Then how can we get the real expression on the stage? On the stage the technique must be the same as in real life, a combination of the physical and emotional.

October 24th:

That an actor or acting gives an impression of compact thoughts, and that the process of acting at the end should embody certain aims. Two moments: the entrance onto the stage and a certain principle. Certain gestures have a purpose. In order to reach his aim, the actor should pass through several stages of development. The impression made upon the audience by certain gestures is so impressive that the audience will always remember it.

Meyerhold's performances in parts are very good, but as complete composition they are not smooth. This is one of the main faults of his theatre as a whole. This is due to the fact that many of his productions are so acutely visual that they give a sharp and irritating impression to the spectator. In his production of *The Wiseman* [M.S. has in mind *The Magnanimous Cuckold*], it was so timed that each movement was fitted into a time sheet. When there are half-hours in which the movement sags it is like the inefficiency of some Moscow cinemas where the film breaks and there are interruptions.

Synthetic Art

Some actors before the Revolution were popular because they played negative roles. For example, *The Bells* and its impression—the Irving/Martin Harvey role—here is the scheme of the actor and creative enthusiasm. The entirely Left Theatre (this is in style not politics) thinks of the looks and then fits the body to the appearance. The Right Theatre (in style not politics), the Art Theatre does the very opposite, disregarding the outward appearance.

When you only have the *result* you arrive at schematicism, for example, the younger and less cultured actors of Meyerhold's theatre. The necessary process of building in any theatre must be visual. The feeling for art is the process by which the result is achieved. The division between the actor and the producer (big masters of the past omitted to show the part played by the producer).

The round table method of the Art Theatre (They sat around the table and imagined the character they were going to play in every possible situation not included in the play—M.S.) The table method divided a play and a part into small pieces. It was too mental and only internal. The actor must get his movements from his mind and his body. In the creative work they do, the actors must use the experience of mankind through the ages. When they think of something their whole body must take part. This is what the actors of the Art Theatre don't realize although they use the stage, but only as the mise en scène for the single group of people on the stage. That is a system of reduction which becomes pathological, as in the case of Leonidov which manifests itself in a fear of the stage. He is afraid to move, and left alone on the stage he does not organize his movements. There is competition between Kachalov and Leonidov when they play the same parts. (This interchange of parts is characteristic of many Moscow theatres.)

The system of education in the Art Theatre encouraged the pathological elements in their natures, particularly in Leonidov. (It is interesting to know that before and even during the War the Art Theatre was steeped in various schools of mysticism, notably that of Sulerzhitsky, an associate of Tolstoy.) Naturally in some Art Theatre actors we do not find anything pathological. The dreaming and feeling methods of the Art Theatre bring about a psychological change in the actors.

In order to find the exact expression on the stage, the actor must know the complete scale of technique. Then you can invent much more interesting movements than if you sit around a table. Sometimes it is impossible for Glizer (She is a leading actress of the Theatre of the Revolution and lived in the apartment next to Eisenstein.) to find the right intonation until she has run about the stage. If you are working on the stage then you get the natural theatre intonation. When you are alone your behavior is quite different than when you are working with actors on the stage. You cannot solve the use of the stage without actively using the space. When you are completely skilled you can sit and think out the movements on the stage (Eisenstein did this in the case of a play by [Natan] Zarkhi which he never produced in the end.), but this is different than the Art Theatre method of contemplation.

Everything can be performed on a different scale: the Japanese painter with his grain of rice, the curtain for *Prince Igor*, the enlargement of Palekh boxes (a certain school of peasant painting). Meyerhold in 1924 was going to produce *Boris Godunov* at the Vakhtangov. They were very suspicious that he would miss something. When Godunov's mistress did not move off the stage, they asked him what he was doing, and Meyerhold answered: "But they live together!"

Now there is the problem of suggestion. Some producers will not take suggestions. Even foolish suggestions may contain a germ of positiveness, and that is what you must extract. When a director cannot incorporate ideas into his plan, then it is a sign of limitation. But the director who takes everything from others is as bad as the man who rejects everything. Actors are very satisfied to have their ideas incorporated.

Typage in the cinema. During that period those types had to do what they did in real life. Natural defects which are simply recorded, and social color by juxtaposition. The same elements were introduced into the theatre — Types. Had to deal with unskilled actors and utilize their natural elements.

It was almost the same thing in the theatre. (In *The Wiseman*, an Ostrovsky play produced by Eisenstein in 1922), the scene in which one character steals a notebook from another character. It was treated as a detective story—the thief was walking on the tightrope (Eisenstein introduced many circus tricks.) and talking to the aunt of the other character, from whom the book had been stolen. The tightrope gave an impression of being in a difficult position, for if you walk quietly on the stage there is no tension. This was convincing in the physical sense although mechanistic. It was a kind of montage of the text. The end of *Battleship Potemkin* on the other hand was in the tempo of the end of traditional American pictures, the rhythm of galloping going after the suffering heroine.

There are two elements of montage: the physical action and the dialogue. The tension spreads an atmosphere over the whole scene. The whole performance of *The Wiseman* was based upon the same principle.

When Meyerhold worked with Stanislavsky (at the beginning of this century) he could not get a sentence which he had to speak. They told him to pick up a match from the floor and that action was the beginning of two lines in the theatre—the real properties and future Meyerhold who thought that every emotion was to be expressed in movement. That match was the origin of activity on the stage. The actors of Meyerhold's theatre are always doing things. Every scene is based upon some action, while the atmosphere of the nineteenth century is introduced by many utensils. All these occupations are the children and the grandchildren of the match.

The same fact can be used in different ways. In the Art Theatre the washing of plates constitutes environment; in the theatre of Meyerhold it is a basis for dialogue. On the other hand, I introduced action in *The Wiseman* which could not happen in any circumstances—the third way of the match. The reality of this fact of taking a match influences your expression of this act. Equally the wire (tightrope) in *The Wiseman* influenced the whole scene.

The reality of tension. What is the reality? What role does it play for every actor? The reality of the actor's performance calls forth different associations in him and helps him. In Biomechanics (Meyerhold's method) you work with a physically heavy thing and it helps the actor to feel his role. Through the action you come to the performance of the role. The whole process need not be shown on the stage for the audience will trust the actor in the conversion.

That is the solving of the problem which the actor must feel on the stage. If he feels one element it will so influence the audience that everything will assume a dynamic actuality. Feeling for the actor depends upon his temperament. The artist must be infatuated with his work so that he has the necessary tension. You must take a single element which calls forth everything.

Though I give you all the theoretical elements it is for you to find the technique of work.

October 25:

...When we speak about the feelings we have to take into consideration: the necessity of possessing emotions. Without them you can create nothing. The artist must be infatuated with the subject, ideas, and emotions which are within it—the most important and the most decisive moments.

THEATRICAL SYSTEMS—
STANISLAVSKY is only concerned with the first of the two elements, MEYERHOLD and the conventional theatre only with the second, the composition. The best representatives of both systems have both elements, though they stress only one of them. STANISLAVSKY, CHEKHOV and MOSKVIN saw that the explosion had to be expressed in a perfect form. MEYERHOLD, in the process of finding the form, came to the emotional explosion. The Art Theatre worked upon the first, the Art Theatre teaches you how to concentrate—*isolation from the public*—the streetcar—*effective remembrance*.

The Art Theatre method has good and healthy roots, but there are the elements of endless dreaming and fantasy—instead of concentrating upon the elements of this room some of the followers think of the next and the next. *The work of preparation is spread over too many things*. The Conventional Theatre, the theatre of composition—The actors of Meyerhold complain that they are taught to do things which they don't feel—Meyerhold's actors say that they are empty. One of the actors of the Theatre of the Revolution told me that Meyerhold says, say "mother" louder; the Art Theatre says, say the word as if the mother is a very long way off.

If Biomechanics are thought of seriously, the method presupposed the existence of feeling. The absolutely right tendency will combine these systems. The Art Theatre system cannot be free from pathological elements because they escape from reality into endless dreams—There are, though, many positive elements. The complete process of creation cannot divorce thought from form.

In actuality, in the Art Theatre there is at one and the same time concentration and the spreading out of consciousness—the case of [Mikhail] Chekhov noticing Eisenstein's boots. When Eisenstein produced *The*

Wiseman he could judge how the acrobats had spent their previous day. The performance is the same psychological process performed in a certain period of time — the subjected essence of everything. But at the same time you must have a form in which the emotions can be expressed. In boxing there are moments in which you hate your opponent — you must hate him in order to beat him.

Movements and form must be definite. Catch what is expressive in experience so that when you are inspired you can select that which is essential. The actor must always be enriched by the *regisseur*—that is, in the technical form. If you have chosen a corresponding form the audience will reflect it; if it is out of harmony the audience will not receive the same emotion. The form must correspond to the general laws of behavior, so that it will emerge in the reaction of the audience. We have on the stage the same laws as there are in life — A magnification of reality upon the stage which appeals to the audience.

October 28:

Daydreams — those in which one plans one's career — There are two kinds of daydreams, one useless, the other useful. Those useless dreams have no basis in the past as in past experience and have no hope of a near future. But the useful kind is immediately linked with the problems in hand and is immediately applied, either in converting abstracts into the concrete, or else putting the concrete idea into action.

The Art Theatre neglect the whole field of dream, planning work and work only upon the material in front of them. The quality of accident always plays an important part — The one slow man whose name was known in *Potemkin*. The dreaming of the Stanislavsky system — the actors think of additional material. In order to find the right state of feeling for the role the feeling has to be repeated. They add any additional thing connected with the whole.

Thus a character enters a room, takes a glass of water and drinks it. In order to characterize that single moment, the actor concentrates upon the character in every circumstance of life, and having done so, gathers all the characteristic features together. The character is imagined in the street, in the theatre and at the horse races — the complete person through different images — A kind of hypnosis and it produces a certain rhythm. The rhythm of a drum induces a certain state of feeling — these dreams create feeling and imagination.

On one hand the Art Theatre has the concentration upon the character, and on the other hand they dwell on reality, the real things that they introduce onto the stage. Instead of introducing the most characteristic elements, they introduce all the lines in the restaurant or the antique shop. A myriad of elements contribute to the whole, but there is a contradiction. The detailed concentration upon the character conflicting with the ever-widening circle of concentration upon the extraneous elements of property. It is a very dangerous theory, for it can be developed beyond the limits of healthy reason. There are other actors—abroad—whose playing is based upon integral feelings. VALESKA GERT is the furthest development of this—She is incapable of repeating a section of her dance. She is the victim of ecstatic introspection.

To Meyerhold this state of feeling has no meaning, though he himself has the emotional basis. The actor must have the ability to get the right state of feeling without thinking of it and express it—by reflex, immediate reaction. There lies Meyerhold's mistake: he mixed up the function of the *regisseur* and the actor. Meyerhold stresses automatic imitation so that he doesn't develop the process of the evolution of the expressive movement.

The cause is individual as well as social. The Art Theatre will discuss a single point for twenty days. One of the most important things I have to do with you (the students) is to make you concentrate on the dominant elements and eliminate the subsidiary.

STUDENT: In the education of the actor, which one element is more dominant than the other, which element must you develop?

EISENSTEIN: Both—All actors must be masters of both kinds of technique. Both schools are one-sided and refuse to consider the elements of the other. In the school of Meyerhold the movement should call forth the corresponding emotions—*movements create a feeling* (exercise in the morning!)

Sometimes movement must be divorced from psychology and emotion, as in the ballet—the dancer would not be able to bear the double strain. The aim of ballet training is to devoid the movement of all emotion.

Now our aim is to create a synthetic school which must embody a natural combination. The whole is connected with dialectical materialism, two opposites coming together in a synthesis—Stanislavsky, anti–Stanislavsky: coming to the new period. *We must take what is essential from each* for today we can appreciate that which is essential. We should be happy that we come in this synthetic age and that we can create it in art. Sometimes the press is a contradiction: they say that the synthetic period is already reached. The fourth Five-Year Plan of the cinema—

CREATION—

There are two aspects in creation—recording emotions and feelings, sometimes we feel and then we record: the conventional [stylized] theatre. You put a gallows on the stage and you have to imagine the rest: the Japanese theatre. On the one hand you have primitive naturalism, on the other Constructivism and conventionalism. The ritualistic element, for instance: they have a naturalistic room, a door, and beyond there is a painted garden and a gold fish dancing in a pond. The strange combination, the limits of the combination—the Vakhtangov Theatre's *Turandot*—the eclectic combination.

The conventional theatre required from actors the movement which feels the stage—Kamerny, abstract. The Kamerny are changing on account of the capital earned by MOSPS [Theatre of the Moscow Oblast Council of Trade Unions], the stylization of MOSPS! They feel the audience with their voices, and so also the Jewish theatre. It is based upon the graphic.

There is the tendency of which Brecht was the leader, the intellectual theatre. The aim of this theatre is to teach the people—they are like Jesuits. From the moral preaching point of view, the school theatre, the didactic theatre—the theatre of the discussion between good and evil (*Saint Joan of the Stockyards*)—Weill and Eisler, emotional elements. Agitprop brigades did the same thing only not so aesthetically as the theatre of Brecht.

In the Greek theatre there were many emotions but emotions disappeared in the Middle Ages and the morality plays appeared. Why did this didactic theatre appear in Germany? In Germany there were many discussions of social problems; in 1923 we thought there would be the Revolution. But the revolutionaries became immersed in the abstract, the mystic Marxism—the psychoanalysis of Reich, his sexual and economic magazine. Those people finding themselves frustrated began discussing, and Brecht became characteristic of the German intellectuals of the last years.

Brecht proves that similar forms of art appear when there are similar social forces exercising an influence. His art is abstract, devoid of emotions, scholastic—it came after the defeat of the Revolution and it is a reflection of the abstract discussions. There is the problem whether actors must play the process or the result. The intellectual cinema has nothing to do with the scholastic theatre of Brecht.

November 1:

. . . There are two interesting points. Why do people go to the circus? Because the circus repeats our physical struggles, with animals, or with the

252   *Documents*

man and forty women (the harem). After the Revolution there was an effort to introduce sense into the circus, but it was without success. Balance is not a thing that can be altered by class consciousness; it is biological consciousness. The circus cannot be changed because it is biological.

A BIOMECHANICAL SESSION
by Harold Clurman

When Harold Clurman departed for Moscow on April 26, 1935, he carried with him a leather-bound book, a gift from his colleagues at the Group Theatre, in which to record his impressions of the Soviet theatre. During his five-week stay in Moscow, Clurman saw thirty-five theatrical productions and met virtually everyone of any importance in the Soviet cultural world. Among the entries he recorded, the notes of a visit to Meyerhold's theatre to observe a class in Biomechanics offer a brief but vivid response by a skeptical American director to Meyerhold's system of actor training.

One year after Clurman's visit to Moscow, the Actors' Committee of the Group Theatre submitted a reorganization plan. In its December 1936 report, the Committee suggested that Biomechanics be added to the training of the Stanislavsky-oriented Group actor. A two-hour-per-week course was placed on their roster. Exactly who would teach Biomechanics was unclear. In fact, no instructor was ever found, but the Group became the first professional theatre company in America even to consider such a program. The following is from Harold Clurman's 1935 Soviet Diary, published for the first time.

May 12, 1935: Got up early to meet Paul Strand. Looked forward to his arrival and was glad to have him in Moscow both because of our friendship and because he would have a word from the Group.... But after I met him and saw him to the hotel I had to rush off to a Biomechanics class at the Meyerhold Theatre. I had seen funny pictures and had heard abstruse explanations of the theory of Biomechanics, neither of which had interested me particularly. But this class, for which the teacher apologized continually, interested me greatly. To put it bluntly, this was the best body work for the actor I had ever seen. After seeing this I could understand why the Russian actor (though the other Soviet theatres do not use Biomechanics exactly, they do use related systems of body training) — why the Russian actors are so fluent and graceful on the stage compared to our own Group actors, who as individuals have just as strong and muscular bodies. The difference is in the *kind* of body training the Russians get.

The Biomechanics exercises are not only excellent in their purely physical elements for training the muscles through tension and relaxation, movement and the stopping of movement, but remarkable for their dramatic elements (without any artiness), for each of these exercises is a kind of play (indeed, they have names such as "The Havoc," "The Meeting," "The Killing"), a play with two characters generally in conflict so that the movement is always related to a partner and demands a constant adjustment of person to person—most often of a man to a woman. One can see at once that these exercises have been devised by a person with a profound sense of theatre. They demand agility and poise, feeling and physical freedom: they are actually a pleasure to see and they must be even a greater pleasure to perform.

Some of the things the students are able to do are extraordinary: a man jumps on another's chest while his partner stands erect: the first man slides off him, slowly, his feet never touch the ground until he gets down on the floor. A man carries a girl on his back like a burden, she lying flat and relaxed all the while. One might suppose that the students are all young giants, but as a matter of fact, our actors are nearly all of them physically better equipped for this work. Those students we saw had only been doing Biomechanics for a little over a year, and had been working on a collective farm before they came to the Meyerhold School. It would be very useful if the Group could teach this system: the actors would not only benefit by it, but they would enjoy it. Besides Biomechanics—done three times a week—the Meyerhold actors also do acrobatics. Acrobatics, of course, are recommended by Stanislavsky as training for the actor. The Group is ready for acrobatics now.

Part IV
Appendices

Glossary of Biomechanical Terminology

ACTING CHAIN. The three obligatory phases making up each element of acting: (1) Intention—the intellectual perception of the task received from outside (author, playwright, director, the initiator of the activity); (2) Realization—the cycle of conscious, mimetic and vocal reflexes; (3) Reaction.

CHECHOTKA. A tap dance step that can be introduced into the PARADE.

DACTYL. The basic signaling device (a sweep of the hands upward followed by two rapid downward claps), it denotes the initiation and completion of the biomechanical exercise. The term is borrowed from poetry: a three-syllable measure consisting of one long followed by two short syllables. (See Chapter 5 for directions on how to execute the DACTYL.)

FIGURE. A neutral word to designate the person executing the biomechanical exercise. For some exercises with partners, the actors (regardless of sex) were divided into "Heavy" and "Light" FIGURES. Each Heavy FIGURE was expected to be able to carry a Light FIGURE in his or her arms. According to the Soviet actress Elizaveta Kogan, for some of the women this proved to be quite a challenge.

FIXATION. The micro-stop at the end of the SETTLING. It also marks the beginning of a new RECOIL. Eisenstein further defines it in his *Expressive Movement* as "The moment when the forces are balanced, after which the expression passes over either into a real act, symbolized by the expression (victory of the reflexive thrust), or into a state of repose (victory of the voluntary stimulus). The teeth bared in fury either will bite, or the lips will close over them; the hand, with fingers crooked symbolizing grasping will either grasp, or the fingers will relax and return to normal."

HOP-STEP. End position for RUNNING. The left foot takes the final RUNNING step. The right foot executes a slight hop (as though stepping up on an imaginary step), and the left foot simultaneously swings back almost cutting the ground (*raser la terre*). This places the runner in the same position as at the beginning of the RUNNING.

258 *Glossary of Biomechanical Terminology*

JUMP-TURN. From the DACTYL position, the runner recoils and jump-turns to the left, landing with his left foot forward, right foot back, thus placing his feet in the position for RUNNING.

PARADE. The entrance and exit of the actors in single file. The actors move at a lively tempo in a half-walk, half-run, usually to the accompaniment of music. The PARADE is also used at the completion of an exercise as a means of moving to a new formation in preparation for the execution of the next exercise.

PARTING. A single handshake which two actors make as part a biomechanical exercise. It occurs following the RUNNING in pairs, either at the beginning of the exercise or preceding the final DACTYL.

POSE. The arrangement of the body in a harmonious whole without a utilitarian objective. Unlike the RACCOURCI, it is static and has no relationship to the general movement.

RACCOURCI. An art term from the French meaning "foreshortening." Meyerhold and Eisenstein used it to mean an instantaneous, expressive moment pulled out from the general movement, a point of break between two movements. It is related to the *mie* of the Japanese theatre. Unlike the POSE, it is always utilitarian and dynamic.

RECOIL. The movement which, in preparation for making a movement in one direction, is made in advance in the opposite direction. One of the basic laws of Biomechanics, it is fundamental in the execution of each movement in an exercise in order to give a feeling of balance. The RECOIL also serves as a signal to the partner of readiness to proceed. Anyone who has watched a snake prepare to strike a victim understands the meaning of this term. The RECOIL is not necessarily of the same magnitude as the subsequent movement. In fact, the danger for the beginner is in a tendency to exaggerate the RECOIL.

All biomechanical movements begin in the same way: RECOIL—SETTLING—FIXATION. This is done for the rhythm of the movement; it is what conveys a feeling of naturalness.

RUNNING: Following the JUMP-TURN, the left is foot forward, the right foot back in preparation for the RUNNING. A recoil, right hand in front, left behind, sets the body in motion for the RUNNING. The RUNNING movement is lively, always on the balls of the feet, heels off the ground, the arms also in motion. The RUNNING ends with a HOP-STEP. For exercises by partners, the RUNNING may be done with hands joined (as in ice skating in pairs).

SETTLING. The slight downward relaxation of the body, or of one of the extremities, at the end of each RECOIL—as if one were on springs.

Notes

Abbreviations used in Notes:

RGALI   Russian State Archive of Literature and Art [Rossiiskii gosudarstvennyi arkhiv literatury i iskusstva], Moscow. Formerly TsGALI (Central State Archive of Literature and Art [Tsentral'nyi gosudarstvennyi arkhiv literatury i iskusstva]).

Stat'i   Meierkhold, V. E. *V. E. Meierkhol'd: stat'i, pis'ma, rechi, besedy* (2 tt.) [V. E. Meyerhold: Articles, letters, speeches, conversations], edited by Aleksandr V. Fevralsky. 2 vols. (Moscow: Iskusstvo, 1968).

Vstrechi   *Vstrechi s Meierkhol'dom: Sbornik vospominanii* [Encounters with Meyerhold], edited by Lyubov' D. Vendrovskaya. (Moscow: VTO, 1967).

Introduction

1. Huntly Carter, *The New Theatre and Cinema of Soviet Russia* (London: Chapman & Dodd, Ltd., 1924), pp. 70–72.

2. Nikolai A. Gorchakov, *Theatre in Soviet Russia*, trans. Edgar Lehrman (New York: Columbia University Press, 1957), pp. 201–204.

3. Edwin Duerr, *The Length and Depth of Acting* (New York: Holt, Rinehart, 1962), p. 470.

4. RGALI, 963-1-38, "Conference on the artistic method of the Meyerhold State Theatre, June 8[–June 11], 1933," p. 83.

5. James Symons, *Meyerhold's Theatre of the Grotesque* (Coral Gables: University of Miami Press, 1971), p. 118.

6. Robert Leach, *Vsevolod Meyerhold* (Cambridge: Cambridge University Press, 1989), p. 52.

7. Ibid., p. 56.

8. Ibid., p. 57, et passim.

9. RGALI, 963-1-38, p. 77.

10. Christine Hamon, "La biomecanique de Meyerhold," *Travail téâtral*, no. 15 (April-June 1974), p. 93.

11. Edward Braun, *Meyerhold on Theatre* (New York: Hill and Wang, 1969), p. 183.

12. Valentin Pluchek, "V sentiabre 1926 goda...," *Teatr*, no. 2 (Feb. 1974), p. 50.

13. See, for example, Igor' Ilinsky, *Sam o sebe* (Moscow: VTO, 1961), pp. 154-162; Aleksandr Gladkov, "Vospominaniya, zametki, zapisi o V. E. Meierkhol'de," *Tarusskie stranitsy* (Kaluga: Literaturno-khudozhestvennyi illyustrirovannyi sbornik, 1961), p. 297. See also Sonia Moore, "Meyerhold: Innovator and Example," in *Stanislavski Today*, ed. Sonia Moore (New York: American Center for Stanislavski Theatre Art, 1973), p. 110.

14. Mel Gordon, "Meyerhold's Biomechanics," *The Drama Review* vol. 18, no. 3 (September 1974), pp. 73-88.

15. "Meyerhold's *The Magnanimous Cuckold*: An Evening of Russian Constructivist Theatre," a recreation of scenes from the original 1922 production held in conjunction with the exhibition "Art of the Avant-Garde in Russia: Selections from the George Costakis Collection." The Solomon R. Guggenheim Museum, New York, December 10-13, 1981; Museum of Fine Arts, Houston, March 25-28, 1982. Scenes from *D.E.* were performed as part of "Constructivist Music and Performance," held at the Kitchen, New York, October 6-16, 1983. "*The Death of Tarelkin*, a Performance-Demonstration," was presented at the City University of New York Graduate Center Mall in conjunction with an exhibition from March 11 to May 24, 1985, of the furniture reconstructed from the 1924 Meyerhold production. For a description of these recreations, see Mel Gordon, "Reconstructing the Russians," *The Drama Review*, vol. 28, no. 3 (Fall 1984), pp. 9-16.

PART I. MEYERHOLD AND EISENSTEIN

1. Meyerhold: From Actor to Revolutionary Director

1. Aleksandr Gladkov, *Teatr. Vospominaniya i razmyshleniya* (Moscow: Iskusstvo, 1980), p. 283.

2. Gladkov, ibid, p. 271.

3. Gordon Craig, "The Russian Theatre Today," *The London Mercury*, vol. 32, no. 192 (October 1935), p. 537.

4. Aleksandr Gladkov, *Teatr*, p. 152.

5. Ibid., p. 260.

6. Ibid., p. 259.

7. Private archive, Moscow.

8. The account of Meyerhold's pre-Revolutionary years is based on the following sources: Vsevolod Meierkhol'd, "Biograficheskie dannie" (1921) in *Stat'i* I, pp. 308-315; Nikolai Volkov, *Meierkhol'd* (Moscow: Zrelishcha, 1923); Nikolai Volkov, *Meierkhol'd* (2 tt) (Moscow-Leningrad: Academia, 1929); Aleksandr Gladkov, *Gody ucheniya Vsevoloda Meierkhol'da* (Saratov: Privolzhskoe knizhnoe izdatelstvo, 1979); Konstantin Rudnitsky, *Meierkhol'd* (Moscow: Iskusstvo, 1981); V. Sadchikov, "Meierkhol'd v Penze," *Teatr*, no. 5 (1972), pp. 124-133.

9. Gladkov, *Godi ucheniya*, p. 24.

10. RGALI, 998-1-625, p. 1ob.

11. Gladkov, *Godi ucheniya*, p. 29.

12. Volkov, *Meierkhol'd*, vol. 1, p. 36.
13. Gladkov, *Godi ucheniya*, p. 38.
14. Gladkov, *Teatr*, p. 283.
15. Volkov, *Meierkhol'd*, vol. 1, p. 172.
16. Cited in Volkov vol. 2, p. 51. In 1909, perhaps inspired by the tour of another Japanese actress, Hanako, Meyerhold drafted an article on the Japanese theatre for *Apollon*. RGALI, 998-1-609, contains notes made in 1909 for the article, and judging from several letters Meyerhold received from the editor, Sergei Makovsky (998-1-1718), the article was apparently written. But it was never published and no copy of it has been located. As further testimony to Meyerhold's keen interest in the Japanese theatre, that same year Meyerhold also translated from German the Japanese Kabuki tragedy *Terakoya*. The one-act play was actually act 4 of a Kabuki play adapted from Bunraku. Written in 1746, the full name of the play is *Terakoya: The Secret of Sugawara's Calligraphy*, by Takeda Izumo, Namiki Senryu, and Miyoshi Shoraku. Meyerhold's translation was staged at the Liteiny Theatre in St. Petersburg, September 18, 1909, and directed by P. Ivanovsky. In the late 1920s Meyerhold wrote to Nikolai Konrad, a prominent Orientalist, asking him to translate a Japanese play for the Meyerhold Theatre. See: RGALI, 998-1-1561, letter dated January 3, 1927, from Nikolai Konrad to Meyerhold; also RGALI, 998-3-73, letter dated March 3, 1928. Nothing ever came of the proposal, however.
17. "Iz pisem o teatre. Berliner Kammerspiele. Regie Max Reinhardt," *Vesy*, Moscow, no. b (1907), pp. 93-98. Republished in *Stat'i*, I, pp. 162-166.
18. V. E. Meierkhol'd, trans., "O stsenicheskoi obstanovke," by Edward Gordon Craig, in *Zhurnal teatra Literaturno-khudozhestvennogo obshchestva*, no. 3 (1909-1910), pp. 16-18; V. E. Meierkhol'd, trans., "Neskol'ko slov o rezhissere i stsenicheskikh postanovkakh," by Edward Gordon Craig, in *Zhurnal teatra Literaturno-khudozhestvennogo obshchestva*, no. 9 (1909-1910), pp. 27-28.
19. Rudnitsky, op. cit., pp. 213-226.
20. *O teatre* (St. Petersburg: Prosveshchenie, 1913). The book was reprinted in V. E. Meierkhol'd, *Stat'i*, I. All subsequent references are to the latter.
21. *Stat'i*, I, p. 111.
22. From Meyerhold's description of his course, "Techniques of Movement on the Stage," in *Lyubov'k trem apel'sinam*, no. 4-5 1914, p. 94.
23. RGALI, 998-1-747, p. 11.
24. See Gerard Abensour, "Meyerhold à Paris," in *Cahiers du Monde Russe et Soviétique*, vol. 5, no. 1 (April–June, 1964), pp. 5-21.
25. Volkov, II, p. 40.
26. Ibid, pp. 40-41.
27. *Stat'i*, I, p. 114.
28. *Lyubov'k trem apel'sinam*, no. 4-5 (1914), pp. 94-98.
29. *Lyubov'k trem apel'sinam*, no. 6-7 (1914), pp. 105-15.
30. *Lyubov'k trem apel'sinam*, no. 4-5 (1914), pp. 90-92.
31. Aleksandra V. Smirnova-Iskander, "V 1917," in *Tvorcheskoe nasledie V. E. Meierkhol'da*, ed. Lyubov' Vendrovskaya, et al. (Moscow: VTO, 1978), p. 245.
32. Braun, *Meyerhold on Theatre*, p. 159.
33. Interview with N. M., *Teatr*, Moscow, October 24, 1913; quoted in Edward Braun, *The Theatre of Meyerhold* (New York: Drama Book Specialists, 1979), p. 146.
34. Stefan Mokul'sky, "Petrogradskie teatry ot Fevralya k Oktyabryu," in *Istoriya*

Sovetskogo teatra, vol. I: *Petrogradskie teatry na poroge Oktyabrya i v epokhi voennogo kommunizma 1917*-1921 (Leningrad: Leningradskoe otdelenie gosudarstvennogo izdatelstva khudozhestvennoi literatury, 1933), p. 58.

35. For a vivid picture of theatrical life following the February revolution, see V. F. Bezpalov, *Teatry v dni revolyutsii 1917* (Leningrad: Academia, 1927).

36. *Krechinsky's Wedding* was actually completed before the February uprising. It premièred on January 25, 1917. *The Case* premièred on August 30, 1917, and *The Death of Tarelkin* on October 23. During that time Meyerhold also rehearsed Rimsky-Korsakov's opera *The Snow Queen* at the Marinsky Theatre (it premièred December 14, 1917) and codirected Ibsen's *The Lady from the Sea* at the Alexandrinsky Theatre (it opened on December 15).

37. Konstantin Rudnitsky, "Zabytaia stat'ya V. E. Meierkhol'da," in *Voprosy teatra* (Moscow: Ministerstvo kul'tury SSSR, Vsesoiuznyi nauchno-issledovatel'skii institut iskusstvoznaniya, soiuz teatral'nykh deyatelei RSFSR, 1990), p. 215.

38. Konstantin Rudnitsky, *Meierkhol'd*, p. 230–31. See also Boris Malkin's brief account in Wiktor Woroszylski, *The Life of Mayakovsky*, tr. Boleslaw Taborski (New York: The Orion Press, 1970), pp. 186–187.

39. Aleksandr Matskin, *Portrety i nablyudeniya* (Moscow: Iskusstvo, 1973), p. 309.

40. Aleksandra Smirnova-Iskander, "Iz vospominanii o Meierkhol'de i studii na Borodinskoi," unpublished manuscript, private archive, p. 88.

41. "Polozhenie o Teatral'nom Otdele Narodnogo Komissariata po Prosveshcheniyu, 19 September 1918, No. 203 (467)" published in *Vremennik Teatral'nogo Otdela Narodnogo Komissariata po Prosveshcheniyu*, Vyp. 1, Petersburg–Moscow November 1918), pp. 24–29. See also *Leonid Sergeevich Viv'en: Akter. Rezhisser. Pedagog. Sbornik*, comp. V. V. Ivanova (Leningrad: Iskusstvo, 1988), pp. 169–175.

42. Ibid, p. 170.

43. *Vestnik teatra*, no. 72–73 (January 4, 1921), p. 20.

44. *Vestnik teatra*, no. 78–79 (January 4, 1921), p. 25.

45. *Tefizkult* (Istoriya vozniknoveniya), *Vestnik teatra*, no. 93–94 (August 15, 1929), pp. 22–23.

2. Meyerhold: From Biomechanics to the Triumph of Socialist Realism

1. Aleksandr Gladkov, "Meierkhol'd govorit," *Tarusskie stranitsy* (Kaluga: Kaluzhskoe knizhnoe izdatel'stvo, 1961) p. 302.

2. "Rezhisserskie masterskie," *Teatral'naia Moskva*, no. 3 (4–6 November 1921), p. 6.

3. B. Yurtsev, "Proletkul't na zavodakh," *Zrelishcha*, no. 8 (17–22 October 1922), p. 23.

4. The discussion on Taylorism in Russia and on Gastev is drawn from the following sources: Mark R. Beissinger, *Scientific Management, Socialist Discipline, and Soviet Power* (Cambridge, Mass.: Harvard University Press, 1988), pp. 20 et passim; Zenovia A. Sochor, "Soviet Taylorism Revisited," in *Soviet Studies*, vol. 33, no. 2 (April 1981), pp. 246–264; Kendall E. Bailes, "Alexei Gastev and the Soviet Controversy over Taylorism, 1918–24," in *Soviet Studies*, vol. 24, no. 3 (July 1977), pp. 373–94; *Aleksej*

Gastev. Proletarian Bard of the Machine Age (Stockholm: Almqvist & Wiksell International, 1983); Richard Stites, *Revolutionary Dreams: Utopian Vision and Experimental Life in the Russian Revolution* (New York: Oxford University Press, 1989), pp. 146 et passim.

    5. These principles are drawn from the following sources: Frederick Winslow Taylor, *The Principles of Scientific Management* (New York: W. W. Norton & Co., 1911); Frank B. Gilbreth and Lillian M. Gilbreth, *Fatigue Study* (New York: Sturgis & Walton, 1916); Frank B. Copley, *F. W. Taylor. Father of Scientific Management* (New York: The American Society of Mechanical Engineers, 1923).

    6. Zenovia A. Sochor, op. cit., pp. 246–250. See also Charles S. Maier, "Between Taylorism and Technocracy: European Ideologies and the Vision of Industrial Productivity in the 1920s," *The Journal of Contemporary History*, vol. 5, no. 2 (1970), pp. 50–51.

    7. As he was described by Nikolai Aseev in his poem "Gastev," quoted in Bailes, op. cit., p. 373.

    8. Of the more than 500 works published in his lifetime, the best known was *Kollektivnaya refleksologiya* (Petrograd: Kolos, 1921). It, along with other Bekhterev works, was included in the Meyerhold Theatre bibliographies (RGALI 998-1-861). As testimony to the international significance of his writings on reflexology, in 1932 Bekhterev's book was published in English translation as *General Principles of Human Reflexology*, and reprinted by Arno Press (New York, 1973).

    9. See James Riordan, *Sport in Soviet Society* (London: Cambridge University Press, 1977), pp. 47–53; Pyotr F. Lesgaft, *Izbrannye pedagogicheskie sochineniya*, comp. I. N. Resheten' (Moscow: Pedagogika, 1988).

    10. *Gosudarstvennyi Institut Fizicheskogo Obrazovaniya imeni P. F. Lesgaft, Spravochnik po 1925–26 god* (Leningrad: GIFO im. P. F. Lesgaft, 1925), p. 33.

    11. Riordan, op. cit., p. 50.

    12. Harold Clurman, "Conversation with Two Masters," *Theatre Arts Monthly* (November 1935), p. 874.

    13. Aleksei Gripich, "Uchitel' stseny," in *Vstrechi*, p. 125.

    14. G. A. Kogan, *Biomekhanika fizicheskogo sklada v 4-kh chastiakh* (St. Petersburg, 1910).

    15. See, for example, Richard Stites, op. cit., p. 161.

    16. "Rezhisserskie masterskie," *Teatral'naia Moskva*, no. 3 (November 4–6, 1921), p. 6.

    17. In conversation with the authors, August 17, 1991.

    18. In conversation with the authors, August 17, 1991.

    19. *Vestnik teatra*, no. 87–88 (April 5, 1921), pp. 2–3. Reprinted in Vsevolod Meierkhol'd, *Stat'i* II, pp. 24–29.

    20. Ibid, p. 28.

    21. "Biomekhanika. Iz besedy s laborantami Vs. Meierkhol'da," *Zrelishcha*, no. 10 (1922), p. 14, a report issued by the Student Information Bureau (STINF).

    22. "Moskovskaya khronika," *Teatr i muzyka*, no. 1–7 (November 14, 1922), p. 23.

    23. Rich., "Nas vosem'desiat," *Ermitazh*, no. 7 (June 27, 1922), p. 8.

    24. *Lev Sverdlin: Stat'i. Vospominaniya*, comp. N. A. Velekhova and A. G. Obraztsova (Moscow: Iskusstvo, 1979), p. 206. The Uzbek Studio later formed the nucleus of the Khamza Theatre, presently located in Tashkent.

    25. For a detailed description of the production see Alma H. Law, "Meyerhold's

Le Cocu Magnifique," Les Voies de la création théâtrale, vol. 6 (Paris: France Editions du CNRS, 1979), pp. 13–43.

26. Ivan Aksyonov, "Prostranstvennyi Konstruktivizm na stsene," in *Teatral'nyi Oktyabr'* (Moscow, 1926), p. 34. The word in Russian is *igra*, from the verb *igrat'*, which can mean both "to play" as in "to play a game," and "to act or play a role." We have tried to be consistent throughout in translating *igra* as "play," though in reading, both meanings should be kept in mind.

27. Aleksandr Gladkov, unpublished manuscript, private archive, Moscow. Meyerhold went on to say, "I thought sometime we would also reach 'higher mathematics.' A beginning was made in *Bubus the Teacher* and *The Inspector General*."

28. Louis Lozowick, "Moscow Theatre, 1920s," *Russian History/Histoire Russe*, vol. 8, no. 1–2 (1981), p. 143.

29. RGALI, 963-1-312, pp. 18–20.

30. Aleksandr Gladkov, unpublished manuscript.

31. For a detailed description of the "Letter Scene," see below.

32. Mikhail Zharov, *Zhizn', teatr, kino* (Moscow: Izd. "Iskusstvo," 1967), p. 171. For a detailed description of the furniture and how it was used, see Alma H. Law, "*The Death of Tarelkin*: A Constructivist Vision of Tsarist Russia," *Russian History Histoire Russe*, vol. 8, no. 1–2 (1981), pp. 145-198.

33. Alpers, *Teatr sotsial'noi maski* (Moscow-Leningrad: GIKHLSI, 1931), p. 32.

34. V. E. Meierkhol'd, "Igra i predigra," *Stat'i*, II, p. 93.

35. Konstantin Rudnitsky, *Rezhisser Meierkhol'd* (Moscow: Nauka, 1969), p. 330.

36. V. E. Meyerhold, "*Uchitel' Bubus* i problema spektaklya na muzyke" (Talk delivered January 1, 1925), in *Stat'i*, II, p. 92.

37. In conversation with Alma Law, 1982.

38. Edward Braun, *Meyerhold on Theatre* (New York: Hill and Wang, 1969), p. 216.

39. "Beseda s orkestrom," RGALI, 998-1-384.

40. Aleksandr Gladkov, "Meierkhol'd govorit," *Novyi mir* no. 8 (1961), p. 217.

41. For an example of a chronométrage, see the chronométrage of performances of *Woe to Wit* in Alma H. Law, "Meyerhold's *Woe to Wit* (1928)," *The Drama Review*, vol. 18, no. 3 (September 1974), p. 92.

42. Aleksandr Gladkov, "Meierkhol'd govorit," p. 218.

43. Edward Braun, op. cit., p. 216.

44. Quoted in Wiktor Woroszylski, *The Life of Mayakovsky*, op. cit. p. 438.

45. B. Ermilov, "O nastroeniyakh melkoburzhuaznoi 'levizny' v khudozhestvennoi literature," *Pravda* (March 9, 1930), quoted in Rudnitsky, *Rezhisser Meierkhol'd*, p. 416.

46. John Freedman, "Nikolai Robertovich Erdman," *Soviet and East European Drama, Theatre, and Film*, vol. 8, no. 2–3 (December 1988), p. 8. See also his book on Nikolai Erdman, *Silence's Roar: The Life and Drama of Nikolai Erdman* (Ottawa: Mosaic Press, 1992).

47. Elena Tyapkina in a taped conversation with Alma Law, October 1, 1978, published in: "Pages from the Past," *Soviet and East European Drama, Theatre, and Film*, vol. 8, no. 2–3 (December 1988) pp. 17–18.

48. Igor' Il'insky, *Sam o sebe* (Moscow: VTO, 1961), p. 200.

49. David Talnikov, "Velikodushnyi rogonosets," *Sovremennii teatr*, no. 9 (1928), p. 184.

50. Ilinsky left and returned to Meyerhold's theatre several times between 1925 and 1935. Erast Garin also left more than once. Among those who parted for good, in addition to Babanova, were Sergei Martinson and Nikolai Okhlopkov.

51. Aleksandr Gladkov in conversation with Alma Law.

52. Aleksandr Matskin, "Igor' Il'insky i ego kniga," *Novyi mir*, no. 1 (1960), p. 265.

53. Konstantin Rudnitsky, *Meierkhol'd*, p. 382.

54. Nikolai Bogolyubov, "Revolyutsionnaya deistvitel'nost'," *Vstrechi*, p. 445.

55. I. Bachilis, *"Vystuplenie* v teatre imeni Meierhkhol'da," *Komsomol'skaya Pravda* (March 11, 1933).

56. "O tvorcheskom metode Teatra imeni Vs. Meierkhol'da," *Rabis*, no. 9 (1931), p. 14.

57. Ibid. pp. 14–15

58. "O zadachakh RAPP na teatral'nom fronte," *Rabis*, no. 35–36 (1931), pp. 25–26.

59. Stenographic notes of V. E. Meyerhold's talk to the actors before a rehearsal of *The Forest*, October 29, 1931. RGALI, 998-1-331.

60. Ibid.

61. "Konferentsiya po tvorcheskomu metodu gosudarstvennogo teatra Meierkhol'da ot 8/VI/33," RGALI, 963-1-38.

62. Ibid., p. 13.

63. Ibid., pp. 73–75.

64. *O Zadachakh RAPP na teatral'nom fronte* (Leningrad: GIKhL, 1932).

65. Ibid., p. 35.

66. Ibid., p. 36.

67. "Konferentsiya...," op. cit., p. 81.

68. Ibid

69. Ibid.

70. Ibid.

71. Reported in Mikhail Gliyarov, "Put' bol'shevika-khudozhnika," *Rabis*, no. 11 (1933), pp. 34–35. See also Aleksandr Matskin, "Vremya ukhoda," *Teatr*, no. 1, (1990), p. 34.

72. Matskin, p. 34.

73. Mikhail Gilyarov, op. cit., p. 35.

74. Lev Snezhnitsky, "Poslednii god," *Vstrechi*, pp. 556–557.

75. Aleksei Bendersky, "Master rabotaet," *Rabis* no. 10 (1934), p. 24.

76. Leonid Varpakhovsky, "Zametki proshlykh let," *Vstrechi*, p. 475.

77. Ibid., p. 475.

78. Ibid., p. 467.

79. "Printsipy spektaklya (1935)," *Stat'i*, II, p. 322.

80. Ilinsky, *Sam o sebe*, p. 294–295.

81. Mikhail Gliyarov, op. cit., p. 35.

82. Transcription of interview by Paul Ryder Ryan with Lee Strasberg, December 28, 1972. An edited version of this interview was published in "Russian Notebook (1934)," *The Drama Review*, vol. 17, no. 1 (March 1973), pp. 106–112. The remarks cited here were not, however, included in the published interview.

83. Pavel Markov, "Pis'mo o Meierkhol'de," *Teatr i dramaturgiya*, no. 2 (February 1934), p. 19.

84. Maria Valentei, in conversation with Alma Law, January 11, 1988.

85. Directive of the U.S.S.R. Central Executive Committee dated September 6, 1936. See "Pochetnye zvaniya," *Teatral'naya entsiklopediya*, ed. P. A. Markov et al., vol. 4 (Moscow: Sovetskaya entsiklopediya, 1965), p. 455.

86. "Muddle Instead of Music," *Pravda* (January 28, 1936).

87. From notes made available to Alma Law by Aleksandr Gladkov. Gladkov was present when the discussion took place at Meyerhold's apartment in 1936.

88. "Meierkhol'd protiv meierkhol'dovshchiny," *Stat'i*, II (March 14, 1936), pp. 330-347.

89. "Vystuplenie na sobranii teatral'nykh rabotnikov Moskvy," *Stat'i*, II (March 26, 1936), pp. 348-358. For a translation of Meyerhold's speech, see Braun, *Meyerhold on Theatre*, pp. 289-98.

90. Ibid., p. 354.

91. Ibid., p. 356.

92. Yury Bakhrushin, "Stanislavsky i Meierkhol'd," in *Vstrechi*, p. 589.

93. Konstantin Rudnitsky, *Meierkhol'd*, p. 418.

94. A. Nefedov, "Yuchite zhit'!," *Teatr*, no. 8 (August, 1937), pp. 120-122.

95. Ibid., p. 122.

96. Platon Kerzhentsev, "Chuzoi teatr," *Pravda*, (December 17, 1937).

97. Platon Kerzhentsev, "O teatre nashikh dnei," *Molodaya Gvardiya*, no. 6 (1929).

98. Braun, *Meyerhold on Theatre*, p. 250.

99. See *Pravda* (January 8, 1938), p. 2. The resolution was also published in *Teatr*, no. 1 (January 1938), p. 1.

100. "Meierkhol'dovshchine ne mesto v sovetskom iskusstve," *Sovetskoe iskusstvo*, no. 2 (1938).

101. Ibid.

102. Mikhail Sadovsky, "Teatral'nyi charodei," in *Vstrechi*, pp. 526-528. The Theatre's final performance was to have been *The Lady of the Camellias* on Saturday evening, January 7, but since the theatre had not yet received the official order on its closing, it went ahead and scheduled the Sunday matinee.

103. *Pravda* (January 8, 1938), p. 2.

104. Aleksandr Gladkov, *Meierkhol'd*, II (Moscow: STD/RSFSR, 1990), p. 232.

105. Ibid., p. 233. See also the chapter on "The Method of Physical Action" in Jean Benedetti, *Stanislavsky: An Introduction* (London: Methuen, 1982), pp. 315-323.

106. For an account of the rehearsals of Griboyedov's *Woe from Wit* Stanislavsky conducted in 1930-1931 as he began working out this new methodology, see Nikolai Gorchakov, *K. S. Stanislavsky v rabote nad p'esoi "Gore ot uma" 1930-31* (Moscow: VTO, 1954).

107. Erast Garin, *S Meierkhol'dom* (Moscow: Iskusstvo, 1974), p. 33.

108. Stanislavsky's notebook, MXAT Museum, K. S. Archive, no. 263. The undated note was written no earlier than 1933-1934. See also Inna Vinogradskaya, *Zhizn' i tvorchestvo K. S. Stanislavskogo. Letopis'*, IV (Moscow: VTO, 1976), p. 488.

109. Boris Alpers. "Sud'ba teatral'nykh techenii," *Teatr*, no. 5 (May 1965), p. 14.

110. Benedetti, p. 318.

111. Ibid., p. 318.

112. Konstantin Rudnitsky, *Meierkhol'd*, p. 421.
113. RGALI, 998-1-130. Cited in Solomon Podol'sky's unpublished manuscript, *Konstantin Sergeevich Stanislavsky i Vsevolod Emilevich Meierkhol'd* (Moscow: 1959), p. 150.
114. Bakhrushin, op. cit., p. 586.
115. Rudnitsky, *Meyerhold*, p. 421.
116. Benedetti. op. cit., p. 321.
117. Bakhrushin, op. cit., p. 589.
118. For an account of Meyerhold's work with Sergei Prokofiev on *Semyon Kotko*, see Harlow Robinson, *Sergei Prokofiev* (New York: Viking, 1987), pp. 358 ff. Meyerhold was arrested only a week before Prokofiev finished the piano score for the opera. It was ultimately staged by Serafima Birman.
119. Sery's account of his meetings with Meyerhold is based on Alma Law's interview with him, May 24, 1991.
120. *Rezhisser v sovetskom teatre. Materialy pervoi vsesoyuznoi rezhisserskoi konferentsii*, ed. A. D. Solodovnikov (Moscow-Leningrad: Iskusstvo, 1940), pp. 16–22. See also Arkady Vaksberg, *Stalin's Prosecutor: The Life of Andrei Vyshinsky* trans. Jan Butler) (New York: Grove Weidenfeld, 1991), pp. 177–181.
121. Ibid., p. 21.
122. Ibid., p. 7.
123. Ibid., p. 82.
124. Typescript of Meyerhold's speech, private archive. All citations are from it. A shamefully edited version of the speech omitting this and subsequent excerpts quoted here was published in *Teatr*, no. 2 (1974), pp. 39–44. Of other writers who have quoted from Meyerhold's speech, only Alexander Kaun seems to have seen the original text (Alexander Kaun, *Soviet Poets and Poetry* [Berkeley: University of California Press, 1943], p. 96).
125. Juri Jelagin, *Temnyi genii* (Vsevolod Meierkhol'd), 2nd enl. ed. (London: Overseas Publication, 1982), pp. 406–410. As a Russian theatre historian recently quipped, "The only thing Jelagin got right in his book was the title."
126. For Meyerhold's own description of his interrogation see Vsevolod Meyerhold, "Petition," transcribed by Marjorie Hoover, in *Soviet and East European Performance: Drama, Theatre, Film*, vol. 9, no. 1 (1989), pp. 19–22.

3. Eisenstein: From Engineer to Revolutionary Filmmaker

1. Diary note dated September 30, 1946, *Eisenstein*, vol. 4 (Moscow: Iskusstvo, 1966), p. 751.
2. See Leonid Kozlov, "A Hypothetical Dedication," *Eisenstein Revisited*, edited by Lars Kleberg and Håkan Lövgren (Stockholm: Almquist & Wiksell International, 1987), pp. 65–92; and Nikita Lary, "Eisenstein's (Anti) Theatrical Art. From Kino-Fist to Kino-Tragedy," *Slavic and East European Arts*, vol. 6, no. 2 (Winter 1990), pp. 88–100.
3. Sergei Eisenstein, *Notes of a Film Director* (Foreign Languages Publishing House: Moscow, n.d.), pp. 9–10.
4. Naum Kleiman in conversation with Alma Law, October 29, 1989.

5. RGALI, 1923-1-1549, p. 64 ob (letter dated October 27, 1920).
6. RGALI, 1923-1-1549, pp. 84 ob., 86, quoted in G. D. Endzina, "Zhil, zadumyvalsya, uvlekalsya...." (Perepiska S. M. Eizenshteina), *Vstrechi s proshlym*, ed. I. L. Andronikov et al. (Moscow: Sovetskaya Rossiya, 1976), pp. 311-12.
7. Sergei Yutkevich, *Sobranie sochinenii v trekh tomakh*, vol. 1, comp. and ed. M. Z. Dolinskii (Moscow: Iskusstvo, 1990), p. 81.
8. Sergei Eisenstein, *Immoral Memories*, trans. Herbert Marshall (Boston: Houghton Mifflin, 1983), p. 79.
9. Ibid., p. 76.
10. Aleksandr Fevralsky, *Puti k sintezu: Meierkhol'd i kino* (Moscow: Iskusstvo, 1978), p. 177.
11. At the beginning of 1922, Meyerhold wrote Eisenstein: "As my reward for paying you such 'homage,' I want you to get started as quickly as possible on the encyclopedia group because it will give you a chance to be in the forefront of GVRM's work. But I'm ashamed to exploit you like this when you are so loaded down with work." V. E. Meyerhold'd, *Perepiska. 1896-1939*, comp. V. P. Korshunova and M. M. Sitkovetskaia (Moscow: Iskusstvo, 1976), p. 213.
12. Aleksandr Fevralsky, "S. M. Eizenshtein v teatre," *Voprosy Teatra* (Moscow: VTO, 1967), pp. 86-87.
13. *Immoral Memories*, pp. 74-75.
14. *Vstrechi s proshlym*, p. 314.
15. Mikhail Zharov, op. cit., p. 174.
16. RGALI, 1923-1-1550, p. 14 ob., quoted in *Vstrechi s proshlym*, p. 314.
17. RGALI, 1923-1-2065, p. 1, quoted in *Vstrechi s proshlym*, pp. 314-15.
18. Sergei Eisenstein, "Montazh attraktsionov," *Lef*, no. 3, (1923), pp. 70-75. For a translation of it and a description of Eisenstein's *The Wiseman*, see: "Montage of Attractions for *Enough Stupidity in Every Wiseman*," trans. Daniel C. Gerould, *The Drama Review*, vol. 18, no. 1 (March 1974), pp. 77-84.
19. "At Rehearsals of *The Wiseman*," see Chapter 9.
20. Rudolf Bode, *Ausdrucksgymnastik* (München, 1922).
21. *Slyshish', Moskva?!* (Moscow/Leningrad: Gos. Izd., 1928). A translation by Liudmila Hirsch of Tretyakov's play in a workers' club version appears in *The Drama Review*, vol. 22, no. 3 (September 1978), pp. 113-123.
22. See, for example, Aleksandr Fevralsky, "Slyshish', Moskva?—Slyshu!," *Pravda* (November 13, 1923). Other reviews appeared in *Izvestia*, *Rabochaya Moskva*, and *Gorn*.
23. See articles by Tretyakov in *Oktyabr' mysli*, no. 1 (1924), and *Lef*, no. 4 (August 1924).
24. Ibid.
25. *Protivogaz* (Moscow/Leningrad: Gos. Izd., 1928). For a description of the production, see Aleksandr Fevralsky, "S. M. Eizenshtein v teatre," pp. 97-99.
26. Jay Leyda and Zina Voynow, *Eisenstein at Work* (New York: Pantheon Books/The Museum of Modern Art, 1982), p. 114.
27. Sergei Eisenstein, *Selected Works: Volume 1: Writings 1922-34*, ed. and trans. Richard Taylor (London: BFI Publishing, 1988), pp. 50-58.
28. Why wasn't the brochure published? According to Aleksandr Fevralsky (in conversation with Alma Law, February 1976), *Lef* wanted an article from Eisenstein, and so he thought up the one on montage witout Tretyakov. Tretyakov was offended

that Eisenstein hadn't told him about this article before it came out in print, and as a result the brochure on Expressive Movement fell by the wayside.

Later, when the question arose of including the manuscript in the six-volume edition of Eisenstein's works, it was decided not to. Although the conception was Eisenstein's (there is in the archives an outline in Eisenstein's hand), the two of them apparently talked through everything together and Tretyakov wrote it down. Thus the decision was reached that it would be more appropriate to include the manuscript in the volume of Tretyakov's writings that was also in the planning stage. However, that volume has not as yet been published. (Naum Kleiman in conversation with Alma Law, January 1988.)

We are indebted to Aleksandr Fevralsky for making available to us a copy of the manuscript of "Expressive Movement" as well as the one on "Biomechanics in the Representational Aspects of Honoré Daumier's Lithographs."

29. In conversation with Alma Law, January 4, 1988.
30. Rostislav Yurenev, *Sergei Eizenshtein: Zamysly. Fil'my. Metod*, Part 1: 1898–1929 (Moscow: Iskusstvo, 1985), p. 53.
31. *Eisenstein*, vol. 4, p. 24.
32. Ibid., pp. 23–24.
33. For details on Eisenstein's break with Proletkult, see the documents published in "Falling out of Proletkult," *Eisenstein 2*, ed. Jay Leyda (Calcutta: Seagull Books, 1985), pp. 1–8.
34. See Ivan Aksyonov, "Sergei Mikhailovich Eizenshtein (Portret khudozhnika)," *Iskusstvo kino*, no. 1 (1968), pp. 106–107; and Aleksandr Fevralsky, "S. M. Eizenshtein v teatre," op. cit., p. 100.
35. Rostislav Yurenev, op. cit, pp. 53–54.
36. Ibid., p. 53.
37. "Zweig. Babel. Toller. Meyerhold. Freud," in *Immoral Memories*, pp. 158–164.
38. The obituary, contained in a letter to Maksim Shtraukh, dated September 17, 1931, appears in Leonid Kozlov, "A Hypothetical Dedication," *Eisenstein Revisited*, op. cit., 1987, pp. 72–75.
39. Eisenstein, vol. 4, pp. 536–604.
40. A. V. Fevral'sky, "S. M. Eizenshtein v teatre," op. cit., p. 100.
41. Gladkov, vol. 2, p. 261.
42. A. V. Fevral'sky, "S. M. Eizenshtein v teatre," op. cit., pp. 100–101.
43. Edward Braun, *Meyerhold on Theatre* (New York: Hill and Wang, 1969), p. 311.
44. Quoted in Yon Barna, *Eisenstein* (Boston: Little, Brown and Co., 1973), p. 61.
45. In conversation with Naum Kleiman, May 23, 1990.
46. Mikhail Sadovsky, "Teatral'nyi charodei," *Vstrechi*, p. 523.
47. Gladkov, vol. 2, p. 221. When Meyerhold staged Vishnevsky's *The Last, Decisive Battle* in 1931, he had great hopes that he had found a playwright to replace Mayakovsky, who had just committed suicide. But they soon broke off their relations following a quarrel over Vishnevsky's next play, *Fighting in the West*. Vishnevsky had defended Eisenstein in the *Bezhin Meadow* affair, and at the time Eisenstein took Vishnevsky out to Meyerhold's dacha in the summer of 1937, the playwright had just written a scenario, *We, the Russian People*, for Eisenstein.

48. Naum Kleiman in conversation with Alma Law, October 27, 1989. Kleiman recalls that among the people Eisenstein called were Dovzhenko (who attended), Tretyakov (he was away), and Esfir Shub.

49. A. V. Fevralsky, "S. M. Eizenshtein v teatre," op. cit., p. 101.

50. Sergej Eisenstein, "Leb wohl," *Yo Ich selbst Memoiren*, ed. Naum Kleiman and Valentina Korshunova, tr. Regina Kuhn and Rita Braun (Vienna: Locker Verlag, 1984), vol. 1, pp. 324–26. The translation here is from the German by Marjorie Hoover; the Russian text of this section of Eisenstein's memoirs has yet to be published in the original.

51. *Immoral Memories*, p. 115. For a color reproduction of Golovin's decor, see Al'fred I. Bassekhes, *Teatr i zhivopis' Golovina* (Moscow: Izobrazitel'noe iskusstvo, 1970), p. 51.

52. Naum Kleiman in conversation with Alma Law, May 23, 1990. For the scenario of *Pushkin: The Love of a Poet*, see Jay Leyda and Zina Voynow, op. cit., pp. 116–122.

53. Naum Kleiman in conversation with Alma Law, May 23, 1990.

54. Sergei Eisenstein, *Immoral Memories*, p. 275.

55. In his memoir of taking the archive (see "Der Schatz," *Yo Ich selbst Memoiren*, vol. 1, pp. 327–331), Eisenstein is mistaken when he implies ("Every night bombs drop here") that the war had already begun. Since Meyerhold's stepdaughter, Tatiana Sergeevna Esenina ("A girl with dark rings around her eyes"), from whom he received the archive, left for Tashkent in early fall 1940, it could only have been before that date, that is, well before the German invasion of Russia.

56. *Eisenstein Revisited*, op. cit., p. 75.

57. Naum Kleiman in conversation with Alma Law, May 23, 1990.

58. For Nikolai Cherkasov's account of working with Eisenstein on *Ivan the Terrible*, see Nikolai Cherkasov, *Notes of a Soviet Director* (Moscow: Foreign Languages Publishing House, n.d.), pp. 104–106. See also Leonid Kozlov, "De l'hypothèse d'une dédicace secrète," *Cahiers du Cinéma*, no. 226–227 (January–February 1971), pp. 57–67, for a more detailed analysis of the physical and psychological resemblance between Eisenstein's conception of Ivan the Terrible and Meyerhold.

59. *Immoral Memories*, pp. 75, 130.

PART II. BIOMECHANICS

4. Introduction

1. Aleksandr Gladkov, unpublished manuscript, private archive, Moscow.

2. At a rehearsal of *Gore umu* (second variant), September 22, 1935, during Mei Lan-fang's visit to Moscow. RGALI, 998-1-390.

3. V. E. Meierkhol'd o sovremennom teatre," *Teatr*, No. 1370 (Oct. 25, 1913), p. 7.

4. K. S. Stanislavsky, *My Life in Art* (Cleveland: World Publishing Co., 1956), p. 466.

5. V. E. Meierkhol'd, "K istorii i tekhnike Teatra," *Stat'i*, I, pp. 141–142.

6. At a rehearsal of *Gore umu*, Dec. 18, 1927, RGALI, 998-1-378.

7. Aleksandr Gladkov, "Repliki Meierkhol'da," *Teatral'naia zhizn'*, no. 5 (1960), pp. 19–20.

8. Boris Alpers, *Teatr sotsial'noi maski*, p. 54.

9. *Stat'i*, II, p. 505.
10. Aleksandr Gladkov, "Meierkhol's govorit," *Neva*, no. 2 (1966), p. 206.
11. Alpers, *Teatr sotsial'noi maski*, p. 54.
12. Diana Loercher, "The Essence of Dance," *The Christian Science Monitor* (September 18, 1978), p. 15.

PART III. DOCUMENTS

8. Meyerhold Documents on Biomechanics

1. *Pechat' i revolyutsiya*, no. 1 (January–March 1922), pp. 305–309. Reprinted in Vsevolod Meierkhol'd, *Stat'i II*, pp. 37–43.
2. "Stenogramma besedy narodnogo artista respubliki V. E. Meierkhol'da so studentami-vypusknikami IV-go kursa GITISa ot 15-go fevralya 1936 goda," RGALI, 998-1-747, p. 16.
3. "Konferentsiya...," op. cit., p. 83.
4. V. E. Meierkhol'd, *Perepiska. 1896–1939*, op. cit., p. 220.

Selected Bibliography

Alpers, Boris. *Teatr sotsialnoi maski* [The theatre of the social mask]. Moscow-Leningrad: GIKhLSI, 1931.
Bode, Rudolf. *Ausdrucksgymnastik*. München: 1922.
―――. *Expression-Gymnastics*. Trans. Sonya Forthal and Elizabeth Waterman. New York: A. S. Barnes, 1931.
Braun, Edward. *Meyerhold on Theatre*. New York: Hill and Wang, 1969.
―――. *The Theatre of Meyerhold. Revolution on the Modern Stage*. New York: Drama Book Specialists, 1979.
Carter, Huntly. *The New Theatre and Cinema of Soviet Russia*. London: Chapman & Dodd, 1924.
Clurman, Harold. "Conversations with Two Masters." *Theatre Arts Monthly*, no. 11 (1935), pp. 871–876.
Eisenstein, Sergei. *Film Form*. Ed. and trans. Jay Leyda. New York: Harcourt Brace, 1949.
―――. *The Film Sense*. Ed. and trans. Jay Leyda. New York: Harcourt Brace & Co., 1942, 1947.
―――. *Immoral Memories, An Autobiography*. Trans. Herbert Marshall. Boston: Houghton Mifflin, 1983.
―――. *Izbrannye proizvedeniya* [Selected works]. 6 vols. Moscow: Iskusstvo, 1964–1971.
―――, and Sergei Tretyakov. "Expressive Movement." Trans. Alma H. Law. *Millennium Film Journal*, no. 3 (Winter/Spring 1979), pp. 30–38.
Fevralsky, Aleksandr. *Desyat let teatra Meierkhol'da* [Ten years of Meyerhold's Theatre]. Moscow: Federatsiya, 1931.
―――. *Puti k sintezy: Meierkhol'd i kino* [Paths to a synthesis: Meyerhold and the cinema]. Moscow: Iskusstvo, 1978.
Fülöp-Miller, René. *The Mind and Face of Bolshevism*. Trans. F. S. Flint and D. F. Tait. New York: Alfred Knopf, 1927.
Garin, Erast P. *S Meierkhol'dom* [With Meyerhold]. Moscow: Iskusstvo, 1974.
Gladkov, Aleksandr K. "Repliki Meierkhol'da" [Meyerhold's rejoinders]. *Teatral'naya zhizn'* [Theatrical life], no. 5 (1960), pp. 19–21.
Golding, Alfred Siemon. *An Essay on Stage Performance: A Translation of Franz Lang's "Dissertatio de Actione Scenica" (1727)*. New York: Theatre Library Association, 1983.
Gordon, Mel. "Eisenstein's Later Work at the Proletkult." *The Drama Review*, vol. 22, no. 3 (September 1978), pp. 107–112.

———. "Meyerhold's Biomechanics." *The Drama Review*, vol. 18, no. 3 (September 1974), pp. 73-88.
———, and Alma H. Law. "Expressive Movement." *Millennium Film Journal*, no. 3 (Winter/Spring 1979), pp. 25-29.
——— and ———. *Meyerhold's Magnanimous Cuckold*. Program booklet for "An Evening of Russian Constructivist Theatre," held in conjunction with the exhibition *Art of the Avant-Garde in Russia: Selections from the George Costakis Collection*, at the Solomon R. Guggenheim Museum, New York, December 10-13, 1981, and at the Museum of Fine Arts, Houston, March 25-28, 1982.
Hoover, Marjorie L. *Meyerhold. The Art of Conscious Theatre*. Amherst: University of Massachusetts Press, 1974.
Ilinsky, Igor'. *Sam o sebe* [About myself]. Moscow: VTO, 1961.
James, William. *The Principles of Psychology*. New York: Henry Holt, 1890.
Kaun, Alexander. *Soviet Poets and Poetry*. Berkeley: University of California Press, 1943.
Law, Alma H. "Meyerhold's 'The Magnanimous Cuckold.'" *The Drama Review*, vol. 26, no. 1 (Spring 1982).
Lawton, Lancelot. *The Russian Revolution (1917-1926)*. London: Macmillan, 1927.
Levshin, Aleksandr. "Na repetitsiyakh *Mudretsa*," in *Eizenshtein v vospominaniyakh sovremennikov* [Eisenstein in the recollections of his contemporaries]. Moscow: Iskusstvo, 1974, pp. 136-150.
Leyda, Jay, and Zina Voynow. *Eisenstein at Work*. New York: Pantheon Books/The Museum of Modern Art, 1982.
Martin, John. "How Meyerhold Trains His Actors." *Theatre Guild Magazine* (November 1930), pp. 26-30.
Meyerhold, V. E. *V. E. Meierkhol'd: stat'i, pis'ma, rechi, besedy* [V. E. Meyerhold: Articles, letters, speeches, conversations]. Ed. Aleksandr V. Fevralsky. 2 vols. Moscow: Iskusstvo, 1968.
Nizhny, Vladimir. *Lessons with Eisenstein*. Trans. and ed. Ivor Montagu and Jay Leyda. New York: Hill and Wang, 1962.
Picon-Vallin, Béatrice. *Meyerhold*. Les Voies de la création théâtrale, no. 17. Paris: CNRS, 1990.
Rudnitsky, Konstantin. *Meyerhold the Director*. Trans. George Petrov. Ann Arbor: Ardis, 1981.
Rudnitsky, Konstantin. *Russian and Soviet Theatre. Tradition and the Avant-Garde*. Trans. Roxane Permar, ed. Lesly Milne. London: Thames and Hudson, 1988.
Schmidt, Paul, ed. *Meyerhold at Work*. Austin: University of Texas Press, 1980.
Seton, Marie. *Sergei M. Eisenstein*. London: Bodley Head, 1952.
Van Gyseghem, André. *Theatre in Soviet Russia*. London: Faber & Faber, 1943.
Volkov, Nikolai D. *Meierkhol'd*. 2 vols. Moscow and Leningrad: Academia, 1929.
Vstrechi s Meierkhol'dom: Sbornik vospominanii [Encounters with Meyerhold]. Ed. Lyubov' D. Vendrovskaya. Moscow: VTO, 1967.

Index

"The Actor of the Future and Biomechanics" 132, 141–144
Adoration of the Cross 24
Aglaraine and Sélysette 21
Akimov, Nikolai 70, 243
Aksyonov, Ivan 43, 131, 264n
Aleksandrov, Grigori 172
Alexander Nevsky 91
Alexandrinsky Theatre (later Pushkin Theatre) 16, 22, 28, 69, 75, 262n
All-Russia Red Stadium 31, 146
Alpers, Boris 47, 97
Altman, Nathan 27
Amar, Jules 145
Andreev, Leonid 21, 50
Anokhin, Petr 145
Apollinaire, Guillaume 23
Appia, Adolph 21
Arensky, Pavel 76
L'Art et le comédien 144
Aseev, Nikolai 263n
At the Gate of the Kingdom 208
Atwater, Wilbur 145

Babanova, Maria 52–54, 265n
Babochkin, Boris 206
Bakhrushin, Yury 68, 69
Bakst, Leon 23
Balagan 15, 170
Barba, Eugenio 7
Basilov, Nikolai 133, 151–160
The Bathhouse 52
The Battleship Potemkin 74, 88, 170, 172, 202, 247, 249
Bebutov, Valery 41, 131

The Bedbug 52, 65
Bedny, Demian 172
Bekhterev, Vladimir 37, 38, 41, 126, 263n
Belenson, Aleksandr 85
The Bells (Émile Erckmann and Alexandre Chatrian) 245
Bely, Andrei 57
Benedetti, Jean 68, 69
Bernhardt, Sarah 167
Bernshtein, Nikolai 41
Bezhin Meadow 69n, 89, 90
Birman, Serafima 70, 267n
Blok, Aleksandr 21, 27
Blyum, Vladimir 28
Bode, Rudolf 82, 85–87, 173–176, 183–185, 191n, 212
Bogolyubov, Nikolai 54, 55, 220
Bolshoi Theatre 42, 63, 66, 89
Boris Godunov (Aleksandr Pushkin) 64, 65, 90–92, 246
Botticelli, Sandro 21
Braun, Edward 7, 49, 50
Brecht, Bertolt 14, 251
Brik, Osip 172
Bubus the Teacher 48, 49

Calderón de la Barca, Pedro 24, 117
Carter, Huntley 3, 225
The Case 27, 262n
Central Institute of Labor (TsIT) 35, 40, 149, 189, 192n
Chaliapin, Feodor 68, 167, 188
Chapaev 206, 207
Chaplin, Charlie 13, 77, 90
Chatrian, Alexandre see *The Bells*

275

Chauveau, Jean-Bapistise 145
Chekhov, Anton 18, 19, 21, 64, 220
Chekhov, Mikhail 7, 57, 167, 241, 248
Chekrygin, Aleksandr 24
Cherkasov, Nikolai 92, 270n
Chevalier, Maurice 54
Chinese Theatre 39, 48, 152, 160, 214
Chronométrage 50, 264n
Cinema Today 85
Circus 13, 26, 31, 39, 82, 170–171, 191n, 251, 252
Clurman, Harold 39, 252–253
Colditz, Carl 180
Columbine's Garter 79
Columbine's Scarf 24
Commedia dell'arte 4, 21, 24–26, 226, 237, 244
Comte, Auguste 145
The Constant Prince 117
Constructivism 2, 4, 33, 38, 39, 42, 43, 65, 71, 77, 81, 142, 224, 233, 243, 251, 252, 260n
Coquelin, Constant-Benoît 95, 131, 144, 167, 171, 203
The Count of Monte Cristo 78
Craig, Gordon 14, 21
Crommelynck, Ferdinand 14, 88; see also *The Magnanimous Cuckold*
The Cry of Life 20

Dalcroze, Émile Jaques *see* Jaques-Dalcroze, Émile
Dalmatov, Vasily 16
Daneman, K.I. 24
Danilovna, Alvina (Meyerhold's mother) 16
d'Annunzio, Gabriele 23
Darwin, Charles 218
Daumier, Honoré 86
The Dawns 30, 33, 243
D. E. (Mikhail Podgaetsky) 8, 45, 126, 220
Dead Souls (Nikolai Gogol) 241
The Death of Tarelkin (Aleksandr Sukhovo-Kobylin) 4, 5, 8, 27, 45–46, 80, 262n, 264n
Death of Tintagiles 20
Degas, Edgar 97
Delsarte, François 228, 232
Demeny, Georges 145

Derzhavin, Konstantin 41
Diderot, Denis 171
Dietrich, Marlene 77
Do You Hear, Moscow?! 83–85, 268n
A Doll's House 30
Don Giovanni 68, 69
Don Juan 22, 49, 60, 75
Donato, Donat 24
Donato, Giacomino 24
Dostoyevsky, Fyodor 17
Dovzhenko, Aleksandr 90, 270n
Du Bois-Reymond, René 174
Duchenne, Guillaume 175
Dumas, Alexandre (*fils*) 60–62, 89, 90, 97, 167, 266n; see also *The Lady of Camellias*
Dumas, Alexandre (*père*) see *The Count of Monte Cristo*
Dunaevsky, Isaac 69
Duncan, Isadora 41, 95, 138, 147
Duse, Eleanora 154

Earth 205
The Earth in Turmoil 47, 227
Eccentricism 45, 79, 80, 127
Edison, Thomas 142
Ehrenburg, Ilya 45
Eisenstein, Julia (Eisenstein's mother) 75, 76, 80
Eisenstein, Mikhail (Eisenstein's father) 75, 76, 92
Eisenstein, Sergei (*and see following two entries*): apprenticeship at Meyerhold's Workshops 77–80, 268n; Communist Party criticisms of 90, 91; death 92; director and teacher at Proletkult 82–84; early years 75; Expressive Movement 1, 2, 8, 74, 75, 82, 83, 85–87, 163, 164, 167, 192, 206, 207, 209, 210, 211, 213, 215, 217, 218, 219, 223, 238, 239, 241, 244, 250, 257; first work as film director 84, 85; rivalry with Meyerhold 74, 75, 87–92, 269n, 270n; service in Red Army 76; teacher at State Institute of Cinematography (GIK) 87, 88, 163, 164, 238–252
Eisenstein, Sergei, films: *Alexander Nevsky* 91; *The Battleship Potemkin*

74, 88, 170, 172, 202, 247, 249;
Bezhin Meadow 69n, 89, 90; *Ivan the Terrible* 81, 86, 91, 92; *October* 244; *Que Viva Mexico* 88, 238; *Strike* 85, 86, 88, 244, 247–249
Eisenstein, Sergei, writings: *Columbine's Garter* (with Sergei Yutkevich) 79; *Expressive Movement* (with Sergei Tretyakov) 85–87, 163, 173–192, 268–269n; "Lecture on Biomechanics March 29, 1935" 163, 164, 204–223; "The Montage of Attractions" 81, 268n; "Notes on Biomechanics" 163–167; "On Recoil Movement" 163, 192–204; "Principles of Movement in Our Theatre" 163, 167, 168; "What Is a *Raccourci* and What Is a Pose?" 163, 165, 168, 169; *The Wiseman* 80–85, 170–173, 243, 245, 247, 249, 268n
Eisler, Hanns 251
Elizabethan Theatre 25, 26
The Emploi of the Actor 131
Engels, Friedrich 200, 203
Enough Stupidity in Every Wiseman 80
Erdman, Nikolai 50, 52, 139, 269n
Erckmann, Émile see *The Bells*
Erik XIV (August Strindberg) 167
Ermilov, Vladimir 52
Ermolova, Maria 18
Esenina, Tatiana (Meyerhold's stepdaughter) 91, 270n
Eurhythmics 42, 76, 191n
The Expression of the Emotions in Man and Animals 218
Expressive Gynmnastics 82, 173
Expressive Movement 173–192; see also Eisenstein, Sergei, writings
Expressive Movement and Creative Power 173

Faiko, Aleksei 48, 49, 243
Fairbanks, Douglas 77
Fairground Booth 21
FEKS (Factory of the Eccentric Actor) 79
A Fervent Heart (Aleksandr Ostrovsky) 65
Fevralsky, Aleksandr 78, 89, 90, 141, 268n, 269n
Fighting in the West 269n

First Workers Theatre of the Moscow Proletkult 42, 76, 80, 81
Flight 243
Fokine, Mikhail 23
Foregger, Nikolai 78, 80, 81, 149, 192n
The Forest (Aleksandr Ostrovsky) 5, 47, 53, 54, 58, 62, 65
Free Theatre Company 30
Freud, Sigmund 88
Fuchs, Georg 20
Fuller, Loie 23
Futurist Theatre 31, 33

Gabrilovich, Evgeny 65; see also *One Day*
Garin, Erast 73, 112, 132, 139–141, 265n
Garshin, Vsevolod 18
Gas Masks 84, 85
Gastev, Aleksei 35, 36, 39–41, 132, 134, 262n, 263n
Gastev, Yuri 40
George, Lloyd 77
German, Yury 54, 55; see also *Prelude*
Gershwin, George 77
Gert, Valeska 250
The Ghosts 20
Gilbreth, Frank 35
Gilbreth, Lillian 35
Gladkov, Aleksandr 7, 14, 15, 17, 43, 67, 89, 264n, 266n
Glizer, Judith 246
Gluck, Christoph Willibald Ritter von 22
Gnesin, Mikhail 24
Goethe, Johann Wolfgang von 55
Gogol, Nikolai 15, 50, 139; see also *Dead Souls*; *The Inspector General*
Golden Guts 88
Goleizovsky, Kasyan 95
Golovin, Aleksandr 22, 91, 270n
Gorbachev, Mikhail 8, 72
Gorchakov, Nikolai 266n
Gorky, Maxim 14, 63
GOSET (State Jewish Theatre) 242, 251
Gozzi, Carlo 25; see also *Turandot* 242, 251
Granovsky, Aleksei 4
Grasso, Giovanni 112, 144, 162
Greek Theatre 251
Griboyedov, Aleksandr 17, 96, 266n;

see also *Woe from Wit* (*Woe to Wit*)
Gromov, Viktor 220
Grosz, George 97
Grotowski, Jerzy 6, 7
Guglielmo (Guglielmo Ebereo of Pesaro) 25

Hamlet 25, 81, 88
Hamon, Christine 6
Hamsun, Knut 208
Hanako (pseudonym for Ōta Hisa) 261n
Hauptmann, Gerhart 20
Heartbreak House 79
Hilker, Franz 181
His Honor Eugène Rougon 205
Hisa Ōta *see* Hanako
Hokusai, Katsushika 136
How the Steel Was Tempered 65
Hueppe, Ferdinand 190n, 191n

I Am a Son of the Working People 69
Ibsen, Henrik 20, 30, 262n
Ilinsky, Igor 7, 30, 32, 77, 220, 265n
Inkizhinov, Valery 26, 99, 165, 171, 220, 225, 226
The Inspector General 15, 50, 62, 67, 71, 77, 88, 139
The Intruder 19
The Iron Flood (Aleksandr Serafimovich) 244
Irving, Henry 245
Ivan the Terrible 81, 86, 91, 92
Ivanov, Vyacheslav 24
Ivnev, Ryurik 27

James, William 36, 37, 39, 87, 164, 167, 207–209
Japanese Theatre 20, 76, 152, 160, 214, 237, 251, 261n
Jaques-Dalcroze, Émile 42, 76, 82, 142, 143, 146, 181, 191n
Jelagin, Juri 71, 267n

Kabuki 13, 20, 39, 48, 95, 97, 171, 196, 237, 261n

Kachalov, Vassily 149, 172, 246
Kamerny Theatre 143, 150, 192n, 241, 251
Kataev, Valentin 69
Katerina, Izmailova (Dmitri Shostakovich) 89
Kaun, Alexander 267n
Kawakami, Otojiro 20
Keffler, Leo 146
Kellermann, Bernhard 45
Kerzhentsev, Platon 40, 65, 66, 68
Khersonsky, Khrisanf 139, 140
Khmelev, Nikolai 89
Kiselevsky, Ivan 16
Klages, Ludwig 173
Kleiman, Naum 86, 90, 269n, 270n
Kleist, Heinrich von 167, 182, 183
Knipper, Olga 18
Kohnstamm, Oskar 199–201
Komissarzhevskaya, Vera 21
Komissarzhevsky, Fyodor 21, 164
Konchalovsky, Pavel 69
Konrad, Nikolai 261n
Korenev, Mikhail 59, 99, 102, 132–138
Kosheverov, Aleksandr 19
Kosheverov, Maria 19
Kozikov, Stefan 133
Krasnaya Presnya *see* Realistic Theatre
Krechinsky's Wedding (Aleksandr Sukhovo-Kobylin) 27, 262n
Krupskaya, Nadezhda 30
Kuleshov, Lev 216
Kustov, Nikolai 99, 205, 206, 219, 236

Laboratory of Theatrical Expressionism 144
The Lady from the Sea 262n
Lady Macbeth of Mtsensk District (*Katerina Izmailova*) 64
The Lady of Camellias 60–62, 89, 90, 97, 167, 242, 266n
Lake Lyul 243
Lancret, Nicholas 25
Lang, Franciscus 195, 196
Lang, Fritz 216, 217
The Last, Decisive Battle 54, 55, 269n
The Last Sacrifice 18
Lawton, Lancelot 225–227
Lazarenko, Vitaly 31
Leach, Robert 5

"Lecture on Biomechanics March 29, 1935" 163, 164, 204–223
Léger, Fernand 14
Lenin, Vladimir 34, 35; *Collected Works* 197
Lensky, Aleksandr 16, 18, 48
Leonardo da Vinci 97
Leonidov, Leonid 231, 245, 246
Lermontov, Mikhail 69; see also *Masquerade*
Lesgaft, Pyotr 37–40, 60, 146
Lessing, Gotthold 195
Levinsky, Aleksei 49
Levshin, Aleksandr 82, 163, 170–173
Life of a Man 21
Lipps, Theodor 187
Lissitzky, El 74
A List of Assets 4, 54
Loiter, Ephraim 42
Lokshina, Khesia 73, 139
London, Jack "The Mexican" 77
Lunacharsky, Anatoly 27, 28, 30, 192n
Lyubov Yarovaya 65

Maeterlinck, Maurice 19, 20, 21, 50; see also *Sister Beatrice*
The Magnanimous Cuckold (Ferdinand Crommelynck) 4, 8, 42–46, 53, 62, 65, 79, 133, 146, 150, 160–162, 260n
Makovsky, Sergei 261n
Malevich, Kazimir 28
Malraux, André 14
Maly Theatre 18, 65, 242
Mandelshtam, Osip 64
Manet, Edouard 97
Marey, Etienne 145
Marinetti, Filippo Tommaso 23
Markov, Pavel 63
Martin, John 228–233
Martinet, Marcel 47
Martinson, Sergei 165n
Marx, Karl 242, 243
Marxism 59, 151, 152
Masquerade (Mikhail Lermontov) 22, 49, 69, 75
MASTFOR 78, 80
Matskin, Aleksandr 54
Mayakovsky, Vladimir 27, 28, 31–32, 52, 65, 74, 77, 172
Médrano Circus 23

Mei Lan-fang 14, 211
Memling, Hans 20, 21, 97
Mensendieck, Bess 175
Meyer, Victor 145
Meyerhold, Artur (Meyerhold's brother) 17
Meyerhold, Emil (Meyerhold's father) 15–17
Meyerhold, Fedor (Meyerhold's brother) 17
Meyerhold, Irina (Meyerhold's daughter) 99, 220
Meyerhold, Teodor (Meyerhold's brother) 15, 17
Meyerhold, Vsevolod (*and see following entry*): apprenticeship in Moscow Art Theatre 18, 19; Communist Party criticisms of 52, 57–60, 62–66, 70–73, 90, 91, 267n; death 73, 267n; development of "Biomechanics" 38–42; director at Imperial theatres 21–24; "Doctor Dapertutto" 24, 25, 28, 75; formalism, campaign against 57–60, 64, 65, 66, 70, 72; GEKTEMAS (State Experimental Theatre Workshops) 153; GVRM-GVTM (State Directors [later Theatre] Workshops) 1, 4, 5, 6, 26, 33, 40, 41, 42, 44, 53, 75, 77, 78, 79, 80, 81, 85, 105, 106, 124, 132, 133, 139, 143, 145, 225; *The Magnanimous Cuckold* production 42–46; Meyerholditis 64, 66; personality 14, 15, 265n; rhythm and movement 49–52; R.S.F.R. Theatre No. 1 30–33, 77, 79; Sixteen Études 25, 26; studio on Borodinskaya 24, 26, 28; "Technique of Stage Movement" 28, 29; Theatre Studio on Povarskaya 20; "Theatrical October" 26–32, 47; "Three-Dimensional Actor" 95–98
Meyerhold, Vsevolod, writings: "The Actor of the Future and Biomechanics" 132, 141–144; *Columbine's Scarf* 24; *The Emploi of the Actor* (with Valery Bebutov and Ivan Aksyonov) 131; *Vs. Meyerhold: On the Theatre* 22, 24
Mikhoels, Solomon 70, 73
Milhaud, Darius 14

Molière, Jean-Baptiste Poquelin 22, 75; see also *Don Juan*
Möller, Robert 177
Molotov, Vyacheslav 64
"The Montage of Attractions" 81, 268n
MOPS *see* Theatre of the Moscow Oblast Council of Trade Unions
Morgan, Barbara 98
Moscow Art Theatre 18, 19, 30, 41, 49, 57, 62, 171, 172, 192n, 208, 241, 242, 245–247
Moscow Two 89
Moskvin, Ivan 248
Le Moteur humain et les bases scientifiques... 145
Mozart, Wolfgang Amadeus 68, 69
Much Ado About Nothing 48
Müller, Joergen 146
Munt, Olga (Meyerhold's first wife) 17, 18
Mystery-Bouffe 28, 31–32, 77

Natasha 14, 65
Nefedov, A. 65, 66
Nemirovich-Danchenko, Vladimir 14, 18, 19, 67, 68, 219
New Economic Policy (NEP) 32, 224
Nezlobin Theatre 196
Nikitin, Leonid 76
Nikolai II 77
Notes of a Director 131
"Notes on Biomechanics" 163–167

October 244
Okhlopkov, Nikolai 64, 233, 243, 264n
Olesha, Yury 4, 54
"On Recoil Movement" 163, 192–204
One Day 65, 90
Orlov, Dmitry 47
Orpheus 22
Ostrovsky, Aleksandr 5, 18, 47, 80; see also *The Forest*; *A Fervent Heart*
Ostrovsky, Nikolai 65
Ostwald, Wilhelm 145

Pallat, Ludwig 181
Le Paradox sur le comédien 171
Pasternak, Boris 64

Pavlov, Ivan 37, 40, 60, 63, 89, 133, 236
Pavlov, Vladimir 57
Petrov, A. 29, 41
Physical Culture 31, 37, 38, 69, 172, 191n
Picasso, Pablo 13, 14
Pisanelle 23
Piscator, Erwin 14
"Play with Objects" 46, 47, 50, 62
Plekhanov, Georgy 57
Pletnev, Vladimir 41
Pluchek, Valentin 7
Podgaetsky, Mikhail see *D.E.*
Podvoisky, Nikolai 30, 146
Popov, Aleksei 73
Popov, Andrei 70
Popova, Lyubov 31, 42, 46; "Struggle and Victory" (with Aleksandr Vesnin) 31
Pozdnev, Arkady 132, 148–151
Pre-acting 42, 48, 49
Prelude 54, 55, 89
Presnyakov, Valentin 24
Prince Igor (Aleksandr Borodin) 246
"Principles of Movement in Our Theatre" 163, 167, 168
Prokofiev, Sergei 16, 69, 70, 267n
Proletkult 42, 76–80, 82–84, 88, 98, 171, 172, 215, 22, 243, 269n
Proletkult Touring Theatre (Pere Tru) 82
Proshek, Josef 146
Prosvetov, Evgeny 42, 76, 82
Przybyszewski, Stanisław 19
Pudovkin, Vsevolod 171, 243
Pushkin, Aleksandr 16, 18, 64, 90, 91; see also *Boris Godunov*
Pushkin Theatre *see* Alexandrinsky Theatre
Puss in Boots 78

Que Viva Mexico 88, 238
The Queen of Spades 64

Raccourci 5, 83, 86, 97–99, 125, 136, 154, 155, 163–166, 168, 169, 171
Radezwill, H. 177
Radlov, Sergei 64, 70

Raikh, Zinaida (Meyerhold's second wife) 52, 53, 60, 67, 73, 80, 90
Ranvier, Louis-Antoine 145
Raoult, François 145
Realistic Theatre 233, 244
Recoil (*Otkaz*) 5, 61, 62, 88, 163, 171, 184, 192–204
Reflexology 36–37, 49, 263n
Reich, Wilhelm 251
Reinhardt, Max 21
Remizov, Aleksei 19
Renoir, Auguste 97
Rigoletto (Giuseppe Verdi) 262n
Rimsky-Korsakov, Nikolai 262n
Riordan, James 38
Rivera, Diego 14, 97
Rossov, Nikolai 16
Rubenstein, Ida 23
Rudenko, Pyotr (Zhorzh or Georgy) 171
Rudnitsky, Konstantin 48
Ryan, Paul Ryder 265n

Sadanji, Ichikawa 196
Sadovsky, Mikhail 90
St. Joan of the Stockyards 251
Salvini, Tommaso 19
Schiller, Friedrich 178, 185
Schluck and Jau 20
Schmidt, Fritz 177
Schnitzler, Arthur 20, 24, 79
Schulte, Robert 191n
The Seagull 19
Sechenev, Ivan 145
The Second Army Commander 54
Seifullina, Lydia 14, 65
Selvinsky, Ilya 54
Semyon Kotko 69, 267n
Serafimovich, Aleksandr see *The Iron Flood*
Sery, Nikolai 69, 70, 73, 267n
Seton, Marie 238–253
Shakespeare, William see *Hamlet*; *Much Ado About Nothing*
Shaw, George Bernard 79
Shebalin, Vissarion 16, 89
Shlepyanov, Ilya 89
Shostakovich, Dmitri 16, 64, 70; see also *Katerina Izmailova*
Shtraukh, Maksim 75, 269n
Shub, Esfir 270n

Sister Beatrice (Maurice Maeterlinck) 21, 97
Smirnova-Iskander, Aleksandra 26, 28
Smyshlyaev, Valentin 77, 82, 171
Snezhnitsky, Lev 60
Snow 19
The Snow Queen 262n
Socialist Realism 6, 62–66, 242
Sokol Gymnastics 120, 144–148
Sokolov, Ippolit 132, 144–149
Sokolova, Zinaida 68
Solovyev, Vladimir 24–26
Spanish theatre 24, 160, 226
Spezielle Muskelphysiologie 174
Stalin, Joseph 20–22, 63, 64, 70–72, 91
Stanislavsky, Konstantin 1, 5, 6, 8, 14, 65, 67–69, 72, 80, 89, 95, 154, 164, 165, 228–233, 236, 241, 242, 247, 248, 266n
Stanislavsky Opera Theatre 67–69, 91
Stanislavsky System 7, 59, 60, 95, 96, 131, 143, 145, 151, 156, 171, 209, 248–250; Method of Physical Action 5, 6
Stavsky, Viktor 243
Stepanova, Varvara 46, 80
Strand, Paul 252
Strasberg, Lee 63, 236–238, 265n
Strike 85, 86, 88, 244, 247–249
Strindberg, August see *Erik XIV*
The Suicide 52
Sukhovo-Kobylin, Aleksandr 27, 45–46, 80; see also *The Case*; *The Death of Tarelkin*; *Krechinsky's Wedding*
Sulerzhitsky, Leopold 246
Symbolist theatre 20, 23
Symons, James 5

Tairov, Aleksandr 14, 78, 131
Takeda Izumo 261n
Talnikov, David 53
Tatarinov, Vladimir 171
Taylor, Frederick Winslow 34–36, 39, 40, 263n
Taylorism 3, 34–36, 38, 40, 141–144, 148–151, 236, 263n
Tchaikovsky, Peter 64
Tefizkult (Theatricalization of Physical Culture) 31, 262n

Telyakovsky, Vladimir 21
Terakoya: The Secret of Sugawara's Calligraphy 261n
The Theatre Courier 30
The Theatre of the Future 20
Theatre of the Moscow Oblast Council of Trade Unions (MOPS) 251
Theatre of the Revolution 4, 225–227, 242, 246
33 Swoons 64, 220
Tieck, Ludwig 78
Tigerstedt, Robert 174, 175
Tolstoy, Aleksei K. 19
Tolstoy, Leo 246
Tonal-Plastics 42, 76, 82, 171
Traube, Moritz 145
Trenev 65
Tretyakov, Sergei 47, 82, 83–85, 163, 172, 268n, 269n; see also *The Earth in Turmoil*
Tristan und Isolde 22
Trotsky, Leon 35
Trust D. E. 45
Tsar Fedor Ioannovich 19
The Tunnel 45
Turandot (Carlo Gozzi) 242, 251
Tyapkina, Elena 73, 264n

Union of Workers in the Arts 27
Urbanovich, Pavel 112, 220
Uzbek Theatre Studio 42, 263n

Vakhtangov, Evgeny 165, 236, 241, 242
Vakhtangov Theatre 246, 251
Vasiliev, Sergei and Georgy 206
Van Gyseghem, André 233–236
Varpakhovsky, Leonid 60, 89
Veil of Pierrette 24, 79
Verdi, Giuseppe see *Rigoletto*
Verhaern, Émil 30; see also *The Dawns*

Vershilov, Boris 68
Vs. Meyerhold: On the Theatre 22, 24
Vesnin, Aleksandr, "Struggle and Victory" (with Lyubov Popova) 31
Villiams, Pyotr 89
Vishinsky, Andrei 70, 72
Vishnevsky, Vsevolod 54, 90, 269n
Viven, Leonid 28, 29, 41
Vsevobuch (General Military Training) 30–31
Vsevoldsky-Gerngross, Vsevolod 168, 196
VTO (All-Russia Theatre Society) 70
VVO (General Military Training) 146

Wagner, Richard 22, 89
Die Walküre 89
The Warrant 50, 139
We, the Russian People 269n
Weber, Edouard 145
Weill, Kurt 251
"What Is a Raccourci and What Is a Pose?" 163, 165, 168, 169
The Wiseman 80–85, 170–173, 243, 245, 247, 249, 268n
Woe from Wit (Woe to Wit) (Aleksandr Griboyedov) 17, 50–52, 58, 62, 88, 96, 266n

Yakko, Sada 20, 21
Yuriev, Nikolai 77–79
Yutkevich, Sergei 79, 89, 246

Zarkhi, Natan 89, 246
Zharov, Mikhail 47, 80
Zlobin, Zosima 59, 67, 73, 88, 205, 219–222
Zola, Émile 205
Zon Theatre 31
Zuntz, Nathan 145
Zweig, Stefan 88

www.ingramcontent.com/pod-product-compliance
Ingram Content Group UK Ltd.
Pitfield, Milton Keynes, MK11 3LW, UK
UKHW041928140426
5217IPUK00014B/363